Globalizing Social Justice

International Political Economy Series

General Editor: Timothy M. Shaw, Professor and Director, Institute of International Relations, The University of the West Indies, Trinidad & Tobago

Titles include:

Lucian M. Ashworth and David Long (*editors*)
NEW PERSPECTIVES ON INTERNATIONAL FUNCTIONALISM

Jeffrey Atkinson and Martin Scurrah
GLOBALIZING SOCIAL JUSTICE
The Role of Non-Government Organizations in Bringing about Social Change

Robert W. Cox (*editor*)
THE NEW REALISM
Perspectives on Multilateralism and World Order

Frederick Deyo (*editor*)
GLOBAL CAPITAL, LOCAL LABOUR

Stephen Gill (*editor*)
GLOBALIZATION, DEMOCRATIZATION AND MULTILATERALISM

Björn Hettne, András Inotai and Osvaldo Sunkel (*editors*)
GLOBALISM AND THE NEW REGIONALISM

Christopher C. Meyerson
DOMESTIC POLITICS AND INTERNATIONAL RELATIONS IN US-JAPAN TRADE POLICYMAKING
The GATT Uruguay Round Agriculture Negotiations

Isidro Morales
POST-NAFTA NORTH AMERICA

Volker Rittberger and Martin Nettesheim (*editor*)
AUTHORITY IN THE GLOBAL POLITICAL ECONOMY

Justin Robertson (*editor*)
POWER AND POLITICS AFTER FINANCIAL CRISES
Rethinking Foreign Opportunism in Emerging Markets

Michael G. Schechter (*editor*)
FUTURE MULTILATERALISM
The Political and Social Framework
INNOVATION IN MULTILATERALISM

Ben Thirkell-White
THE IMF AND THE POLITICS OF FINANCIAL GLOBALIZATION
From the Asian Crisis to a New International Financial Architecture?

Thomas G. Weiss (*editor*)
BEYOND UN SUBCONTRACTING
Task Sharing with Regional Security Arrangements and Service-Providing NGOs

Robert Wolfe
FARM WARS
The Political Economy of Agriculture and the International Trade Regime

---

International Political Economy Series

Series Standing Order ISBN 978–0–333–71708–0 hardcover
Series Standing Order ISBN 978–0–333–71110–1 paperback
(*outside North America only*)

You can receive future titles in this series as they are published by placing a standing order. Please contact your bookseller or, in case of difficulty, write to us at the address below with your name and address, the title of the series and the ISBN quoted above.

Customer Services Department, Macmillan Distribution Ltd, Houndmills, Basingstoke, Hampshire RG21 6XS, England

Globalizing Social Justice
The Role of Non-Government Organizations in Bringing about Social Change

By

Jeffrey Atkinson

and

Martin Scurrah

with

Jeannet Lingán,
Rosa Pizarro

and

Catherine Ross

© Jeffrey Atkinson and Martin Scurrah 2009
Chapter 7 © Catherine Ross 2009
Chapter 8 © Martin Scurrah, Jeannet Lingán and Rosa Pizarro 2009
Foreword © Jeremy Hobbs 2009

All rights reserved. No reproduction, copy or transmission of this publication may be made without written permission.

No portion of this publication may be reproduced, copied or transmitted save with written permission or in accordance with the provisions of the Copyright, Designs and Patents Act 1988, or under the terms of any licence permitting limited copying issued by the Copyright Licensing Agency, Saffron House, 6–10 Kirby Street, London EC1N 8TS.

Any person who does any unauthorized act in relation to this publication may be liable to criminal prosecution and civil claims for damages.

The authors have asserted their rights to be identified as the authors of this work in accordance with the Copyright, Designs and Patents Act 1988.

First published 2009 by
PALGRAVE MACMILLAN

Palgrave Macmillan in the UK is an imprint of Macmillan Publishers Limited, registered in England, company number 785998, of Houndmills, Basingstoke, Hampshire RG21 6XS.

Palgrave Macmillan in the US is a division of St Martin's Press LLC,
175 Fifth Avenue, New York, NY 10010.

Palgrave Macmillan is the global academic imprint of the above companies and has companies and representatives throughout the world.

Palgrave® and Macmillan® are registered trademarks in the United States, the United Kingdom, Europe and other countries

ISBN-13: 978-0-230-22113-0   hardback

This book is printed on paper suitable for recycling and made from fully managed and sustained forest sources. Logging, pulping and manufacturing processes are expected to conform to the environmental regulations of the country of origin.

A catalogue record for this book is available from the British Library.

A catalogue record for this book is available from the Library of Congress.

10 9 8 7 6 5 4 3 2 1
18 17 16 15 14 13 12 11 10 09

Printed and bound in Great Britain by
CPI Antony Rowe, Chippenham and Eastbourne

Contents

Foreword — vi
Preface — viii
Acknowledgements — xi
Explanation of Terms Used — xii
List of Abbreviations — xv

1. Types and Tactics — 1
2. Challenges and Questions — 30
3. Oxfam and its Global Campaign on Trade — 52
4. Case Study: Garment Workers in Sri Lanka — 67
5. Case Study: Trade and Agriculture in India — 94
6. Oxfam's Global Extractive Industries Campaigning — 118
7. Case Study: Natural Gas Project in Peru — 133
   Catherine Ross
8. Case Study: Jobs and Health in Peru — 166
   Martin Scurrah, Jeannet Lingán and Rosa Pizarro
9. Legitimacy, Accountability and Voice — 207
10. Conclusions — 236

Index — 245

Foreword

Increasing globalization has meant that democratic space has shrunk, and with it has come the concentration of power in global institutions, global business, and global media, often to the detriment of national governments' sovereignty. Yet at the same time, civil society organizations, including non-government organizations (NGOs), have been able to seize opportunities offered by globalization – the internet, rapid global communications, use of online campaigning technology communications and the role of global media – to increase democratic space across national boundaries, in ways that compliment national level campaigns and increase the leverage of local NGOs.

This book documents how NGOs have repositioned themselves in this dynamic context. Nearly all major global development networks, including Oxfam International, now engage in some level of campaigning and advocacy, many from a rights based approach. However we are all at different stages of the process. Moving from a traditional project based focus to integrating global, national and local campaigns and programmes, requires major managerial and cultural change, and ensuring that both programme partners and donors understand the rationale. And increasingly our partners are embracing advocacy, and expecting the same of their international NGO partners.

This book brings some uncomfortable truths to the fore, as well as positive learnings. It is a practical book for active campaigners, written by two experienced practitioners who bring a powerful ethical framework to their analysis. Jeff Atkinson and Martin Scurrah's book is based largely on case studies of campaigns with which they are familiar, and is grounded in the nuts and bolts of social change.

It focusses on the campaigning work of Oxfam, and its strength is that it is written by Oxfam insiders, who have been both actors in, and witnesses of, the organization's embrace of globalized campaigning over the last 20 years. Despite this, they bring objectivity to their analysis with an emphasis on understanding what actually works and what does not.

Yet for all the practical focus, the authors successfully link their experiences to the main ethical dilemmas. They explore legitimacy and voice, responsibility and accountability, changing North-South power dynamics and the broader challenge to civil society activism by vested interests.

At the heart of this is the question of power and the right to voice. As some Indian NGOs say, 'nothing about us without us'; how do we balance the practicalities of global campaigns with the need to respect the voices of local actors and avoid occupying their political space? As the authors note, this comes down to the nature and quality of partnerships, something Oxfam has not always got right.

Increasingly, the relationships between large global NGOs and national and local partners will be about 'political' alliances, and less about funding. Indeed Oxfam's campaigns now are all strongly grounded in alliances, such as the Global Call and Action against Poverty.

Many campaigns are about holding duty bearers – multilateral institutions, national governments and transnational or large national businesses – accountable for their responsibilities and promises. International NGOs are also powerful and should be held accountable to the highest standards if they are demanding this from others. There needs to be as much emphasis on downward and lateral accountability (i.e. to partners and allies) as there is to donors and the general public. A good start is the regular publication of independent evaluations, such as those done for Oxfam's Make Trade Fair campaign.

'Globalizing Social Justice', which delves deeper into the campaign narratives and explores the learning from these cases, is a major contribution to improving that accountability.

Jeremy Hobbs
Executive Director
Oxfam International
Oxford, UK

Preface

This is a book about civil society organizations (CSOs) and their role in modern society as advocates for change. In particular it is about those CSOs, including non-government organizations (NGOs), that have a social justice agenda, a concern with poverty, inequality, injustice, climate change, human rights, environmental degradation, etc, in the poorer countries of Africa, Asia and Latin America. It looks at the way in which they attempt to bring about positive change in the lives of the poor, the exploited or the abused by exerting influence at a local, national and international level – either directly themselves or through advocacy coalitions, including those that stretch across national borders linking organizations in the under-developed 'South' with those in the more affluent 'North'.

The book takes a case study approach in that it looks in detail at a number of particular campaigns, of varying degrees of success, at how they were run, what strategies they used, what problems they encountered, what worked in terms of achieving the campaign's objectives, and what did not, and why. It also uses these detailed case studies to illustrate and expand on some of the underlying issues, challenges and problems facing the organizations that undertake such advocacy.

Writing on these issues and the role of CSOs and NGOs in society is a relatively new phenomenon, despite the fact that such organizations have been around for centuries. Until the mid-1990s, there was almost no serious academic writing about the role of CSOs and NGOs. But their rise in prominence during the last few decades, and their increasing influence on governments and inter-governmental bodies has prompted serious challenges to their legitimacy, their accountability, their accuracy and their role in society, by those who oppose them or are challenged by them. This in turn has prompted serious consideration of these issues by those interested in this new phenomenon of civil society as a third force in international affairs, in addition to business and government, and in their advocacy role as a possible contribution to global governance in the future. As a result, the last decade has seen a dramatic increase in interest in the subject, manifested in the appearance of an extensive literature, and even entire university courses, looking at civil society and its role in national and global governance.

Most of this literature has been produced by academics and other commentators or analysts. This book is somewhat unique in that it is written by NGO insiders. The authors have between them over half a century of accumulated experience working for NGOs, most of it involved in advocacy and campaigning around various issues in a range of countries in Asia and Latin America. The case studies described in the book are ones in which the authors had some personal involvement, often from the periphery but close enough to give them access to detail and to the players involved. This is the reason for the book having a practical as well as the theoretical aspect to it, looking at what works and what does not in bringing about social change and why, and at the pitfalls for NGOs in advocacy and campaigning.

But the basic aim of the book is to look at the more fundamental questions around the role of civil society and NGOs – at the issues of legitimacy and accountability, as well as internal democracy, participation and responsibility within advocacy networks. On each of these issues, the case studies are drawn on extensively to illustrate the nature of the problem and how it is manifested in practice, and to provide examples of appropriate or inappropriate responses.

The case studies in the book have an element in common in that they all involved the international NGO Oxfam. As such they collectively provide a look at one particular international NGO involved in transnational advocacy and at how it operates, an insider's view of this new and significant type of activity by a typical Northern-based NGO. Oxfam International is a confederation of a dozen or so national NGOs, all bearing the name Oxfam, that are involved in development assistance programmes in the South, and have come together in recent years to harmonize their programmes and to advocate together on issues of common concern. While it operates within advocacy networks involving other organizations, the internal relations within this confederation, between the different affiliated organizations, and between their head offices in the North and their numerous field offices in various Southern countries and regions, mean that it operates more like a network than a unified organization. Hence it could be said that Oxfam International not only operates within transnational advocacy networks, but is itself akin to a transnational advocacy network.

The book falls into four parts. The first two chapters are an introduction to civil society organizations and their advocacy campaigns, and describe the different types of organizations that engage in such activities and the tactics they use, and give a brief overview of some of the major challenges and issues that they face. This is followed by three chapters that look in detail at two campaigns in South Asia (Sri Lanka and India) that were part of Oxfam International's global 'Make Trade Fair' campaign. This latter was a major global initiative that ran for five years from 2002 to 2006 in various countries around the world and involved a number of new and innovative approaches to transnational campaigning and advocacy. The next three chapters look at Latin American examples and in particular at campaigns around the impact of extractive industries (mining, oil, gas) on local communities in Peru, and at the national and international networks that were formed to support them. They demonstrate how transnational advocacy can be and is employed to achieve changes and influence decisions both in the North and the South. The last two chapters look in more detail at the issues and challenges facing CSOs and NGOs in undertaking advocacy and, using the case studies as illustrations, draw some conclusions about what can and should be done, and the future of civil society advocacy.

Acknowledgements

The authors would like to thank the author and co-authors of the Peruvian case studies, and all of our colleagues in the various Oxfam affiliates who gave their time and willingly shared their knowledge, experience and advice to enable this book to be produced. We would also like to thank the many people working with CSOs in Sri Lanka, India and Peru that were involved in these campaigns, who also gave generously their time and shared their experiences and insights.

We thank the Economic and Social Research Council (ESRC) in the United Kingdom for providing the funding that enabled us to undertake the work on which this book is based. The ESRC is a research and training institute that addresses economic and social concerns, and aims to provide high-quality research on issues of importance to business, the public sector and government. In 2006 and 2007 it provided funding to enable each of the authors separately to undertake a Practitioner Fellowship at a UK institution, as part of the ESRC's Non-Governmental Public Action Programme. Martin Scurrah thanks the International NGO Training and Research Centre (INTRAC) and the Department of International Development at Oxford University for providing institutional affiliation and the Pratt-Boyden family for their hospitality. Jeffrey Atkinson would like to thank the Institute for Commonwealth Studies at the University of London for hosting him in 2007 to undertake his Practitioner Fellowship.

The La Oroya and Camisea case studies in Chapters 7 and 8 were undertaken with support provided by the Ford Foundation to Oxfam America and the Common Property Institute (*Instituto del Bien Común*) through the project, 'Anticipating the Challenges for Indigenous Peoples in the New Millennium' (*Avizorando los Retos de los Pueblos Indígenas en el Nuevo Milenio*), donation No. 1030–1479. Rosa Pizarro's participation was made possible by support from Oxfam America. An earlier Spanish language version of Chapter 8 was translated into English by Barbara Fraser.

Jeffrey Atkinson
Melbourne, Australia

Martin Scurrah
Lima, Peru

December 2008

Explanation of Terms Used

North and South: 'The South' is a shorthand term used to refer collectively to the poorer countries of Africa, Asia and Latin America. It is an alternative to the term 'developing countries', which is more an aspirational than accurate description of many of these nations. The term is derived from the fact that the majority of these poorer countries are located in the Southern Hemisphere. Likewise, the more affluent industrialized or 'developed' countries of Europe, North America, etc are referred to collectively as 'the North' because they are predominantly in the Northern Hemisphere.

Civil society organization (CSO): Civil society organizations are organizations in which ordinary citizens come together to advance an interest or concern that they have in common, and about which they feel so strongly that they want to take collective action. They are formal and informal not-for-profit organizations, associations, networks and community groups, each with their own issue or area of concern. They include everything from labour unions and farmers' cooperatives, through women's groups, consumer associations and historic preservation groups, to professional or academic associations. They do not include government or business organizations.

Non-government organization (NGO): Non-government organizations are a sub-set of CSOs. They are more formally organized and constituted, usually self-governing, private, and not-for-profit. In this book the term is restricted to organizations that have an explicitly social justice agenda, whose primary concern is the improvement of the lives of the poor, the promotion of human rights, or environmental protection. Examples include environmental groups such as Friends of the Earth, aid and welfare organizations such as Oxfam or the Salvation Army, human rights organizations like Amnesty International, etc. NGOs provide services and/or undertake advocacy to promote particular causes or to bring about particular changes. They are usually governed by a board of trustees rather than by the elected representatives of a constituency, and typically receive a significant proportion of their income from voluntary donations. All NGOs are CSOs, but not all CSOs are NGOs. Representative groups such as labour unions or farmers' associations that are the elected representatives of their constituencies would not normally be classed as NGOs. It is this issue of representation that differentiates them. Organizations of local people who have come together because of a shared problem or grievance are also CSOs but not NGOs.

International Non-Government Organizations (INGOs): These are NGOs that are based in one country but have most of their operations in other countries. It refers particularly to NGOs based in the North whose primary concern is the situation in the countries of the South. Thus, for example, the environment organization Groundwork UK is a national NGO, whereas Friends of the Earth International is an INGO.

Non-state actors: A very general term that includes all organizations apart from government. It is broader than CSO in that it includes business and industry organizations.

Transnational advocacy networks: A group of cooperating NGOs and other civil society organizations that simultaneously pursue advocacy activities in different political arenas in a joint effort to challenge the *status quo* in the interests of greater equity, sustainability or respect for human rights.

Political arenas: Spaces in which political decisions are made. Most are geographic, for example, a particular country, but they can also be institutionally bound, for example, a particular government or the negotiating space within an institution such as the World Trade Organization.

Advocacy versus popular campaigning: The difference between these two is that popular campaigning involves large numbers of people, anyone with an interest or concern about a particular issue, whereas advocacy is generally done by those with specialized knowledge and access to decision makers. For example, an environment group is involved in popular campaigning when it organizes a street demonstration, or urges large numbers of its supporters to write letters to the government or a company. It is undertaking advocacy when official representatives of the organization sit down across the negotiating table with government or company representatives to argue a case or negotiate a deal. 'Advocacy' has a similar meaning to 'lobbying' except that the latter generally refers to efforts to influence governments or inter-governmental bodies, whereas advocacy is more general and includes efforts to influence a company or other organization or group of people. The term 'campaign' is used for the totality of these activities. Thus a campaign will generally involve a variety of activities including popular campaigning, advocacy, media work, etc.

List of Abbreviations

ACC	Acción Ciudadana Camisea (Camisea Citizen Action)
ADA	Asociación de Delegados Ambientales (Association of Environmental Delegates)
AIDA	Asociación Interamericana de Defensa Ambiental (Interamerican Association for Environmental Defense)
AIDESEP	Asociación Interétnica para el Desarrollo de la Selva Peruana (Interethnic Association for the Development of the Peruvian Jungle)
ALaRM	Apparel-industry Labour Rights Movement, Sri Lanka
ANP	Natural Protected Areas
BOI	Board of Investment
CAF	Corporación Andina de Fomento (Andean Development Corporation)
CAOI	Coordinadora Andina de Organizaciones Indígenas (Coordinator of Andean Indigenous Organizations)
CCC	Clean Clothes Campaign
CCD	Covenant Centre for Development
CDES	Centro de Derechos Económicos y Sociales (Center for Economic and Social Rights)
CEAS	Comisión Episcopal de Acción Social (Bishop's Social Action Commission)
CECOEDECON	Center for Community Economics and Development Consultants Society
CECONAMA	Central de Comunidades Nativas Machiguengas (Machiguenga Indigenous Communities Federation)
CEDHA	Centro de Derechos Humanos y el Ambiente (Center for Human Rights and the Environment)
CEDIA	Centro de Desarrollo para el Indígena Amazónico (Center for the Development of the Amazonian Indigenous)
CENTAD	Centre for Trade and Development, New Delhi, India

CI	Conservation International
CIDH	Comisión Interamericana de Derechos Humanos (Interamerican Human Rights Commission)
CIEL	Center for International Environmental Law, Washington, DC
COICA	Coordinadora de Organizaciones Indígenas de la Cuenca Amazónica (Coordinator of Indigenous Organizations of the Amazon Basin)
COMARU	Consejo Machiguenga del Río Urubamba (Machiguenga Council of the Urubamba River)
CONACAMI	Confederación de Comunidades del Perú Afectadas por la Minería (Confederation of Communities Affected by Mining in Peru))
CONAIE	Confederación de las Nacionalidades Indígenas del Ecuador (Confederation of Indigenous Nations of Ecuador)
CONAM	Consejo Nacional del Ambiente (National Environmental Council)
CONFENIAE	Confederación Nacional Indígena de la Amazonía Ecuatoriana (National Indigenous Confederation of the Ecuadorean Amazon)
CSO	Civil society organization
CUTS	Consumer Union & Trust Society
DIGESA	Dirección General de Salud Ambiental (Ministry of Health's Office of Environmental Health)
DGAA	Dirección General de Asuntos Ambientales (Office of Environmental Affairs)
DRP	Doe Run Perú
DRR	Doe Run Resources
ECA	Export Credit Agency
ECO-ANDES	Peruvian environmental and development NGO
EIA	Estudio de Impacto Ambiental (Environmental Impact Assessment)
EPZ	Export Processing Zones
ESAN	Escuela de Administración de Negocios para Graduados (Graduate School of Business Administration)
ESIR	Environmental and Social Impact Report
ESRC	Economic and Social Research Council
E-Tech	Environmental Technology International
EU	European Union

Ex-Im Bank	Export-Import Bank
FECONAYY	Federación de Comunidades Nativas Yine Yane (Yine Yane Indigenous Communities Federation)
FID	Final Investment Decision
FIPSE	Federación Interétnica del Pueblo Shuar del Ecuador (Shuar People's Interethnic Federation of Ecuador)
FoE	Friends of the Earth
FoEI	Friends of the Earth International
FTZWU	Free Trade Zone Workers Union
GTCI	Grupo Técnico de Coordinación Interinstitucional (Inter-institutional Technical Coordination Group)
G-20	Group of 20 developing countries in the WTO
GUF	Global Union Federations
GVE	Global Villages Engineers
HIPC	Highly Indebted Poor Countries
HRO	Human rights organization
IBFAN	International Baby Food Action Network
ICBL	International Campaign to Ban Landmines
ICFTU	International Confederation of Free Trade Unions
IDB	Inter-American Development Bank
IFC	International Finance Corporation
IOC	International Olympic Committee
ILO	International Labour Organization
IMF	International Monetary Fund
INGO	International non-government organization
IRN	International Rivers Network
ISO	International Organization for Standardization
JAAF	Joint Apparel Associations Forum
LNG	Liquid Natural Gas
MEM	Ministerio de Energía y Minas (Ministry of Energy and Mines)
MFA	Multi-Fibre Agreement
MINEM	Ministerio de Energía y Minas (Ministry of Energy and Mines)
MINSA	Ministerio de Salud (Ministry of Health)
MOSAO	Movimiento por la Salud de La Oroya (Movement for the Health of La Oroya)
MTF	Make Trade Fair
NGO	Non-government organization
NOVIB	Oxfam Novib (Oxfam in the Netherlands)
OA	Oxfam America

OECD	Organization for Economic Cooperation and Development
OI	Oxfam International
OPIC	Overseas Private Investment Corporation
OSINERG	Organismo Supervisor de la Inversión en Energía (Energy Investment Supervisor)
OSINERGMIN	Organismo Supervisor de la Inversión en Energía y Minería (Energy and Mining Investment Supervisor)
PAMA	Programa de Adecuación y Manejo Ambiental (Environmental management and adjustment programs)
PSI	Public Service International
RST	Regional Strategic Team
SALT	South Asia Labour and Trade
SNMPE	Sociedad Nacional de Minería, Petróleo y Electricidad (National Mining, Petroleum and Energy Society)
SPDA	Sociedad Peruana de Derecho Ambiental (Peruvian Environmental Law Society)
STAR	South Asia Trade and Agriculture group
TGP	Transportadoras de Gas del Peru (Techint)
TNC	The Nature Conservancy
UK	United Kingdom of Great Britain and Northern Ireland
UN	United Nations
UNES	Unión para el Desarrollo Sustentable de La Oroya (Consortium for the Sustainable Development of La Oroya)
UNICEF	United Nations Children's Fund
US, USA	United States of America
VANI	Voluntary Action Network of India
WHO	World Health Organization, an agency of the United Nations
WTO	World Trade Organization
WWF	World Wide Fund for Nature, formerly World Wildlife Fund
YUVA	Youth for Unity and Voluntary Action
YWCA	Young Women's Christian Association

1
Types and Tactics

In December 1997, a landmark ceremony took place in the Canadian capital Ottawa, in which 122 governments signed a treaty banning the use, stockpiling, production, and transfer of landmines. This was the culmination of 20 years of campaigning by non-government organizations and others in many countries to have these weapons banned. Hundreds of thousands of landmines had been planted and forgotten by combatants in various conflicts, past and present, and long after the conflict had finished they continued to kill innocent civilians, often children, who stumbled across them in fields.

The campaign began around 1980 when a group of 76 governments agreed on a protocol to limit the use of anti-personnel mines. But the protocol was not particularly effective, and landmines continued to kill and maim. Then civil society organizations took the lead in pushing for an international ban, despite the vehement objections of the world's major military powers. Several civil society organizations – Handicap International (France), Human Rights Watch (US), Medico International (Germany), Mines Awareness Group (UK), Physicians for Human Rights (US), and Vietnam Veterans of America Foundation (US) – joined together in 1992 to form the International Campaign to Ban Landmines (ICBL). Throughout the 1990s, they campaigned and, as a result, public support grew steadily. By 1999 the ICBL had over a thousand non-government organizations (NGOs) in its network spread over more than 60 countries, all of them connected by email, faxes, and occasional conferences, and all of them campaigning vigorously in their own countries for public and government support.[1]

In the meantime the Canadian Government, frustrated by lack of movement at an inter-governmental level and working with the NGO campaigners, convened a meeting in Ottawa in October 1996 to try to revive the process. In the event, over 75 governments attended, but some of the more important players, the United States, China, Russia, the UK, and Japan, were not among them. However the NGOs and sympathetic middle-power governments persisted. Finally in December 1997 their efforts were rewarded when the Convention on the Prohibition of the Use, Stockpiling, Production, and Transfer of Anti-personnel Mines and on their Destruction was finally signed, setting a limit of four years for the destruction of the stockpiles of anti-personnel mines and ten years to clear anti-personnel mines from the signing states' territories. It was a remarkable victory. Civil society organizations, working with medium-sized nations, had been able to bring a major international treaty into effect, without the support of the superpowers.

The last few decades have seen a remarkable growth in this type of activity – civil society organizations and networks challenging and influencing the policies and practices of governments, international institutions and even corporations. Some observers have maintained that this represents a whole new dynamic in national and international politics, a third force matching the power and influence of governments and business. But as these civil society organizations and networks have grown more numerous and prominent, and more effective in exerting influence, a reaction has also grown, an increasing political and media debate about their legitimacy and what role they can or should play in society.

Civil society organizations and the South

The term 'civil society organizations' is used to describe any type of organizations, other than government or business, in which ordinary citizens come together to advance an interest or concern that they have in common, and about which they feel so strongly that they want to take collective action. They are formal and informal not-for-profit organizations, associations, networks and groups, each with its own issue or area of concern. The more formally organized and constituted ones, usually referred to as Non-Government Organizations (NGOs), often dominate the conversation about civil society, but in fact that are just part of a larger picture, a sub-set of the more general term 'civil society organizations' (CSOs). This book is particularly concerned with CSOs and NGOs that have an explicitly social justice agenda, whose primary concern is to improve the situation of the poor and oppressed, to fight for the recognition of basic human rights, or to preserve the natural environment for those who depend on it, including future generations. This type of concern naturally leads these organizations to a focus on the so-called 'developing countries' of Africa, Asia and Latin America for it is there that those problems are most acutely felt. (As many of these countries are not in fact 'developing' economically, a better collective term for referring to them is 'the South', which arises from the fact that they are predominantly in the southern hemisphere).

Environmental organizations, for example, such as Greenpeace or Friends of the Earth, have naturally acquired an interest in what is happening in the countries of 'the South' because what happens to the environment there, for example to the Amazonian rainforests, affects us all. Environmental problems do not respect national boundaries. For most such organizations, this interest includes a concern for the people who live in the forests as well as the forests themselves, for people and social issues as well as for the natural environment. Many environment groups have a physical presence in the South. Friends of the Earth International (FoEI) for example, which began in the 1970s as a network of four organizations in Europe and North America, now has some 70 national member organizations spread over every continent including Africa, Asia and Latin America. The degree of interest or involvement in the situation in the global South varies however between member organizations of the network. FoE Germany for example focuses mainly on domestic issues, while FoE United Kingdom has a strong international emphasis. FoEs based in the South, such as WALHI (FoE Indonesia) or GroundWork (FoE South Africa), naturally tend to focus on domestic issues, which are by definition Southern.

Human rights organizations have always had a focus on the South, working to prevent arbitrary arrests, disappearances, torture, etc and supporting the victims of such abuses. An example would be the Zimbabwe Human Rights Association (ZimRights) based in the capital Harare, which amongst other things, lobbies the Zimbabwe Government 'to commit itself to good governance through ratifying important international human rights instruments, and to rededicate itself to its commitment to observe, protect and respect human rights and dignity of the individual through constantly reminding it of its international obligations'. This kind of work is difficult and dangerous and those undertaking it often end up as victims themselves. Support at an international level can be essential in such circumstances. The organization most prominent in this regard is Amnesty International, whose 2.2 million members and supporters in 150 countries exert influence on governments, political bodies, companies and inter-governmental groups by mobilizing public pressure through mass demonstrations, vigils, and direct lobbying as well as online and offline campaigning.[2] It is a centralized federation of some 50 national member organizations or 'sections' with an international secretariat in London. During the last decade there has been a strong growth of Southern members, who now comprise about half the sections.

Because supply chains in many industries are now organized on an international scale, with production concentrated in the cheap-labour countries of the South, labour unions have also had to become international in their perspective and transnational in their advocacy. In the South, unions are often struggling to survive in the face of repression from hostile governments. In the more industrialized countries of Europe and North America ('the North') they face other challenges, including falling membership, but are still well organized and relatively strong. When the unions speak, they do so with the considerable authority that comes from their membership. And unlike most of the other civil society groups mentioned here, they do so as representatives, as the legitimate voice of workers for whom they have been elected (in most cases) to speak. There is currently a regrouping of unions occurring internationally in the form of stronger global alliances of national unions organized by sector. For example the unions that represent public sector workers have come together to form a global federation, Public Service International (PSI), which now has 650 member unions in 160 countries, North and South, and represents more than 20 million workers in that sector. The International Textile, Garment and Leather Workers Federation brings together unions in 110 countries who represent workers in those industries. Among its aims are to 'undertake solidarity action in support of unions in the sector whose trade union rights are being denied' and to 'lobby inter-governmental organizations and other relevant institutions to ensure that the interests of workers in the sectors are taken into account in decisions made at international level'. Such Global Union Federations (GUFs) have existed for a long time but their roles and influence have changed significantly in recent years in response to the globalization of production.

As the global search for natural resources leads mining, oil and gas, timber and other companies into the more remote regions of the South, they have begun to compete for the lands and natural resources of indigenous peoples hitherto protected from such impacts by their isolated geographical locations. The resulting conflicts between national and multinational companies on the one hand and indigenous peoples on the other has resulted in the creation of indigenous peoples' organizations, particularly in Latin America. These are ethnic and regional civil society organizations, national federations and increasingly international organizations, such as COICA (Coordinator of Indigenous Organizations of the Amazon Basin) that unites national federations from nine countries in a common effort to defend their territories and cultures. Its Andean highlands equivalent, CAOI (Coordinator of Andean Indigenous Organizations), brings together more than 400 indigenous groups with the aim of defending their rights, fighting for the survival of their culture, and enabling them to exchange experiences in their quests for solutions to their various problems. They have accomplished such things as allowing indigenous peoples to be educated in their native languages, and establishing an Amazon Indigenous University. Similar multinational indigenous organizations, such as the Inuit Circumpolar Council, which represents approximately 160,000 Inuit living in Alaska, Canada, Greenland and Russia, have emerged in the North. Just as trade unions in their time organized locally, nationally and internationally in defence of their members against the exploitation of their labour, today we see a similar effort by indigenous peoples in both the North and the South to defend themselves against the dispossession of their land and natural resources and the erosion of their cultures.

Throughout Africa, Asia and Latin America there are large numbers of NGOs dedicated to economic development, to reducing chronic poverty and improving the economic and social situation of the poor in their country. They vary enormously from small groups of a few dedicated individuals working in their local area to large organizations like the Grameen Bank in Bangladesh, whose operations are on the scale of a large corporation. Because they work in countries where funds are scarce, most of these development NGOs in Southern countries depend for their funding on donor organizations in the North. In addition to their direct development work, many undertake advocacy in their local area of operation in order to change policies, practices or attitudes that impinge negatively on what they are trying to achieve. For example an NGO in southern Africa working to assist people affected by the HIV/AIDS epidemic might also undertake a campaign to change the attitude of people towards those who are HIV-positive, or policies that discriminate against them, or might lobby the government to provide better health services. In some cases these local organizations will link with national level bodies working on the same issues, who in turn may be linked to international networks engaged in transnational advocacy.

Northern development NGOs, such as Oxfam, Save the Children or World Vision, have traditionally seen their role as supporting the grassroots development work of Southern NGOs by assisting financially and in other ways projects that address people's basic needs and rights to water, food, shelter, a livelihood, etc. They have also traditionally provided emergency food, water, health care and other assistance to the victims of famines, floods, tsunamis and other natural and man-made disasters. Although headquartered in the North, where their funding base is, these organizations will usually have offices in the Southern countries where their development assistance or relief programmes are located, reporting to the head office in the North. But the realization that such development and humanitarian relief work by itself was never going to bring about lasting improvements if they did not at the same time tackle the structures that created and perpetuated poverty, injustice and the denial of basic rights, led them several decades ago to take on advocacy as well. British academic Alan Hudson describes it thus:

> In the early 1990s policy-makers in leading Northern NGOs began to acknowledge that despite the fact that more public money than ever before was channelled through NGOs, their impact on the ground was still temporary, small-scale and subject to fluctuations of policies, prices, interest rates and exchange rates at an international level. In response to this, leading NGOs began to consider a range of strategies of 'scaling up' in order to make more of a difference. Over the course of the 1990s, NGO thinking and increasingly practice, swung behind efforts to develop more effective forms of trans-national lobbying and advocacy.[3]

For some years, debates raged within these NGOs about whether this was a wise thing to do. Would it be seen as too political by their traditional donors and hence undermine their financial viability? Was advocacy and campaigning a distraction from their 'core business' of meeting people's immediate basic needs? However by the early 1990s there was a growing sense that the dichotomy between these two – meeting basic needs and working for systemic change – was a false one, and that sustainable poverty reduction required a range of simultaneous approaches and strategies in different arenas, from the household and local community right through to corporate boardrooms and international forums. It is now generally accepted by development NGOs in the North and the South that advocacy to change the policies and practices of governments, corporations and institutions that negatively impact on development should be part of their work – but that this advocacy work should draw on their traditional work of improving the lives of those living in poverty and contribute to its objectives. There has been a tendency in recent years for like-minded development NGOs to come together, as the labour unions have done, into international federations. Oxfam International is one example of this, a confederation of 13 national level organizations that carry the Oxfam name. Other development NGOs, such as CARE, Save the Children, World Vision, Plan International and Medecins Sans Frontieres have also formed international networks of national level agencies, with varying degrees of centralization and programme harmonization.

As well as these more visible NGOs, there are others in both the affluent industrialized North and the 'developing' South that do not have development assistance programmes but instead focus entirely on research and advocacy. These policy and advocacy NGOs include for example the World Development Movement in the UK, which says it aims to tackle the underlying causes of poverty by 'lobbying decision makers to change the policies that keep people poor'. It researches and promotes positive alternatives, and seeks to mobilize consumers, shareholders and governments to hold multinational companies accountable, and to reform institutions such as the World Trade Organization. Amongst other things, it won a High Court victory in the UK to stop the British aid budget from being used to support the arms trade. Much of its work is done in partnership with other organizations in the UK and around the world.[4]

An example in the US would be the Bank Information Centre, a Washington DC-based NGO whose aim is to influence the World Bank and other international financial institutions to ensure that the projects and programmes that they fund in the South promote social and economic justice and ecological sustainability. Its core goal is to enhance the ability of local communities and civil society organizations in project and programme affected areas to protect their rights and influence development strategies, projects, and policies. It undertakes and supports transnational advocacy using three major strategies: information services and capacity building; project and policy monitoring; and policy reform of the Multilateral Development Banks. It is a principal source of information for affected communities and their supporters working to address the negative impacts of projects and programmes.

There are also several such policy and advocacy NGOs in the South – for example, the Third World Network, based in Malaysia, which describes itself as 'an independent non-profit international network of organizations and individuals involved in issues relating to development, the Third World and North-South issues. Its objectives are to conduct research on economic, social and environmental issues pertaining to the South; to publish books and magazines; to organize and participate in seminars; and to provide a platform representing broadly Southern interests and perspectives at international fora such as the UN conferences and processes'.[5] In neighbouring Thailand, there is a similar but more radical organization, Focus on the Global South, which 'combines policy research, advocacy, activism and grassroots capacity building in order to generate critical analysis and encourage debates on national and international policies related to corporate-led globalisation, neo-liberalism and militarisation'. Its central aim is deglobalization, 'the transformation of the global economy from one centred around the needs of transnational corporations, to one that focuses on the needs of people, communities and nations and in which the capacities of local and national economies are strengthened'.[6]

Organizations such as Third World Network, Focus on the Global South and COICA have an important role to play in that they provide voices from the South, enabling those in the South to speak for themselves rather than have Northern organizations speak for them. For no matter how well intentioned the latter are, they are speaking at one extra step removed from those about whom they speak, and what they say will inevitably be affected or filtered by their own Northern priorities and agendas. But it is their Northern voice that is most likely to be heard in the corridors of power. A classic example of this were the initial campaigns to stop the destruction of the Amazonian rainforests, an issue that was vigorously taken up by US environmental groups who tended to portray it in terms of rainforest and species conservation, with little mention of the people who depend on the Amazon's resources for their livelihoods. In 1990 the Amazon Alliance was set up to counter this neglect of the human aspect by the groups that were having the most influence on Amazonian affairs. It is an alliance between COICA and environmental and indigenous rights organizations that aim to promote cooperation in the defence of both the rights of the indigenous peoples *and* the natural resources and biodiversity of the Amazon. It established an office in Washington DC, and has managed to persuade many (but not all) Northern NGOs to broaden their advocacy message.

Organizational structures

Civil society organizations come in all shapes and sizes, with different structures, different issues, different political philosophies and ideologies, different influencing strategies, priorities and tactics. Some are centralized hierarchical structures while others are just loose informal networks. Some are sophisticated lobbyists in national and international arenas, while others focus on service delivery, with advocacy and influencing a secondary activity confined to their local area. Some are quiet and reformist, while others are loud and deliberately confrontational. Classifying them into meaningful groupings is quite difficult. But one of the more useful attempts at doing this is that by analyst John Clark who classifies them according to the degree of centralization in their organizational structures.[7] He distinguishes five basic types:

Centralized organizations: organizations with a global headquarters or secretariat, and national offices in other countries, which have some autonomy at the local level – for example the Catholic Church, Greenpeace, and Human Rights Watch.

Federations: networks made up of national members with a common name and charter but with a degree of national self-determination. They typically have strong global boards, comprising members' delegates, that make binding decisions, and their secretariats are largely responsible for implementation. Examples include Amnesty International, the Anglican Church, and World Wide Fund for Nature.

Confederations: looser structures in which the members are autonomous but agree to a set of common ground rules and work together on specific activities in which there is mutual advantage. Examples are Public Service International, Oxfam International (see Chapter 3), and Friends of the Earth International.

Informal networks: fluid networks that come together on a self-selecting basis. Any group having broadly similar aims can join, but membership bestows few advantages and demands few responsibilities. Examples include the International Campaign to Ban Landmines, International Baby Food Action Network (IBFAN) and Jubilee 2000. Another example is Social Watch, a network of mainly Southern development, human rights, labour, women's, etc groups that came together during preparations for the World Summit on Social Development in Copenhagen in 1995. It raises issues in international forums, and monitors the implementation of major commitments made by governments and international agencies at UN summits by publishing an annual Social Watch Report.

Social movements: These are not true organizations but amorphous and fluid groupings of activists, civil society organizations and supporters in which the bonds are common grievances or convictions. They connect people and organizations through communities of interest around shared concerns and often vaguely defined alternative visions of society, rather than through organizational structures. They may be national in character, but are often international, such as the climate change movement, or protest movements relating to globalization or the war in Iraq.

An interesting form that has emerged in recent years is the mass global protest movement.[8] These are loose global networks that can bring out huge numbers of people to demonstrate around international events, such as at a meeting of the World Trade Organization, or the day of protest against the war in Iraq that brought an estimated 16 million people out onto the streets of cities around the world on 15 February 2003. They are polycentric, loosely connected, apparently leaderless networks that communicate largely through email lists and a network of websites, with occasional face-to-face organizing and planning meeting at events such as the World Social Forum. They have amorphous identities and encompass individuals and groups with a diverse range of issues, positions and goals, which while generally of a radical anti-capitalist nature can range from anarchist to animal rights. They often seem to be purposely vague and all-embracing in terms of political position in order to involve as many people as possible, and to enable people with a diverse range of positions to take part in large political actions. In a sense it is their way of organizing that gives them their identity rather than the issues for which they stand – spontaneous, all-embracing and emphasizing individual action. They reach large numbers of people, especially young people who would not readily identify with established groups, but who feel strongly about some cause and want to act. They use the Internet and cyberspace as organizing spaces for people with a vaguely defined common ideological position to share information, ideas, and news of forthcoming events.

There are some tensions between this type of movement and the more conventionally structured NGOs and their advocacy networks that run single-issue, centrally organized campaigns aimed at obtaining policy and practice changes from institutional targets. The mass protest movements tend to see the latter as at best ineffective and at worst as agents of capitalism legitimizing the institutions that are causing the problems they are trying to solve. NGOs on the other hand will often want to distance themselves from the 'chaos and carnage' of mass demonstrations, but at the same time will be aware that the media attention that they generate is elevating their cause to a level of attention that they themselves could never achieve.

The advantage of the mass protest movements, apart from being able to bring out large numbers of people at key moments, is that they provide a way for those who are otherwise excluded from political decision making to express their views. They are an answer to the problem of political exclusion. On the other hand it is not clear whether they have enough organizational coherence to be sustainable, or whether their message is too diverse and vague to be politically effective. They have not been able to gain credibility in the eyes of the media, which tends to only highlight violence by demonstrators, nor to be taken seriously by decision makers.

Another way of classifying civil society organizations, according to Clark, is by the degree to which they help citizens to achieve a voice for themselves, or speak on behalf of citizens.[9] He combines two variables – the degree of organizational decentralization, and the degree to which decision making lies with volunteers and members (via elected committees of representatives) or with professional staff in international secretariats – and comes up with four broad categories of organization:

1. strongly member-controlled, with decisions taken largely locally (such as trade unions or international peasants' movements);
2. strongly member-controlled, but major decisions largely reached internationally (such as Amnesty International or some of the new social movements);
3. secretariat-driven, with volunteers less powerful, and decisions taken largely at local levels (such as most faith-based organizations and consumers' associations);
4. secretariat-driven, with volunteers less powerful, and decisions largely reached globally (such as Greenpeace, Oxfam, or Third World Network).

Each type has its advantages; the former are more representative and democratic, while the latter usually have faster, clearer decision-making processes and appear more professional, because they do not feel obliged to sound out their members on policy positions and strategies to be adopted, and can swiftly adapt as circumstances change, without being hampered by cumbersome consultation processes.

These various types of organization may come together on occasions to form advocacy alliances or networks, bringing their different attitudes, philosophies, structures and skills to what is hopefully a coordinated effort to achieve a common goal. The power relationship, information flows, levels of autonomy etc within such an advocacy network will depend to a significant degree on the type of network structure that is adopted. Jennifer Chapman of the London-based New Economics Foundation identifies three basic types of network structures, which she calls pyramids, wheels and webs.[10] 'Pyramids' have a coordinating secretariat that organizes and disseminates information centrally to the network during the campaign. 'Wheels' have one (or perhaps several) focal point or hub for decision making and information exchange but information also flows directly from member to member (around the rim, so to speak). 'Webs' have no focal points, and so information flows to and from all members in an unstructured way, as for example in a social movement. The advantages and disadvantages of these different forms of network structures are analogous to those of the different organizational structures described above by Clark. For example, the advantage of the 'pyramid', according to Chapman, is that it is dynamic, quick to act, able to speak for its many member organizations, and hence better able to speak to high-level decision makers. Its disadvantages are that members may feel a loss of individual identity, and strengthening of grassroots CSOs may be neglected as the network speaks for people instead of assisting them to speak for themselves. The 'wheel' type of network structure on the other hand leaves greater independence at the grassroots level and has better information exchange, but it can be slow to change and less able to show a united front or common position. 'Webs' are the best of the three types in terms of information flows and exchange, but can be slow to act and ineffective in terms of policy change because they are so disunited.

Some notable campaigns

Campaigns by civil society organizations and networks for social change have been around for centuries. Early examples include the temperance movement and the fight for women's suffrage in the nineteenth century. Some of these even had a North-South character, such as the movement in the eighteenth and nineteenth centuries to abolish slavery. But the type of international campaign that depends on media publicity and rapid communication is a more recent phenomenon, going back decades rather than centuries. There have been countless such campaigns on different issues, with different strategies and different degrees of success. Described below are a few that have become more well known. They are not necessarily typical but they do illustrate the approaches and tactics that are discussed in this book.

One of the earliest of these more modern North-South advocacy campaigns was that on the *marketing of infant formula*. This challenged the Nestlé corporation, one of the world's largest food corporations, over its aggressive marketing of breast-milk substitutes to mothers in poor countries who could not afford the formula powder, did not have access to clean water to mix it with, and often did not understand the importance of sterilization. As a result, it was claimed, millions of babies in poor countries, who could have been saved if they had been fed at the breast, died from malnutrition or disease. The issue was first brought to public attention in 1973 by the magazine New Internationalist, and in 1974 the British NGO War on Want published a booklet titled 'The Baby Killer'. In Switzerland, the home of Nestlé, the Third World Action Group translated this into German with the title 'Nestlé Kills Babies'. This outraged the Nestlé corporation, which sued the Group for defamation and libel and won. But in the process, Nestlé had inadvertently highlighted the issue to its own detriment. The judge fined the Group a token amount, and commented that Nestlé 'must modify its publicity methods fundamentally'. The widespread publicity led to the launch in 1977 of a boycott of Nestlé products in the US, which soon spread to Europe, Australia, Canada, and elsewhere.

In 1979, the World Health Organization (WHO) and United Nations Children's Fund (UNICEF) hosted an international meeting which called for the development of an international code on the ethical marketing of infant formula, as well as action on other fronts to improve infant and young child feeding practices. Six of the campaigning groups who were at this meeting formed a coalition, the International Baby Food Action Network (IBFAN), which still operates today. In 1981, pressure from the campaign contributed to the World Health Assembly of the WHO adopting an 'International Code of Marketing of Breastmilk Substitutes'. This Code bans the promotion of breast-milk substitutes and restricts the advising of parents to health workers. It limits manufacturing companies to providing scientific and factual information, rather than promotional material, to health workers and sets out labelling requirements.

In 1984, the IBFAN campaign achieved a major victory when it obtained from Nestlé a commitment to major changes in its promotional practices. The company agreed to implement the WHO Code, and the boycott was officially suspended. However in 1989 IBFAN alleged that baby-milk companies were still flooding health facilities in the South with free and low-cost supplies, and the boycott was relaunched. It still continues, coordinated by the International Nestlé Boycott Committee based in the UK. In Europe, many universities, colleges and schools have banned the sale of Nestlé products from their shops and vending machines, and in the UK hundreds of businesses, faith groups, health groups, consumer groups, local authorities, trade unions, education groups, politicians, and celebrities support the boycott. Company practices continue to be monitored by IBFAN, which now consists of more than 200 groups in over 100 countries.

This campaign was significant in that it was one of the first to be directed at a corporation, and to use consumer pressure in the North to bring about positive changes in the South. It gained widespread publicity and support because there was a clear issue that the average person in the street could easily understand, a clearly identified 'villain' or 'villains', and a clear solution to be advocated for, three key elements that assist any advocacy campaign.

Equally successful was the campaign to ban landmines mentioned above. A remarkable aspect of that campaign was the degree to which civil society and state actors worker together. As Canadian Foreign Minister Lloyd Axworthy said, the Ottawa process worked 'because new synergies were created. This was not simply a question of consulting NGOs or seeking their views. We have moved well beyond that. What I am talking about is a full working process between governments and civil groups'.[11] In October 1997 the International Campaign to Ban Landmines was awarded the Nobel Peace Prize, 'as much for how it carried out its mission as for what it accomplished'.[12] The prize committee expressed its hope that the campaign, with its working partnership between governments and civil society, would serve as a model in the future. The publicity that resulted from the Nobel Peace Prize, and from the death of Princess Diana who was an active and high profile supporter, has been used by the campaign to build public support. However, while an impressive number of nations have now signed the Convention, the US, China and Russia have not (although they have agreed to cooperate with it on de-mining and victim assistance) and landmines continue to be planted and innocent victims to be killed and maimed.

Once the agreement was signed, public support and funding for the campaign diminished somewhat, in the mistaken belief that the problem was now largely solved. As can often happen in campaigns that focus on obtaining a particular agreement or legislative change, the less dramatic aspect of ensuring that the agreement is implemented was neglected, which meant that the success of obtaining the agreement may not be translated into gains for mine-affected people. As analyst Michael Edwards reminded NGOs in a 1999 article: 'social change is a long haul, not a sprint, and anyone who is not prepared to run the marathon is in the wrong business'.[13] The infant formula campaign for example obtained agreement to its Code in 1981 but is still fighting for its proper implementation today, nearly 30 years later.

Once again this campaign on landmines had the three key elements that assist popularity and success – a clear and easily understood issue, a clear 'villain' (the landmines themselves) and a clear solution or aim (the international ban). A somewhat similar campaign, to ban the sale of small arms, has not been so lucky as it has had to contend with a less clear-cut issue, arising from the fact that the use of such weapons is seen as legitimate for security reasons in many circumstances and, unlike landmines, their ownership and use is culturally acceptable in many countries.

Another campaign that did not have a clear or easily understood issue but which has nevertheless been relatively successful is the Jubilee 2000 campaign to rid developing countries of the crippling burden of debt. Here was an issue that appeared to be complex and technical and did not have the advantage of the dramatic images of malnourished babies or limbless child victims of landmines, but which nevertheless was able to get its message across to the public and enlist widespread support. The issue was that many poor countries, unable to keep up payments on the massive debts they owed to Northern governments and banks, had got themselves into a vicious circle of ever-increasing debt. Resources that should have been spent on essential services, infrastructure and economic development were being allocated to debt repayment instead. Many had fallen into a situation of dependence on international financial institutions for financial assistance, which came with harsh conditions but did little to ease their debt burden.

The campaign, which took its name from the biblical idea of the Jubilee Year when people enslaved by debt are freed, lands are returned and communities are restored, called for a debt-free start to the new Millennium, including a cancellation of the unpayable debts of the world's poorest countries by the year 2000. In 1996, under pressure from the campaign, the World Bank and International Monetary Fund did in fact introduce an initiative to ease the burden of some countries. Called the Highly Indebted Poor Countries (HIPC) initiative it involved indebted countries agreeing to introduce economic reform in return for receiving some debt write-off. However, it did not provide anywhere near enough relief, and was a very slow process with a heavy price to pay for very little reward. It was a case of too little, too late.

A turning point in the campaign came at the meeting of the heads of the G8 nations in Birmingham, England in 1998, when more than 70,000 campaigners turned up and formed a human chain around the city centre, in a bid to urge world leaders at the G8 Summit to 'drop the debt'. Despite trying to keep campaigners at arm's length, the host of the meeting, British Prime Minister Tony Blair, found it necessary to break off from the official talks at one point to meet with the Jubilee 2000 organizers. While nothing particularly significant was achieved at the meeting, it did at least put debt onto the G8 agenda. A second turning point occurred when the rock star Bono of the group U2 became involved and publicly supported the campaign. In 2002, he travelled to Africa with the US Treasury Secretary Paul O'Neill, to tour some of the countries worst affected by debt and see at first-hand some of the problems it caused. The trip helped convince the US and other world leaders that debt cancellation could have a dramatically beneficial effect on millions of vulnerable people, and could be an effective first step towards the elimination of chronic poverty.

The campaign did not achieve its ultimate goal of a debt-free Millennium, but something over US$100 billion of debt has been cancelled for 20 or so countries. However hundreds of billions of dollars of debt still remain, and the campaign continues. Since 2000, the Jubilee debt campaign has continued to be a major force in the movement to cancel international debt, with chapters in a number of countries around the world working together to influence the governments of Northern nations as well as the World Bank and International Monetary Fund. In June 2008 for example, campaigners in Britain formed a giant white band around Parliament Square in central London to call on the British Government to cancel more debts, ahead of the G8 meeting in Japan the following week. Nearly 11,000 paper chain links saying 'Drop the Debt' in English and Japanese had been signed by people around the UK in the preceding weeks, as part of activities to mark ten years since the Birmingham G8 meeting.

Analysts who were themselves involved in the Jubilee 2000 campaign have identified what they felt were the key factors in its success:

– The expertise and sophistication of its critiques and policy alternatives, which generated confidence among the public and the media.

- The growing use of the Internet, which facilitated inexpensive, wider and more timely dissemination of information and interventions in the policy process.
- The effective popularizing of a complex issue, framed in moral terms. Most of the debt was contracted by non-elected governing elites who misspent the funds, making it immoral to require that debts be repaid at the expense of cutbacks in education and health care.
- Adroit use of the psychological effects of the Millennium, which placed greater public pressure on policy makers to act with a sense of urgency.
- The failure of creditors' own policies and programmes to reduce debt and poverty, which increased the acceptability of proposals for reform.
- Successful mobilizing of media attention and the use of prominent personalities in support of debt relief.
- Flexibility. By refusing to back specific formulations for debt relief, the campaign was able to use each new commitment from creditors as a basis for demanding that they go even further.[14]

They also identified as a challenge the fact that the Jubilee 2000 network reflected the same North-South imbalances that it criticizes in international economic policy, in terms of access to resources, information, and global decision making. The key actors in Jubilee 2000, whether in the South or the North, are still a small number of largely city-based NGOs and religious groups, many of whom lack strong links with grassroots constituencies. But in the end, radicals and reformists were able to work together, as the movement held back from trying to force a common position across the global coalition, and instead worked to use this diversity creatively without compromising goals.

The Jubilee debt campaign was unprecedented in terms of the number of people it involved. Its global petition gathered over 24 million signatures from 166 countries around the world (and created two new Guinness World Records in the process). It also had a significant impact on the way international institutions and governments thought about and responded to the debt crisis. In the late 1980s the idea of cancelling a country's debt was considered economic 'heresy', but by the late 1990s with a re-focus on poverty reduction, it was accepted as 'dogma', thanks in large part to the Jubilee 2000 campaign. The campaign had successfully introduced a new perspective, which is now widely accepted and has changed the terms of debate around national debt.

Civil society tactics

All of these campaigns had several important characteristics in common. They addressed political issues that were being largely ignored or opposed by governments at the time, which meant that growing popular concern could not be channelled through normal political means. They addressed issues that were international in scope and hence beyond the realm of any individual government. They created international networks and advocated simultaneously at different levels, local, national, and international. They involved defending the interests of the weak against those of the powerful. And they sought to arouse public support in order to influence the policies and practices of governments or corporations that were susceptible to public opinion.

Since they are not powerful in the normal sense, the civil society organizations and networks that run these advocacy campaigns must resort largely to persuasion and public pressure to bring about change. Clark distinguishes three broad approaches:

- Seeking to win the argument; showing that that something being done at present is wrong, or that there is a better approach that could be taken.
- Seeking to demonstrate that there are large numbers of people who demand or expect change.
- Insinuating or inflicting damage, either physical damage to property, or preventing activities, or damaging reputations through negative publicity.

He calls these 'the head, heart and fist schools of action'.[15] Academics Keck and Sikkink provide a different but perhaps more useful typology of tactics that civil society organizations use to persuade and pressure. These they call *information politics, symbolic politics, leverage politics* and *accountability politics*.[16] A single campaign may use several of these at the same time, as will be seen in the case studies given later in this book.

Information politics is the tactic of quickly and credibly generating politically useful information and moving it to where it will have the most impact. A classic example of this was the infant formula campaign, which used research reports from Southern countries that showed that aggressive promotion of infant formula was leading to a decline in breastfeeding and an increase in child mortality. This information was then repackaged and dramatized for use in the North in order to shame the companies into stopping their anti-breastfeeding promotions. It was the appearance of the Third World Action Group's booklet 'Nestlé Kills Babies' that caused Nestlé to respond in such a dramatic fashion. In situations like this, civil society organizations are acting as alternative sources of information that hopefully will influence decision makers, providing alternative points of view that would otherwise not be heard. But of course information can easily be ignored by those who do not want to hear it. It has to be presented in a way that demands attention, as the British and Swiss NGOs did in the case of the baby food booklets. Often, as in that case, the facts are expressed in stark terms with a clearly identified problem, culprit and solution. As Keck and Sikkink say:

> Activists interpret facts and testimony, usually framing issues simply, in terms of right and wrong, because their purpose is to persuade people and stimulate them to act. An effective frame must show that a given state of affairs is neither natural nor accidental, identify the responsible party or parties, and propose credible solutions. These aims require clear, powerful messages that appeal to shared principles, which often have more impact on state policy than advice of technical experts.

One technique often used by campaigners to get across a clear, powerful message is the 'killer fact', the simple one-liner that sums up the problem in a short, sharp and dramatic way. For example: '1.5 million infants die unnecessarily each year because they are not breastfed, while companies continue to promote artificial feeding that undermines breastfeeding'.[17] In its campaign on the rights of women workers in the garment industry, Oxfam used the line: 'Some of the world's most expensive clothes are made by some of the world's poorest women'.

Symbolic politics is the tactic of using symbols, actions or stories to make sense of a situation for an audience that is frequently far away. A good example is the use by indigenous people in the Americas of the 500th anniversary of the voyage of Columbus to the Americas in 1992. Another is the symbol of a chain used by the Jubilee 2000 campaign to represent the bond of debt that was constraining many developing countries. Chains featured prominently in their campaign materials, and in their public events such as the action at the G8 Summit in 1998.

Another example is the human story. In the case of the landmines campaign for example this might be a story of a particular child that stepped on a mine and lost a leg, and of how she now has to live. Such stories not only sum up and symbolize the problem in a simple and concrete way that anyone can understand, but they also give the problem a human face and allow the reader to empathize with a fellow human being who is suffering. Such stories are very useful for campaigners, and have to be actively sought out and accurately recorded. However in this process there is a risk that a certain amount of filtering and translating can take place. Campaign organizers in the North may identify what kinds of stories would be useful for the campaign, and approach their network colleagues in the South to find and record them. But because of socio-economic and cultural differences, language translation and the highlighting of certain aspects, there can be a large gap between the story's original telling and its retellings. Affected people in other words can lose control of their story. There is a serious obligation on the part of those who use such stories in their campaigning to do so in a way that does not distort the truth, or degrade the people concerned. This of course applies to visual images as well as the written word.

Leverage politics, as defined by Keck and Sikkink, involves calling upon powerful actors to affect a situation where weaker members of a network are unlikely to have influence. Keck and Sikkink identify two main types – material leverage and moral leverage.

Material leverage is a tactic often used with Southern governments. A campaign which has been unable to influence the government may call on its Northern allies within its networks to try to influence powerful Northern institutions that provide aid or loans or military assistance to that government. This is only possible when the providers of such assistance, which may be a Northern government or financial institution, attach social standards to it, typically human rights or environmental standards. This is why, for example, when a proposed free trade agreement between the United States and Peru was being debated in the US Congress, Peruvian civil society institutions formed an alliance with the trade union and environmental movements in the United States to persuade the Democratic Party, which controlled the Congress, to include in the agreement a series of conditions safeguarding environmental, labour and other standards. If subsequently the network members in the North can demonstrate to the satisfaction of the provider that the problem they are trying to tackle involves the recipient Southern government abusing their environmental, labour or other standards, then the threat of withdrawal of the aid, loans, trade preferences, etc is brought to bear on the Southern government.

In extreme cases where it can be demonstrated that the abuses are widespread, persistent and serious, such as those of the Mugabe government in Zimbabwe, stronger measures may be brought to bear, such as trade sanctions or the withdrawal of bilateral diplomatic relations.

This tactic is also used with companies, for example, those that employ workers in the South under poor conditions, manufacturing products for export. In this case those supporting the workers may call upon network allies in the North, where the products are marketed, to threaten boycotts of those products, if they can be identified, or to exert other forms of consumer pressure on the companies selling those products. The leverage in this case is a threat to the sales of the brand-name company and to its good reputation in the market, which hopefully will prompt it to put pressure on its supplier in the South to clean up any sweatshops and improve workers' conditions. In the 1990s the civil society activists in Indonesia and their Northern allies concerned about the Freeport copper mine in the Indonesian province of Irian Jaya, and the environmental damage and human rights abuses that were resulting from its operations, brought this to the attention of the US government agency that was proving political risk insurance for the mine. One of the conditions for the insurance provided by the Overseas Private Investment Corporation (OPIC) was that the project insured was not causing environmental damage. The accusations by the Indonesian activists and their Northern allies prompted OPIC to conduct its own investigation, which found that the mine 'created and continues to pose unreasonable or major environmental, health or safety hazards with respect to the rivers that are being impacted by the tailings, surrounding terrestrial ecosystem and the local inhabitants'.[18] As a result OPIC cancelled the company's political risk insurance – which unfortunately proved to be only a temporary win as the mine continued to operate more or less as before.

Moral leverage involves 'naming and shaming', and depends on the target valuing its reputation. A classic example was the baby food campaign where a company that projected an image of being a clean and caring supporter of mothers with young babies was called a 'baby killer'. As well as being offensive to the company it was also potentially very damaging commercially. The targets most sensitive to moral or reputational leverage are companies with a well-known brand name, whose reputation is worth money to them. But even a large mining company like Rio Tinto or BHP Billiton which does not sell products to the general public can be damaged by a bad reputation, for example, a bad environmental record, which can make mining leases more difficult to obtain, insurance more expensive, dedicated staff more difficult to recruit, and can undermine staff morale. The extent to which governments are also sensitive to this kind of leverage varies considerably. For some, being held up to international scrutiny as a government that violates its international obligations or does not live up to its own claims, will be enough to motivate a change of policy or behaviour. For others this will not work at all.

By using their transnational networks in this way to leverage more powerful institutions such as Northern aid donors or brand-name companies, weak groups in the South can gain influence far beyond their ability to influence their targets directly. They do this by creating a threat to something of value to the target – money, trade, prestige, good name etc. This is sometimes referred to as the 'boomerang strategy'. Civil society groups that are unable to influence a local target, be it a company or the government, will go around it to their allies in the North who are able to influence a powerful intermediary. And thus the influence and pressure returns to the local target from another direction and with more force.

In this process network relationships are key. For the members in the South the network provides access, leverage and information. For those in the North the linkages with the Southern members provides credibility and a mandate. As Mary Kaldor says of these transnational civic networks: 'They represent a kind of two-way street between Southern groups and individuals, or rather the groups and individuals who directly represent victims....with the so-called Northern solidaristic "outsiders". The former provide testimony, stories and information about their situation and they confer legitimacy on those who campaign on their behalf. The latter provide access to global institutions, funders or global media as well as "interpretations" more suited to the global context'.[19]

Accountability politics involves holding powerful actors to their previously stated policies or principles, or to the obligations involved in conventions they have signed. A government that for example has signed on to International Labour Organization conventions on the basic rights of workers can be accused of not fulfilling its obligations if those rights are being abused within its jurisdiction. An international financial institution that attaches social conditions to its loans can be held accountable if a project it has funded fails to meet those standards. A transnational company that has an internal code of practice, or commitments to industry-wide standards, can be held to account when it does not implement or meet those standards. For example,

IBFAN has for years used the fact that Nestlé and the other infant formula companies have publicly committed themselves to uphold the standards of the WHO Code. They apply pressure to the companies by monitoring and documenting breaches of the Code, and publicizing them. Likewise those involved in the anti-sweatshop campaign directed at the Nike sportswear company highlight the fact that the company has a code of practice for its suppliers whose standards are sometimes breached. Clearly such tactics are not always effective.

Occasionally the process can be taken beyond just 'naming and shaming' in this way by using an official complaints mechanism. In 2005 a group of NGOs were able to bring a complaint against a company that ran detention centres on behalf of the Australian Government for people who arrived in that country by boat, without visas and claiming refugee status. The company claimed that the way it treated the detainees under its control was 'guided by respect for the human rights and fundamental freedoms as laid out in the Universal Declaration of Human Rights'. The NGOs however maintained that holding people in detention without trial, and with no legal limit on the length of their detention, was a violation of their basic human rights and fundamental freedoms. Also keeping children who had committed no crime in detentions in these centres was a violation of the Rights of the Child. Fortunately respect for these fundamental rights forms part of the Organization for Economic Cooperation and Development (OECD) Guidelines on Multinational Enterprises, which the Australian Government had signed, and which have a formal complaints mechanism attached. The NGOs involved were therefore able to lodge a formal complaint with the Australian Government calling on it to take steps to remedy the situation in line with its commitments under the OECD Guidelines. As a result an official investigation was initiated in 2007, which found that the company was in fact in breach of its own standards and those of the Guidelines. This helped create pressure for the abolition of these centres, and of the mandatory detention of those who reached Australia's shores claiming refugee status.

Growth of civil society advocacy

The last few decades have seen a marked increase in the extent and scope of transnational advocacy by civil society organizations using some of these tactics. A reason for this commonly put forward in the literature is the emergence of global issues of popular concern that national governments cannot deal with effectively by themselves because of their cross-border global nature – nuclear testing, the drugs trade, third-world debt, the impact of economic globalization, and more recently climate change and international terrorism. In the absence of any 'global government' and with inter-governmental efforts being less than effective, people have turned to international non-government movements and networks instead. One has only to think of the level of organization, activity and impact of the non-government environmental movement, compared with that of government or inter-governmental environment organizations to see why this might be so. As civil action is seen to be effective, more causes turn to it as a way of bringing about change, and its scope and extent increases.

Connected to this, as either a cause or an effect, is the remarkable growth over recent decades in the number of non-government organizations with an international focus. The statistics of the Union of International Associations show that the number of international NGOs listed in their database has grown from a mere 2,795 in 1972 to 20,928 in 2005–2006.[20] This is a seven-fold increase in the last 30 years – or to put it another way, 86 per cent of the international NGOs operating in 2005–2006 have been formed in the last 30 years. Likewise in Southern countries there has been a related dramatic growth in the number of (mainly development oriented) NGOs. In Nepal, for example, the number of NGOs registered with the government grew from 220 in 1990 to 1,210 in 1993; in Tunisia, from 1,886 in 1988 to 5,186 just three years later. In 1996, the largest ever survey of the non-profit sector found over a million such groups in India, and 210,000 in Brazil.[21] It is the linking of these two groups of civil society organizations, in the North and in the South, that gives rise to transnational advocacy.

Another reason often put forward is the increasing availability of new forms of communications technology that has aided contact between North and South. Twenty years ago it could take a week or two for a letter from a Southern organization to reach its allies in the North. Now most have cell-phones and access to email, which means that contact is easier, information exchanges can be almost instantaneous, and international discussion on campaign strategies can be done at modest cost. Civil society organizations have in general been quicker and more agile than governments or business in utilizing this new technology, which has meant that they are very adept at using 'information politics' and getting information, evidence, political intelligence and news of events to where it can have most effect.

Adding to this picture – as either a contributing factor to the increase in transnational advocacy or a consequence of it – is the increased tendency of governments and international institutions to consult with and involve NGOs. Institutions like the World Bank and the IMF that have been criticized for their secrecy and weak accountability, and many governments in liberal democracies, have found that consulting or involving NGOs is good public relations in that it signifies a willingness (real or apparent) to be open. There is also an increasing awareness in such institutions that genuine openness can be useful for decision makers, in that it exposes them to alternative viewpoints, which they may or may not accept, but which lead to policy that is at least better informed, more rigorously tested, less likely to lead to conflicts and problems, and hopefully more innovative and less constrained by institutional orthodoxy. The World Trade Organization (WTO) for example in its guidelines on relations with NGOs says that the organization 'should play a more active role in its direct contacts with NGOs, who as a valuable resource can contribute to the accuracy and richness of the public debate'.[22]

But while this has given some NGOs greater influence it has also posed challenges and problems for them. When you are outside in the street demanding to be heard, all you really need are political slogans for the placards. But once you are invited in to sit at the table and expound your views, you need well worked out positions with sound arguments and convincing evidence, and for some NGOs this is something altogether new. Many civil society organizations of course refuse to accept the seat at the table, on the basis that it is just playing into a public relations ploy and legitimizing an institution that should be de-legitimized or abolished. This difference of views has caused serious rifts within civil society, between advocates and activists, between those willing to dialogue with targeted institutions and those not, between the 'reformers' and the 'abolitionists', with the latter accusing the former of breaking ranks, selling out or being co-opted. Many of the larger Northern NGOs, including Oxfam, have taken the reformist approach, which has made them less than popular with some of the more radical sections of civil society.

According to Salamon and Anheier: 'The existence of a vibrant non-profit sector is increasingly being viewed not as a luxury, but as a necessity, for peoples throughout the world. Such institutions can give expression to citizen concerns, hold governments accountable, promote community, address unmet needs, and generally improve the quality of life'.[23] Some see this growth in organized civil activism as a fundamental change in the dynamics of national and international politics, as the power of governments, and to some extent corporations, is countered by this new third force. Keck and Sikkink in their book *Activists Beyond Borders* maintain that the growth of civil society activism and transnational advocacy is changing the concept of state sovereignty. In the past, this concept meant that the state was subject to no other state, had full and exclusive powers within its borders, and that how it behaved towards its citizens, disposed of its natural resources, or ordered its economy were matters for it alone. But transnational advocacy presumes the opposite, that it is both legitimate and necessary for states or non-state actors to be concerned about the treatment of the inhabitants of another state. This has meant that the limits of what are legitimate interests of outsiders and what are not, has become fuzzy and contestable. Also the 'boomerang strategy' mentioned above and used by many transnational advocacy networks challenges state sovereignty with its assumption that it is legitimate to use international institutions and other governments to bring pressure on a government to change its domestic practices.[24]

Whether the erosion of national sovereignty is a good or a bad thing is an issue on which civil society actors have varying opinions. Those in the North tend to see it as a positive thing that will make it easier for marginalized people to gain their rights *vis-à-vis* repressive governments. For human rights advocates an erosion of national sovereignty means that individuals suffering abuse can more legitimately seek outside help against the actions of their own state. For environmental activists it means that protection of the 'global commons' can be placed above narrow national interests. Those in the South, however, often have a different view, seeing the principle of national sovereignty as a political defence against efforts by foreign powers and institutions to impose their policies and approaches on their societies. While they may not trust their own government to do the right thing, they trust foreign institutions and governments even less. Hence for some, the erosion of national sovereignty is a worrying thing.

It has been contended that in the new globalized political situation where people and capital, not to mention pollution, diseases, drugs and enthno-national conflict, flow freely across national borders, while the mandate of national governments is confined to within their borders, there is a need for a new form of international governance – a set of rules, norms and institutions that govern behaviour across national boundaries. This, says analyst Michael Edwards, will inevitably involve civil society as well as government and business. There will not be a single framework of international law applied through national governments, but a patchwork quilt of agreements negotiated between governments, corporations and civil society organizations at different levels.

At a time when governance must contend with increasingly international problems, the authority of states is being challenged by the rising power of private actors, both for-profit and not-for-profit...pluralistic regimes are the only alternative we have in a climate where global government remains politically unfeasible. The future of global governance lies in a fairer distribution of power through the international system, expressed through a wider variety of channels, and with many more checks and balances. NGOs are an essential component of these checks and balances. As I have argued elsewhere, the regimes of the future are likely to he composed of a small core of negotiated minimum standards, surrounded by a much larger array of voluntary regulations and other, non-coercive means of influencing destructive behaviour.[25]

This is not to say that civil society and NGOs can or should replace national governments. Rather their role is to supplement them within a democratic framework. As a group of prominent international NGOs have said in their recently established Accountability Charter: 'International NGOs can complement but not replace the over-arching role and primary responsibility of governments to promote equitable human development and well-being, to uphold human rights and to protect eco-systems'. Civil society organizations are generally speaking not representational. Although there are exceptions, most are not elected, and therefore cannot speak as the representatives of any group, which makes their involvement in decision making problematic. While governments have to balance a variety of often conflicting interests in society, NGOs are special interest groups that are concerned with one only. And unlike governments, which must face elections, and businesses, which must face their shareholders, it is not always clear how NGOs are held accountable to society as a whole. These fundamental issues of the role of civil society organizations are dealt with in more detail in the next chapter.

But despite these questions, civil society organizations and NGOs have the potential to play a key role in governance – by providing ordinary citizens with a bigger say in decisions that affect their lives, and for those living under non-democratic regimes, perhaps the only means of having their voice heard.

Notes

1. A. M. Florini (2001) 'Transnational Civil Society', in M. Edwards and J. Gaventa (eds) (2001), *Global Citizen Action* (Boulder CO, USA: Lynne Rienner Publishers).
2. Amnesty International website www.amnesty.org date accessed June 2008.
3. A. Hudson (2001) 'NGO's transnational advocacy networks: from legitimacy to political responsibility?' *Global Networks*, vol 1, number 4, p. 333.
4. World Development Movement website www.wdm.org.uk/about/index.htm date accessed June 2008.
5. Third World Network website www.twnside.org.sg date accessed June 2008.
6. Focus on the Global South website www.focusweb.org date accessed June 2008.
7. J. Clark (2003) *Worlds Apart. Civil Society and the Battle for Ethical Globalisation* (Bloomfield, CT, USA: Kumarian Press) p. 112.
8. For a fuller analysis of these, see W. L. Bennett 'Social movements beyond borders: understanding two eras of transnational activism', in D. della Porta and S. Tarrow (eds) (2005) *Transnational Protest and Global Activism* (Lanham, MD, USA: Rowman & Littlefield).
9. J. D. Clark (ed.) (2003) *Globalizing Civil Engagement: Civil Society and Transnational Action* (London and Stirling VA: Earthscan) p. 8.
10. J. Chapman (2001) 'What makes international campaigns effective? Lessons from India and Ghana', in M. Edwards and J. Gaventa (eds) (2001) *Global Citizen Action* (Boulder CO, USA: Lynne Rienner Publishers).
11. R. Boswell (1997) 'Mines treaty boosts spirits at lost causes', *The Ottawa Citizen*, 5 December.
12. J. Frandsen (1997) 'International campaign to ban landmines receives Nobel Peace Prize', *Gannett News Services*, 9 December.
13. Stockier McGuire *et al.* (1999) 'Its not a pretty picture', *Newsweek*, March 8.
14. C. J. L. Collins, Z. Gariyo and T. Burdon (2001) 'Jubilee 2000: Citizen action across the North-South divide', in M. Edwards and J. Gaventa (eds) (2001), *Global Citizen Action* (Boulder CO, USA: Lynne Rienner Publishers).
15. J. Clark (2003) *Worlds Apart. Civil Society and the Battle for Ethical Globalisation* (Bloomfield, CT, USA: Kumarian Press) p. 104.
16. M. Keck and K. Sikkink (1998) *Activists Beyond Borders* (Ithaca and London: Cornell University Press) pp. 18–25.
17. IBFAN website www.ibfan.org date accessed June 2008.
18. Correspondence from Overseas Private Investment Corporation to the Freeport-McMoran mining company, cited in the shareholders' resolution by the Seattle Mennonite Church, April 1997.
19. M. Kaldor (2003) *Global Civil Society: An Answer to War* (Cambridge, UK: Polity) p. 95.
20. Union of International Associations www.uia.org/statistics date accessed June 2008.
21. M. Edwards (2000) *NGO Rights and Responsibilities. A New Deal for Global Governance* (London: The Foreign Policy Centre) p. 9.
22. World Trade Organization (1996) *Guidelines for Arrangements on Relations with Non-governmental Organizations.* Decision adopted by the General Council on 23 July 1996. WT / L / 162.

23 L. M. Salamon and H. K. Anheier (1998) *The Emerging Sector Revisited: A Summary*. Revised Edition. (Baltimore: Institute of Policy Studies, John Hopkins University Press) p. 19.
24 M. Keck and K. Sikkink (1998) *Activists Beyond Borders* (Ithaca and London: Cornell University Press) p. 36.
25 M. Edwards (2000) *NGO Rights and Responsibilities. A New Deal for Global Governance* (London: The Foreign Policy Centre) pp. 12–13.

2
Challenges and Questions

As the prominence and influence of civil society, and of NGOs in particular, has increased, so too has the scrutiny, questioning and criticism of their role – by academics, politicians, the media and especially by those whom they are attempting to influence. Civil society advocates have in a sense become the victims of their own success. The *New York Times* for example in 2003 declared that: 'non-governmental organizations are now part of the power structure too', and because they receive donations from the public and advocate for certain policies, 'these groups owe it to the public to be accountable and transparent themselves'.[1] In that same year the London-based magazine *The Economist* ran an essay titled 'Who guards the guardians?' in which it suggested that NGOs should be audited:

> Non-governmental organisations, as many charities are pompously described these days, often escape the sort of scrutiny that they themselves like to apply to governments and companies. But NGOs are human organisations too, with all the scope for laziness, inefficiency and even corruption that any group of people risks falling into if it lacks either self-discipline or external scrutiny.[2]

Sometimes the comments are much sharper and more critical, as for example the following, also from *The Economist*:

> The increasing clout of NGOs, respectable and not so respectable, raises an important question: who elected Oxfam, or, for that matter, the League for a Revolutionary Communist International? Bodies such as these are, to varying degrees, extorting admissions of guilt from law-abiding companies and changes in policy from democratically elected

governments. They may claim to be acting in the interests of the people – but then so do the objects of their criticism, governments and the despised international institutions. ... In the West, governments and their agencies are, in the end, accountable to voters. Who holds the activists accountable?[3]

One of the more common accusations is that NGOs are poorly accountable to those in the South whose interests they claim to promote, a criticism that comes from those in the South as well as those in the North. For example, just after the Ministerial Meeting of the World Trade Organization (WTO) in Seattle in 1999, at which there were widespread public demonstrations by civil society groups, a South African newspaper had this to say:

> Especially offensive in Seattle were the groups which – while owing their salaries to rich country protectionists – insisted they were standing up for the interests of the developing world against its rape by the WTO and the multinational corporations...... The actual citizens of the organization's 135 members, of which 120 are democracies, were mostly represented at the meeting, having elected the governments that appointed and instructed the delegates. To whom exactly were the NGOs accountable?[4]

The prominent US bureaucrat John Bolton, writing in 2000 before he joined the Bush Administration, warned that NGOs with their 'extranational clout' were special interest groups projecting themselves as legitimate actors in decision making along with elected governments. 'Civil society also sees itself as beyond national politics, which is one of the reasons its recent successes have such profoundly anti-democratic implications'.[5] But while there are a number of valid and important questions that NGOs have to answer regarding their legitimacy and accountability, it has to be recognized that there is another agenda running here as well. As analysts Jordan and van Tuijl have said:

> [W]eaknesses in NGO accountability are being used as cover for political attacks against voices that certain interests wish to silence. NGO accountability has become a 'wedge issue' that appears incontestable across different constituencies on the surface but disguises deep and often undeclared divisions of interest beneath...... It is no accident that hostility to NGO involvement in global governance forms a key element of neo-conservative thinking in the US. Stronger NGO

accountability mechanisms won't do away with politically motivated attacks like these, but they would surely help to expose them for what they are. Nevertheless, in such politicized climates, deeper innovations in NGO accountability may be more difficult to achieve because the results – gained through increasing openness to public scrutiny – may be used to destroy the organization or close off its access to influence and resources, rather than as an incentive to improve its performance.[6]

This is not to suggest that all criticism of NGOs is politically motivated in this way. There is much that is constructive and useful, if not always particularly friendly. For example the World Trade Organization in a 2005 report noted that NGOs that were lobbying for greater access were 'often neither especially accountable nor particularly transparent themselves'. It added that: 'While there is now a broad recognition among member states of the United Nations of the substantial and proven benefits of non-governmental participation in inter-governmental debate on global issues, there are continuing concerns about the legitimacy, representativity, accountability and politics of non-governmental organizations'.[7]

In recent years academics have also been adding their voices to this debate about the role of NGOs in society and their legitimacy and there has been an upsurge in literature on the subject. What all this amounts to is that the role and legitimacy of NGOs has been called into question and is now regarded as a legitimate topic for public discourse and academic debate – one to which NGOs themselves are perhaps not paying sufficient attention.

Legitimacy

Among the many challenges and questions, perhaps the most significant is: whom do NGOs represent? Where does their mandate come from since, in most cases, they are not elected by anyone? Do they, as is sometimes claimed, speak on behalf of the world's poor and exploited? Does their involvement in political decision making inject the voice of the latter into those processes and make them more democratic, or are they just another special interest lobby group pushing its own political agenda? Academic Kenneth Anderson in a 2000 article challenged the idea that international development NGOs represent the poor, maintaining that they are generally not well connected in any direct way to the masses of poor people and, by virtue of the way they operate globally rather than locally, are fundamentally elite organizations:

> International NGOs collectively are not conduits from the 'people' or the 'masses' or the 'world citizenry' from the 'bottom up'. They are, rather, a vehicle for international elites to talk to other international elites about the things – frequently of undeniably critical importance – that international elites care about. The conversation is not vertical, it is horizontal...... They.....are pressure groups, political lobbying groups, and they do not confer democratic legitimacy, least of all upon the profoundly undemocratic organs of the international system.[8]

Some civil society bodies, for example labour unions and some farmers' organizations, can claim to be representatives and to speak on behalf of, and with a mandate from, the workers, farmers, etc who elected them. But for most civil society bodies, including international NGOs, this is not the case. By what right then do these latter speak out in the way they do about the poor and exploited or the victims of human rights abuses, if they have no mandate to represent them? In 1999 a research project asked 32 UK-based NGOs on what basis they claimed legitimacy for their advocacy work, and came up with a variety of answers.[9] Some claimed it on the basis of their organization's history, track record and reputation, while others relied on the fact that what they were advocating for was a basic right, a moral or ethical principle or value set down in an international charter. A third basis was the organization's democratic structure that extended internationally, while a few also felt legitimized by their UK supporter base. But far and away the most common basis for claiming legitimacy, mentioned by half the NGOs, was the programmes that they were involved in the South and the direct links they had with organizations there that gave them expertise and experience.

But not everyone it seems is convinced by this. As Edwards *et al.* put it: 'Claiming the right to speak out simply because an NGO has projects or contacts on the ground is unlikely to be acceptable to a sceptical audience in the media among other observers, and – most importantly – a more critical local population'.[10] It is not just the fact of having contacts and relationships with organizations in the South that gives an NGO legitimacy but the nature of those relationships – an issue that is explored in more detail later in this chapter.

There is an argument that says that an organization does not have to be representational to legitimately express its views in national and international political debates. According to this argument, there are two ways to gain legitimacy and the right to have a say: through the normal democratic process of election, which gives representational status and the right to participate in decision making – and through effectiveness, which only confers the right to be heard. Effectiveness means basically being recognized by other legitimate bodies as having useful knowledge and skills to bring to the debate, solidly rooted in research and experience and sensitive to the views of those whose welfare is being debated. In the case of those advocating for the poor, this would mean having a working style that exposes the organization to the perspectives of poor people. However it should be stressed that this route to legitimacy gives 'a voice but not a vote'. It conveys the right to speak, to have views heard, but not the right to take part in the final decision. Thus for example in the case of the negotiations around the landmines ban, the NGOs involved were able to legitimately express their views as forcefully as they could, even though they did not in any formal sense represent landmines victims or anyone else, because those views enriched and assisted the public debate. But the final decisions on the wording and signing of the treaty were with governments alone, as the elected representatives of the citizens of the countries that used landmines.

This is the normal situation that has long been the case in national level politics in democratic states. Decision making lies with a democratically elected government as the direct representative of the citizenry, but influenced to a greater or lesser degree by a variety of non-state pressure groups with a multitude of complementary or competing positions. It is the interaction of these competing views in a democratic society that provides its checks and balances. And this could well be a model for a more democratic environment at the international level as well. Edwards and Gaventa write:

> [T]ransnational civil society is far from democratic, and few networks have democratic systems of governance and accountability. Nevertheless, the increasing voice of civil society groups on the world stage adds an essential layer of checks and balances into the international system, while helping to ensure that excluded views are heard.[11]

What international development NGOs such as Oxfam are claiming is a voice, not a vote – and this claim is dependent on their policy positions being solidly rooted in research and experience and sensitive to the views of those they wish to help. But this leaves the question of how to ensure this, of how an organization like Oxfam can demonstrate this. Does their involvement with the poor through their grassroots programmes give them sufficient legitimacy? How do they ensure that the positions they are advocating are sensitive to the views of the poor, given that the poor do not speak with one voice, and are not an undifferentiated mass with the same interests and aspirations? These and other questions are addressed in the case studies later in this book.

Accountability

Related to this is the question: to whom are NGOs accountable for their actions and in particular for their advocacy activities and strategies? To whom do they have to answer for their performance, and who holds them to account if things go wrong? In most cases this is not clear, and therein lies a problem. Academic Jan Aart Scholte believes that most civil society groups 'have operated very limited and unimaginative accountability mechanisms in relation to their own activities', and that this leaves them vulnerable and open to challenge, as authorities can use it to reject their legitimacy in global governance.[12] Analyst Michael Edwards believes that the key issue is accountability to those in the South rather than to donors, funders or supporters in the North:

> Where transparency is poor and networks are dominated by voices from the North, accountability to the grassroots is likely to be weak, but this is far from a theoretical question. What if the NGOs who protested so loudly [at the World Trade Organization meeting] in Seattle turn out to be wrong in their assumptions about the future benefits that flow from different trading strategies – who pays the price? Not the NGOs themselves, but farmers in the Third World who have never heard of Christian Aid or Save the Children, but who will suffer the consequences for generations. The same strictures apply to pro free-traders too of course, but NGOs cannot use this as a defence.[13]

NGOs are good at critiquing and pointing out what is wrong with the policies or practices they are campaigning on, but less good at coming up with workable alternatives that would improve the situation. They do not always have the specialist knowledge or the comprehensive vision needed to do so. As one author put it: '"We know what we don't like, but we don't know what might work better" could be the mantra of the NGO community. Humility doesn't come easy to organisations that have been used to occupying the moral high ground'.[14] If and when an NGO's alternative policy or practice recommendations are inappropriate or have unforeseen negative consequences for those it is trying to help, who is held accountable?

Edwards believes that the accountability of NGOs must be strengthened, both upwards to donors and members and downwards to the poor and those whom it is attempting to assist. He advocates a deal by which NGOs are given greater participation in global governance 'in return for transparency and accountability on a set of minimum standards for NGO integrity and performance, monitored largely through self-regulation'.[15] Academic Peter Spiro proposes a deal in which states accept formal inclusion of non-state actors in international decision making in order to 'hold NGOs, as repeat players, accountable to international bargains'.[16] A system similar to this, in which access is traded for transparency and accountability, already exists in the United Nations (UN) in the form of an accreditation system for non-state actors wishing to input into UN processes. The UN offers different levels of accreditation for NGOs, with each category providing a different level of access to UN documents, status at the General Assembly, and ability to submit written statements, place items on an agenda, etc. To be eligible, NGOs must meet certain criteria, including a democratically adopted constitution, a representative structure, evidence that they derive most of their resources from national affiliates or members, and a description of their finances and activities. A 2004 report commissioned by the UN on its relations with civil society organizations wants to take this further, suggesting that it's engagement with the latter should be conditional on their having in place their own codes of conduct and other self-policing mechanisms that heighten organizational quality, governance and balance. It suggests that the UN should work with civil society bodies to define standards of governance, such as those for transparency and accountability.[17]

A specific proposal for such a self-policing mechanism, in this case for human rights organizations (HROs), has been put forward by Robert Blitt.[18] He proposed that the major HROs jointly establish a set of standards for their 'industry' to which all other HROs could then volunteer to commit themselves. The standards would include professional and financial integrity, best practices for research, fact-finding and reporting, and protocols for issuing public retractions. Adherence to the standards would then be monitored and incentives for good performance created in the form of annual ratings for each HRO. Blitt adds that 'while individuals may remain free to establish fly-by-night HROs, recognized HROs will have an authoritative and objective tool that can be harnessed to credential themselves in the eyes of the media, governments, intergovernmental agencies, courts and the public at large'.

Many international development NGOs already have something like this in place, voluntary self-regulating sets of standards, adherence to which brings credibility, and non-compliance a financial cost. For example, the Australian Council for International Development, the peak body for development NGOs in that country, has a voluntary, self-regulatory industry code of conduct covering organizational governance, management, financial control and reporting that 'sets out standards and requirements to which signatories to the Code are bound and against which complaints and compliance is assessed'. An incentive for compliance is that NGOs wishing to access Australian Government funding for their aid programmes are required to formally adopt and demonstrate compliance with the Code. This particular code is strong on upward accountability to donors, but a little vague on downward accountability to the poor. It does however specify that, amongst other things, signatory organizations should: 'give priority to the needs and interests of the people they serve; encourage self-help and self-reliance among beneficiaries and thus avoid creating dependency; involve beneficiary groups to the maximum extent possible in the design, implementation and evaluation of projects and programs'.

Accuracy

Another accusation commonly levelled at NGO advocates is inaccuracy. They are often accused of presenting a picture of a situation that is ill-informed and distorted, or crude and over-simplistic, driven more by passion and sensation rather than loyalty to the facts. They are criticized for being either well-meaning but naïve 'do-gooders' who have been misled by some scheming group with whom they are working, or at worst of being unreliable and deceptive, or even downright liars.

It is true that NGO campaigners sometimes do get the facts wrong. A classic example was Greenpeace's 1995 campaign over the Shell company's plan to scuttle its redundant offshore oil storage facility, the Brent Spar, in the ocean with large amounts of oil still on board. Greenpeace in its public statements grossly over-estimated the amount of oil that might leak into the surrounding ocean, which made it easier for its critics to write off the whole campaign. As soon as it became aware of the error, Greenpeace proactively corrected and apologized, but the incident became notorious and the story persisted – that Greenpeace had got it wrong over the entire Brent Spar issue.

Some writers have maintained that distortions creep in because an NGO simply does not have an in-depth, nuanced, or sophisticated understanding of the issues involved, nor perhaps the time or resources to do the research necessary to gain an understanding. As former World Bank employee and NGO analyst John Clark has said:

> NGOs aren't always well equipped for thorough research, and the events they try to affect may be fast moving. Most think it is better to take opportunistic chances to achieve real change and be approximately right rather than to be scrupulously accurate and miss the boat. Some take it too far, however, and sound off on the flimsiest of evidence and worry about the consequences latter (the 'load, fire, aim' school); others deliberately exaggerate to excoriate a favourite target.[19]

Another writer, Caroline Harper of Save The Children Fund UK, puts it down to the confrontational approach that many advocacy NGOs adopt, which does not allow them to take on board alternative views: 'Confrontational advocacy strategies require NGOs to come up with clear-cut answers to complex questions. Although many do have considerable knowledge and experience, this approach may fail to recognize the validity of different knowledge claims'.[20]

But more often the problem is not so much inaccuracy as oversimplification. In their attempts to capture public attention and galvanize supporters into action, campaigners may use simple and often dramatic terms and phrases that present things in black and white terms when in fact there are often many shades of grey. There is a principle in campaigning that says that a well-designed campaign should be able to be summed up in a single powerful proposition, a simple statement that sets out the problem, the culprit and the solution. For example:

'Innocent people are being killed and maimed by landmines left over from previous conflicts. Landmines are an inhumane and indiscriminate weapon. They should be banned'.

'Chronic debt is causing undue hardship to the poor in developing countries. Creditors are being unreasonable in their demands for repayment. They need to write-off some or all of this debt'.

There will always be a temptation to forgo nuances, rigour and complexity for clarity, drama and impact. Thus for example in a campaign against 'sweatshops', workers in the footwear or garment industry in a Southern country may be portrayed as poor exploited victims of heartless employers and scheming merchandizing companies, when in fact the wages and conditions in those factories, while not good, may be better than in any other industry in the country, with workers queuing up to get them. The problem is that what works for 'rallying the troops' in a campaign can be alienating for those with whom the campaigners might want to negotiate – while what is needed to be brought to the negotiating table in the way of positions and arguments is too complex and detailed to motivate supporters and the public.

The debt campaign is another example in which there was a temptation to paint too simplistic a picture, of greedy Northern banks and governments insisting on their repayments while health clinics and schools in indebted countries were closing, children were going hungry, etc. Jubilee 2000's call for Southern countries' debt to be simply written off was often met with an official response that this was grossly oversimplified and unrealistic and ignored some basic questions. If the debt were simply written off, how would the debtor governments ever get credit again? And why should profligate governments and corrupt elites be 'let off the hook' in this way? The campaign, to its credit, was able to find a workable balance between the need for a simple and powerful campaign proposition, and a realistic solution to the problem. Its call for a debt free new millennium implied the outright cancellation of debt, but the text of its petitions and campaign literature called for the reduction of debts to levels that countries could afford, and included practical and realistic ways of achieving this.

Insider versus outsider strategies

Campaigns are not all about 'rallying the troops'. Usually there will come a point when it becomes necessary to sit down with the other side and negotiate. The mass rally in the streets, the striking workers at the factory gate or the demonstrators outside a government building may at some point be asked to send representatives to present their case and possibly to negotiate a deal. NGOs that are pursuing a letter-writing or media campaign in the North may be asked to sit down with representatives of the company, government or institution and talk. Some NGOs see such dialogue as their primary strategy, gaining direct access to decision makers and working from the inside of the system to convince them to change their policies by the force of argument and evidence, backed up by the possibility of a popular campaign against them if the talks break down. This 'insider' strategy is favoured by many NGO advocates, injecting one's views, arguments and evidence from the inside – as against the 'outsider' strategy of demonstrating one's power through mass demonstrations in the street.

Which is the better approach? Those who use 'insider' tactics tend to say that both have their place, that the demonstrations in the streets by other civil society organizations help create an atmosphere in which the targeted body is more willing to dialogue, and gives weight to their position and their arguments at the negotiating table. Some who favour the 'outsider' approach however condemn the other as dangerous, as undermining solidarity, or as legitimizing an institution or group of people that has no legitimacy. Most civil society organizations however will use both at different times depending on the circumstances, and on how resistant or open the target is – the operative principle being to 'engage where you can, and confront where you must'. A workers' union in a factory for example may organize a strike or demonstration when management refuses to negotiate, but when they do agree to talk, will go inside and sit at the negotiating table. A study of advocacy campaigns by the Overseas Development Institute found that: 'Most successful examples have included some sort of continuous and long-term engagement with the government, rather than outright confrontation. In some cases a mix of confrontation to raise the profile of the issue, and engagement to provide solutions has proved to be useful'.[21]

One of the arguments against 'insider' strategies is that, while it can mean greater access to decision makers, it can also be used by the latter to undermine a campaign. Those on the other side of the negotiating table are aware and will use the fact that people who are relating to them on a person-to-person basis in a negotiation process are less likely to be aggressive, that keeping the NGOs or unions talking means they are less likely to be taking action against you, and that being seen to be open and consultative will do your company, government or institution no harm at all. 'Insider' approaches can also lead to co-option. Being invited to the table can be very flattering for some, and mixing with the powerful in this way very satisfying. If there is money or travel on offer from the targeted body as well, this can add to the temptation. There is a danger that the NGO will become seduced by this, and that the 'insider' strategy of constructive engagement will become instead a cosy and non-threatening co-existence. It is not unknown for corporations in particular, to use co-option as a tactic to protect the company's reputation while allowing it to carry on business as usual. A variation of this used by some companies operating in the South is to fund a community outreach programme that provides services, infrastructure, training or other benefits to the communities affected by, or workers involved in, their operations, and to out-source the running of those programmes to friendly cooperative NGOs. Long-time anti-sweatshop activist Jeff Ballinger saw how effective this was for the Nike sportswear company:

> Got problems with critical NGOs? Start your own, and engage them in partnership! That is what Nike did with the 'Global Alliance for Workers and Communities' (GA), which dished out millions of dollars to NGOs willing to help.... As Paul Hawken, an entrepreneur turned environmentalist and green-biz theorist, observed after a failed attempt to work with Nike, there was an 'almost biological' process under way, by which major corporations co-opt those critical groups they can draw into partnership, and isolate and marginalize those they cannot.... Don't bother looking for the GA on the web. Nike pulled the plug as soon as it had convinced enough people that it had joined the ranks of the 'most responsible'.[22]

Co-option is the very opposite of legitimacy and accountability. The co-opted organization is far removed from the affected group on whose behalf it is supposed to be acting, and is closer to the targeted company, government or institution than it is to them. Accountability is non-existent, for otherwise it would be soundly condemned by those to whom it is accountable.

Whose voice is heard?

The issues of legitimacy, accountability and accuracy are the ones that most often feature in the public criticisms of NGO advocacy by those who oppose them. But there are others that emanate from the more constructive and thoughtful analysts of civil society, issues that centre around questions of democracy and participation in transnational advocacy networks, of whose voice is heard and whose is not in advocacy and campaigns. These networks by their nature involve organizations in the South as well as the North, but there is an issue of whether both have an equal say in how the campaigns are designed and run, or whether Northern organizations dominate. While they preach democracy and participation, do Northern NGOs practice it themselves in their advocacy networks? Given that the campaigns are usually about improving the lot of an affected group in the South, do the latter have a say in what is done or said on their behalf? Are the voiceless given a voice, or do others simply speak for them? Can the affected group determine who their NGO advocates in the South or the North will be; can they decline to be 'represented' by a particular NGO?

A campaign in the 1990s against World Bank financing of the Arun III Dam in Nepal illustrates the problem. This was a large hydroelectric dam project scheduled to be built in a remote area of Nepal, the Arun valley, which was sparsely populated, but contained an eco-system rich in biodiversity. The dam project, supported by the Government of Nepal and the World Bank, was intended to generate the electrical energy required for two major cities in Nepal, plus a surplus that could be sold to India across the border. The project was first brought to international attention by a local Nepali NGO that worked on microhydroelectricity production, and which opposed the dam on the basis that it was inappropriate to the country's energy needs and would obliterate the potential for small-scale schemes. The international organizations that took it up in the North however tended to emphasize the environmental damage that the project would cause to the valley, and the innocent tribal inhabitants of the valley who would be swamped or pushed aside by this huge dam. This latter image was very effective in capturing media attention in the North, and resulted in congressional discussions in the United States and parliamentary debates in Germany and the UK. Other Northern NGOs became interested because the project coincided with the creation of the World Bank's new Inspection Panel, and provided a perfect test case for the effectiveness of this mechanism. A submission was put to the Inspection Panel that said that by funding the Arun Dam project, the Bank was violating its own policies on the economic evaluation of projects, on energy, information disclosure, the environment, resettlement, and indigenous people.

For the people living in the valley however, or at least the majority of those who spoke out and made their views known, the problem was not the dam itself but the fact that its potential benefits were not going to reach them. They were concerned about a decision to change the original plans for the road leading to the dam so that it no longer passed close to their villages. They were not opposed to the dam as long as it brought employment, and made it easier for them to market their crops. But this message was lost in the international and even national level messaging.[23] This was not so much a case of Northern NGOs crowding out the voice of Southern NGOs, but of both neglecting the voice of those most directly affected, the people in the valley. In Nepal there were two NGO coalitions working on this campaign, the Alliance for Energy and the Arun Concerned Group, but an NGO evaluation of the campaign found that they 'acted more in the international arena and significantly at the national level, but perhaps very little where the dam was to be built and the people were to be affected'.[24] Their connections to the inhabitants of the valley were not as strong as they should have been, and hence the voices of the latter were not effectively heard at the national or international level.

The Government of Nepal objected that, as the democratically elected representative of the people, it was the only body with a mandate to speak on behalf of its citizens, and the only one with a responsibility for the country as a whole rather than just one valley – and that it was not the role of legislators in other countries to be discussing or opposing a decision that it had made about a domestic issue. A counter argument was however put that, as the dam was being funded by World Bank money which came from Northern taxpayers via their governments' aid budgets, groups in the North should have some say in how it was spent. The Inspection Panel carried out a review of the project and concluded that the Bank had in fact failed to follow its own policies in many respects. As a result, in April 1995, it was announced that the World Bank was no longer going to provide funding for the Arun Dam, thus effectively killing the project. This was seen as a victory by the international NGOs, but it is doubtful that the inhabitants of the valley saw it that way.

John Clark argues that NGOs in the South will always tend to be more influenced by their Northern allies than by the affected groups, as long as they are financially dependent on those Northern allies: 'If Northern NGOs finance a large proportion of the budget of Southern NGOs, they will continue to call the shots. They may agree that their partners' voices should be heard in international forums, but since it is Northern funding, they select which voices are heard'.[25] It is in fact increasingly common to hear Southern voices at international fora and even in Northern media, but they are often those chosen by, and funded by, Northern partners. The inequality between Northern and Southern members in terms of access to financial resources is a major factor contributing to the lop-sided relationship within advocacy coalitions. Nevertheless there are many instances in which Southern CSOs and NGOs have taken a different stance in opposition to their Northern colleagues and have aired their opposing views in the North. A classic example was the campaign in the mid-1990s around the replenishment by rich governments of the funds of the International Development Association, the low interest loan arm of the World Bank. North American NGOs, claiming to represent a Southern consensus, campaigned against replenishment on the grounds that social and environmental safeguards attached to the loans were too weak. In contrast, Southern NGOs (mainly from Africa) insisted that the replenishment of the fund go ahead regardless of these weaknesses, since foreign aid was desperately needed. The Camisea case study in Chapter 7 describes how a united coalition of CSOs in Peru persuaded Northern allies to change their position of outright opposition to a proposed natural gas project in favour of supporting a unified campaign to condition the project's funding.

There is a case for advocacy by transnational NGO alliances to be done differently, with more emphasis on equal participation; stronger links between local, national and international action; and a more democratic way of deciding on strategy and messages. One author put this in terms of a move away from 'paternalistic advocacy', in which Northern NGOs dominate and Southern organizations are merely the providers of information and legitimacy, to 'participatory advocacy' in which Southern CSOs are involved in broadening the political space in their own countries so that the voices of the poor can be heard – to 'people-centred advocacy' in which affected groups negotiate for their rights on their own behalf. 'The role of the Northern NGO will then be to act in solidarity – sharing its resources where it can, helping when it is invited to do so, and generating a climate of support for pro-poor policy change within its own immediate constituency'.[26]

Having affected groups negotiate on their own behalf does not mean leaving them to their own devices to fight for themselves in the North, to do their own advocacy with Northern governments and institutions. Rather, Northern allies would do this on their behalf but with affected groups fully involved in the process. An effective coalition will recognize that different groups have abilities and expertise in different political arenas, and will allow advocacy in each arena to be guided by those with the specialist knowledge and mandate in that arena – but with input and advice from those operating in other arenas. Hence Southern groups will basically determine objectives and strategies in the South, and Northern NGOs will do so in the North.

There is also a practical issue involved here. Being participatory and democratic, consulting and finding agreement amongst stakeholders can be a time-consuming and often difficult business. In what are often fast-moving campaigns, many Northern NGOs tend to keep it to a minimum in order to give themselves greater flexibility and the ability to quickly adapt messages and positions to changing circumstances and to seize new opportunities. But there is a price to be paid for this, in that it leaves them open to accusations of being at best insensitive towards those in the South, and at worst inconsistent and hypocritical, preaching the need for greater democracy to others but not willing to practice it themselves. And it can leave the Southern members of the network or coalition marginalized and disempowered. There is in other words a trade-off to be made between speed and flexibility on the one hand and more democratic and developmentally sound processes and outcomes on the other. Different networks will make different decisions about which is more important and what balance they will find between the two.

Supportive, people-centred advocacy can be particularly time consuming if it involves having to organize a disorganized affected group, build their capacity to articulate their problem in a way that will be understood by officials, and their confidence and ability to demand their rights in a constructive way. Advocacy led by an NGO on the other hand is much simpler, quicker and more flexible. It has been argued that the growth of NGOs and their influence may be pushing this grassroots organizing and people-centred advocacy to the margins, and in the process disempowering affected groups, who now increasingly have their grievances and rights articulated and fought for by others in distant arenas, via a process over which they have little control. In the case of workers' rights in the South for example this means that, instead of organizing and fighting for their own rights themselves at the factory and national level, the emphasis is on NGO-run campaigns in the North in which consumers pressure brand name companies, or Northern NGOs negotiate with the representatives of those companies for better conditions in suppliers' factories.

There are strong arguments in favour of grassroots people-centred advocacy. As Jordan and van Tuijl have said: 'The underlying function of advocacy is often to enhance the self-respect of weaker communities, to improve their self-confidence, constitute integrity and promote mutual trust: all essential ingredients to develop a healthy community. It is often overlooked that NGO advocacy also entails a fight against cynicism and despair to which powerless communities tend to fall victim, in the face of massive political and practical obstacles impairing them to improve their lot'.[27] Grassroots people-centred advocacy can, in the long run, also be more effective, in that it is more likely to lead to changes that are sustainable. While the specialist NGO advocates may be more efficient in bringing about a change of policy by a company or government, there has to be at the same time a means of ensuring that the policy change is put into effect and continues to be implemented and respected. And one change of policy or practice by itself will not be enough. There will usually be a myriad of others that need to be tackled and followed up at the same time – a constant responding to the multiple symptoms of a more fundamental problem, which is the lack of political or negotiating power of the affected group and their exclusion from decision making that affects their lives. The more sustainable approach is to focus on the fundamental problem and build the capacity of the affected group to analyse the causes of their problem, to work together effectively, to gather evidence and to speak with one clear voice – and their collective power to demand their rights and hold their government to account.

Political responsibility

One of the more interesting and useful contributions to the literature on participation and accountability within North-South advocacy networks comes from civil society analysts Jordan and van Tuijl. In a 2000 paper they introduced the concept of 'political responsibility' as a more useful alternative to those of 'accountability' and 'representation'.[28] The concept of accountability to those whom the network seeks to assist, they said, implies formal obligations, but within transnational advocacy networks there are no formal mechanisms to enforce obligations, and so to discuss it within such networks is to suggest something that does not yet exist. Likewise while acknowledging that NGOs are in fact representing interests when they take up an advocacy issue in their own political arena on behalf of some affected group, they say that representation 'does not provide a sufficiently viable conceptual or practical approach to come to terms with power relations and responsibilities as they emerge in the context of transnational NGO advocacy campaigns'. The sheer fact of participation in a global campaign, they say, involves a political responsibility toward others engaged in the campaign but operating in a different political arena. 'In general, advocacy NGOs reveal truths that are not liked by vested interests and power holders. Being involved in NGO advocacy therefore entails taking risks:

politically, legally, mentally and physically in the South as well as in the North. Managing these risks invokes a political responsibility toward other groups active in the campaign'.[29]

They suggest that the concept of 'political responsibility' is a more useful one for assessing the quality of relationships within a network, and describe it as: 'a commitment to embrace not only goals in a campaign but to conduct the campaign with democratic principles foremost in the process'. The level of political responsibility within an advocacy network or campaign is assessed by such things as how compatible the different objectives of the campaign are in different political arenas, what happens with information, and how strategies, risks and funds are managed. They identify four basic types of transnational campaigns according to the level of political responsibility exhibited.

A *cooperative campaign* is one in which there is a high level of political responsibility. The objectives pursued by different members of the network in different political arenas are compatible, intertwined and mutually reinforcing. There is a fluid and continuous flow of information among all involved, which is frequent, globally distributed, easily accessible and freely shared. Advocacy agendas and strategies are set in close consultation with the groups who are supposed to benefit from the campaign, and are continuously reviewed. There is joint management of political responsibilities by all CSOs involved, and the level of political responsibility toward the most vulnerable actors is optimal. Risks are assumed only to the extent that they can be born by the most vulnerable.

An example of a *cooperative campaign* is that around the Bujagali Dam in Uganda, described by Juliette Majot of the International Rivers Network (IRN).[30] This was a campaign to stop an inappropriate large-scale dam project supported by the World Bank that was run by several local Ugandan organizations and assisted by several NGOs in the US, including the California-based IRN. According to Majot, the campaign had the following characteristics:

- The IRN worked jointly with the local organizations in order to publicize their views internationally and strengthen the local campaign, but also to contribute lessons from Bujagali to the broader international debate on the best approach to providing affordable electricity for poor communities.
- When, what, how and by whom the different tactics would be employed was planned and decided jointly by the local and international NGOs.

- There was daily or weekly communication between the campaigners.
- There was no formal written agreement between the NGOs about roles, deadlines, functions or responsibilities, just an informal one, which required ongoing electronic communication.
- Neither the local nor international NGOs entered into each other's internal organizational decision-making processes or debates – in order to respect autonomy and minimize international NGO influence.
- Because it was so sensitive, media and public outreach strategies were developed and implemented together.

A campaign in which the level of political responsibility is medium rather than high is classed by Jordan and van Tuijl as a *concurrent campaign*. In this case the objectives pursued by various members of the network in their own political arenas are different but compatible. Information flows are regular but multiphased, freely shared, but more tightly directed than in a cooperative campaign. There is a frequent review of strategies and co-existing management of political responsibilities by varying combinations of NGOs involved at different levels.

A *disassociated campaign* is one in which the level of political responsibility is low. These are campaigns in which network members operating in different political arenas are advocating on the same issue but their advocacy objectives are beginning to clash. There is typically a regular but infrequent flow of information, which is difficult to access and is shared with reservation – and which is often lopsided in that more information flows from the South to the North than *vice versa*. There will be occasional but uncoordinated reviews of strategies, and the management of political responsibilities and risk among the different NGOs involved will tend to be in their own political arena only.

A *competitive campaign* is one in which there is in effect no political responsibility taken. In this type of campaign there will be a parallel representation of opposing objectives by different NGOs in different political arenas. Advocacy on one level may actually be having an adverse or counter-productive impact at another level. There will be a serious lack of information exchange and coordination among the NGOs involved, resulting in an absence of accountability and a failure to embrace political responsibilities. Typically there will be no joint review of strategies or management of political responsibilities, and no recognition of risks, which may result in human rights violations or other negative impacts on affected communities.

The example that Jordan and van Tuijl give of a *competitive campaign* is that of the Huaorani indigenous people in Ecuador against US oil companies operating in their area, whose activities had resulted in leaking pipelines, oil fires, violence and intimidation, and damage to rainforests and tribal communities. International activists who joined the campaign tended to focus on saving the rainforests, while at the local and national level the battle was about human rights rather than the environment, about protecting the lives and rights of the indigenous peoples. At various points in the campaign these differing approaches got in each other's way. In the campaign against the oil company Conoco for example, which ran from the late 1980s to the mid-1990s, the US- and European-based activist groups took up a variety of political positions ranging from opposition to Conoco to support for the company as the best option in a bad situation. Many of these positions were taken without consultation with the Huaorani, who were difficult to contact deep in the forest, or were based on limited information from national level groups in Ecuador. Information flows between the different actors in the campaign were limited – and decisions on strategies were based on political feasibility rather than on what the Huaorani communities requested. Deals were agreed by Northern actors that undermined the rights of indigenous peoples to manage their own land, including an attempted deal by one representative of a US indigenous rights organization that would have allowed the company to build a road right through Huaorani territory. Money raised by Northern NGOs in the name of the campaign was sometimes not shared with the cash-strapped groups working directly with the affected people or with the Huaorani themselves. Decisions taken at the international level without consultation in effect restricted the negotiating abilities of the indigenous communities – and undermined a fledgling alliance between the indigenous peoples and national level Ecuadorian environmental organizations.[31]

In the case studies that follow, this typology based on the level of 'political responsibility' is used as an analytical tool to assess the level of democracy, participation and 'downwards accountability' in each of the campaigns studied.

Notes

1 *The New York Times*, 21 July 2003.
2 *The Economist*, 18 September 2003.
3 *The Economist*, 25 September 2000.
4 *Business Day*, 8 December 1999.
5 J. R. Bolton (2000) 'Should we take global governance seriously?' *Chicago Journal of International Law*, vol 1, pp. 205–216.

6 L. Jordan and P. van Tuijl (eds) (2006) *NGO accountability. Politics: Principles and Innovations* (London: Earthscan).
7 World Trade Organization (2005) *The Future of the WTO*. Report of the Consultative Board to the Director General ('The Sutherland Report') (Geneva: WTO).
8 K. Anderson (2000) 'The Ottawa Convention banning landmines: the role of international non-government organizations and the idea of international civil society', *European Journal of International Law*, vol 11, pp. 91–120.
9 A. Hudson (2001) 'NGO's transnational advocacy networks: from legitimacy to political responsibility?' *Global Networks*, vol 1, number 4, pp. 337–338.
10 M. Edwards, D. Hulme and T. Wallace (1999) 'NGOs in a global future: marrying local delivery to worldwide leverage', *Public Administration and Development*, 19, p. 133.
11 M. Edwards and J. Gaventa (eds) (2001) *Global Citizen Action* (Boulder CO, USA: Lynne Rienner Publishers) p. 7.
12 J. A. Scholte (2004) 'Civil society and democratically accountable global governance', *Government and Opposition*, vol 39, number 2, p. 230.
13 M. Edwards (2000) *NGO Rights and Responsibilities: A New Deal for Global Governance* (London: The Foreign Policy Centre) p. 19.
14 Edwards (2000) *op cit.*, p. 26.
15 Edwards (2000) *op cit.*, pp. 5, 19.
16 P. J. Spiro (2002) 'Accounting for NGOs', *Chicago Journal of International Law*, vol 3, pp. 161–169.
17 United Nations (2004). *We the People: Civil Society, the United Nations and Global Governance*, Report of the Panel of Eminent Persons on United Nations-Civil Society Relations (the Cardoso Report) (New York: United Nations).
18 R. C. Blitt (2004) 'Who Will Watch the Watchdogs? Human Rights Non-Government Organizations and the Case for Regulation', *Buffalo Human Rights Law Review*, vol 10, p. 261.
19 J. Clarke (2003) *Worlds Apart: Civil Society and the Battle for Ethical Globalisation* (Bloomfield, CT: Kumarian Press) p. 102.
20 C. Harper (2001) 'Do the facts matter? NGOs, research and international advocacy', in M. Edwards and J. Gaventa (eds) (2001) *Global Citizen Action* (Boulder CO, USA: Lynne Rienner Publishers) p. 252.
21 E. Mendizabal (2006) *Good News for Troubled Contexts. Lessons Learned from Case Studies on How Civil Society Organizations Influence Policy Processes* (London: Overseas Development Institute) p. 22.
22 J. Ballinger (2007) 'Co-opt and isolate', *New Internationalist*, number 407, December.
23 J. Clark (2001) 'Ethical Globalization: The Dilemmas and Challenges of Internationalising Civil Society', in M. Edwards and J. Gaventa (eds) (2001) *Global Citizen Action* (Boulder CO, USA: Lynne Rienner Publishers) pp. 23–24.
24 Participatory Research in Asia (1997) *Study of Social Policy Mapping of NGOs in South Asia* (New Delhi: PRIA).
25 J. Clark (2001) 'Ethical Globalisation: The Dilemmas and Challenges of Internationalising Civil Society', in M. Edwards and J. Gaventa (eds) (2001) *Global Citizen Action* (Boulder CO, USA: Lynne Rienner Publishers) p. 23.
26 D. Eade (2002) *Development and Advocacy* (Oxford UK: Oxfam GB) p. xiv.

27 L. Jordan and P. van Tuijl (2000) 'Political Responsibility in Transnational NGO Advocacy', *World Development*, vol 28, number 12, p. 2052.
28 Jordan and van Tuijl (2000) *op cit.*, pp. 2051–2065.
29 Jordan and van Tuijl (2000) *op cit.*, p. 2053.
30 J. Majot 'On trying to do well: practicing participatory democracy through international advocacy campaigns', in L. Jordan and P. van Tuijl (eds) (2006) *NGO Accountability: Politics, Principles and Innovations* (London: Earthscan).
31 Jordan and van Tuijl (2000), *op cit.*, which was in turn based on J. Kane (1995) *Savages* (New York: Vintage Books).

3
Oxfam and its Global Campaign on Trade

Oxfam is typical of present-day NGOs for whom advocacy is a key element in their approach. For most of its early history the organization focused on emergency relief and development assistance projects. It began in Britain in 1942 as the Oxford Committee for Famine Relief, campaigning for food supplies to be sent through an allied naval blockade to starving women and children in enemy-occupied Greece during the Second World War. In the years after the war, it grew to become a major NGO in the fields of emergency relief in disaster situations, and long-term development in poor communities around the world. Other similar organizations associated with the British organization grew up in other Northern countries (e.g. Oxfam Canada), and in 1995, these came together to form the Oxfam International confederation. Today the 13 affiliated organizations of this confederation work in over 100 countries, with more than 3,000 local organizations who strive to help people living in poverty to exercise their human rights, assert their dignity as full citizens and take control of their lives. Oxfam's efforts are focused on three areas: long-term development programmes aimed at reducing poverty and combating injustice, assistance to people affected by natural disasters or conflict, and advocacy and campaigning to raise awareness of the causes of poverty and press decision makers to change policies and practices that reinforce poverty and injustice. 'Experience of the real issues confronting poor people is linked to high-level research and lobbying aiming to change international policies and practices in ways which would ensure that poor people have the rights, opportunities and resources they need to improve and control their lives'.[1]

Each of the affiliates that make up the Oxfam International confederation is an independent and autonomous entity.[2] But in exchange for the right to use the Oxfam name, which has considerable marketing and other advantages, and the benefits of sharing resources, information and expertise with the other affiliates, each has agreed to abide by certain rules and obligations. These range from always using the standard Oxfam logo in the standard shade of Oxfam green on all printed material, through to actively contributing to international Oxfam advocacy campaigns and keeping to mutually agreed policy positions in their public pronouncements in these campaigns.[3]

One of the reasons why these organizations came together in 1995 was to better coordinate their development assistance programmes in Asia, Africa, Latin America, etc, which up till then had been run separately in an uncoordinated and sometimes duplicating manner. But another perhaps more powerful reason was to coordinate their various advocacy activities. Conscious of the fact that many of the institutions and organizations that they wished to influence in their quest to reduce poverty – the World Bank, World Trade Organization, transnational companies, etc – were international in nature, the affiliates felt that they too needed to be international in the way they organized their advocacy. One of the first activities carried out under the name of Oxfam International was the establishment of an advocacy office in Washington DC from which the World Bank and International Monetary Fund (IMF) could be more effectively lobbied and influenced.

But coordinated advocacy required more than just a joint office. The next step was to establish common aims and objectives for this joint advocacy, with common policies and strategies and coordinated activities. The idea was to have all the Oxfam affiliates around the world saying the same thing at the same time, via the media, popular campaigning, lobbying, etc to the same targets. The first attempt at this in the late 1990s was a campaign called 'Education Now' whose aim was to increase the access of girls and women in the South to education by increasing the funding that donors and governments devoted to schools and teachers. As a joint Oxfam campaign it was only partially successful, in that it was not taken up as actively as it might have been by affiliates.[4] The second attempt however, the 'Make Trade Fair' (MTF) campaign was altogether more ambitious and demanded a much greater commitment by all affiliates. It was expected that not only their advocacy staff would be involved but also their campaigners, their supporters, media liaison people, marketing departments, etc, plus their staff in field offices in Asia, Africa, Latin America, etc. The motivation at this stage was not just the need to correct some injustice that needed urgent attention, but also to see if this collection of diverse organizations and people spread around the globe could in fact act together as an influencing force on international bodies and processes that were too big for any individual Oxfam. In other words the process was as important as the outcome.

The topic for this new larger campaign was determined through a process of internal consultation and discussion. Various issues were put forward as being of urgent importance and argued for by different people and sections within the affiliates. But this was a time of increasing interest in the World Trade Organization (WTO) – the massive demonstrations at the Seattle WTO Ministerial Meeting had happened only a few years before – in the activities of sportswear companies that supposedly bought their products from 'sweatshop' manufacturers, and in 'fair trade' products such as coffee, tea and chocolate. Trade-related issues were on people's minds, and hence 'trade rules and practices' won the day as the topic for the campaign. The central message of the campaign was to be that trade has the potential to lift millions out of chronic poverty, but that potential is not being realized because the rules and practices of trade are rigged in the interests of the richer and more powerful nations and trading companies, and to the disadvantage of the poor. Its aim was to change the way in which the rules of international trade were set in the WTO, and the way in which some transnational companies traded, that disadvantaged the poor and the vulnerable in the South.

But trade is a big and multifarious subject and the issues involved quite complex. In order to make the campaign more concrete and accessible, it was decided to highlight certain examples of trade that illustrated the central message. The examples chosen were the international trade in pharmaceuticals, coffee beans, ready-made garments and agricultural products. Hence within the overall 'Make Trade Fair' campaign there were to be these sub-campaigns, on particular illustrative aspects of trade. Each became the focus of the campaign for a few months, with the launch of reports, lots of media work, popular campaigning and lobbying on that particular topic. The work on agricultural trade and the WTO negotiations on agriculture however had several such peaks of activity during the course of the campaign.

One of the ideas that influenced the design of this campaign was that there were 'tipping points' in public discourse, points at which the weight of public opinion becomes such that an issue is generally accepted by all, and little or no further dialogue is required. The movement against slavery, for example, reached such a point in the mid-19th century, after which it was no longer necessary to argue the merits or evils of the institution as it was generally accepted that it had to go. The struggle to allow women to vote also had a 'tipping point' in the early decades of the 20th century, after which women's suffrage became generally accepted. We are probably reaching such a point at the moment with the acceptance of global warming as a reality. It was hoped that the 'Make Trade Fair' campaign could also reach such a point where it was generally accepted that the rules and practices of trade had to be reformed so that they benefited rather than exploited the poor. One of the key strategies for doing this was to generate a massive global petition with tens of millions of names on it from all over the world that would represent a loud and forceful cry from the peoples of the world for the rules and practices of trade to be changed and made fair. For this reason it was called the 'Big Noise' petition. The idea was to some extent successful in that it was taken up in scores of countries around the world and by December 2005 had gathered nearly 18 million signatures. Whether it or the campaign in general ever generated a 'tipping point' in public discourse about trade is however debatable.

Oxfam as a network

In April 2002, the various Oxfams around the world, under the banner of Oxfam International, launched the 'Make Trade Fair' campaign in 25 countries. It was to run for the next five years, until mid-2007, after which it ran down and elements of it were incorporated into other campaigns. During those five years, the way in which the various parts of the Oxfam confederation operated and interacted, it can be argued, was more like that of a transnational network than a unified organization.

As well as its head office, located in its Northern home country, each affiliate has a number of field offices in the Southern countries in which it operates. In any particular country, say India, there will be field offices of several different Oxfams, who will to different degrees be working together on their field programmes of development assistance, perhaps emergency relief, and on their advocacy campaigns. So the staff of a field office of a particular affiliate in say India or Sri Lanka will be relating to the field offices of other affiliates in that country, as well as to its own head office – and of course to the partner organizations and allies with whom it is working in that country. They are in other words involved in a complex matrix of relationships and responsibilities. Also parts of this matrix are the Oxfam International offices. These do not belong to any one affiliate but are funded jointly by all. Located in key centres of power, such as Washington DC, New York, Brussels, and Geneva, their role is to support the advocacy work of affiliates and field offices by maintaining contact with and lobbying organizations such as the World Bank, United Nations, European Commission and World Trade Organization that are targets of Oxfam advocacy, gathering information, acting as a conduit into these organizations, and so on. This is part of a general trend among international NGOs that focus on transnational advocacy – the opening of advocacy offices in cities that are strategically important from an advocacy point of view.

The 'Make Trade Fair' campaign was to a large extent centrally planned. The shape and form of the campaign, its topic, targets, policy positions, strategies, timing, etc, were determined by bodies with representation from all affiliates. But within this centrally determined overall framework there was scope for flexibility and variation at an affiliate, region or country level. An affiliate always had the option of not taking up a particular activity or aspect of a campaign, for example because it did not have the resources to run with it, or the issue was not appropriate or relevant in their political context. What the campaign was advocating for in Brussels or London may be inappropriate or counter-productive in Washington, and perhaps completely irrelevant in Canberra, in which case it was simply not pursued in those countries. Also there were always issues related to the campaign that were of importance in one country, say the USA or Australia, but nowhere else, and which would be taken up by those affiliates only. The degree or flexibility was even greater for field offices in the South, in recognition of the fact that they have their own often quite difficult political situation to deal with – and a field programme that should not be put at risk or forced to close down because of what Oxfam said or did in its advocacy campaign. Oxfam offices in the South had the ability to control, and where necessary veto, what was said in the international campaign about the country or region in which they were operating.

In working on the international campaign, this array of Oxfam organizations and offices with this degree of independence interacted with one another in ways that were not unlike those of a transnational advocacy network. They worked on a common issue, with commonly held policy positions and coordinated activities, but they did so in their own way, depending on their particular role in the network, and their own priorities and political circumstances. In terms of the different network structures proposed by Chapman (see Chapter 1) this was a 'wheel' type structure with a central hub, but also interaction 'around the rim' between different parts of the network. For example when trying to influence the WTO trade negotiations, the Oxfam International (OI) office in Geneva, where the WTO is based, would provide political intelligence about what was happening and what various governments were proposing or arguing in the negotiations. Some field offices would be providing research on what the actual or potential effects of such proposals would be on the poor, plus human-interest stories that could be used in the media. Inter-affiliate groups would confer by email and teleconference to determine Oxfam policy positions, as well as lobbying, campaigning and media strategies. And affiliate head offices in the North would, if they chose, lobby their own governments that are members of the WTO, raise awareness in their own media, and perhaps run letter-writing and other campaigning activities in their home countries. Some offices in the South might do the same.

The design and overall supervision of the 'Make Trade Fair' campaign was in the hands of a Trade Campaign Working Group (later Project Group), which consisted of representatives of Oxfam affiliates and regions as well as specialists such as media and popular campaigning people. It met periodically face-to-face and in between via emails and teleconferences. As the campaign developed other inter-affiliate coordinating groups were formed – a Trade Policy Group to research and develop common policy positions; a Media Group which coordinated the activities of the media liaison people in the various affiliates; and a Popular Mobilization Group made up of the people responsible for popular campaigning in their respective countries. Members of these groups tended to be staff based in the North, in affiliate head offices, although as time went by representatives from the Southern regions in which Oxfam operated were incorporated.

For operational purposes, Oxfam International divides the world into regions – East Asia, South Asia, Southern Africa, Central America Mexico and the Caribbean, etc. In each of these Southern regions there are moves to bring the diverse programmes of the individual Oxfam affiliates in the region together into a coherent whole. To achieve this, a Regional Strategic Team has been established in each of them. The degree to which the development assistance and emergency response programmes of the various affiliates has been 'harmonized' in this way varies from region to region. But the advocacy programmes by and large are well integrated. Nearly all of the advocacy and campaigning that is done by Oxfam in these Southern regions is done jointly, under the supervision of the Regional Strategic Team and under the name of Oxfam International.

The way in which all of these different groups operated together can be illustrated by a typical campaign event – the launch of an Oxfam International briefing paper on some aspect of the WTO negotiations.

The need for this paper and the strategy for its use would be determined by the Trade Campaign Project Group. The research for it would be commissioned by the Trade Policy Group, using the resources of the Geneva office and various relevant offices in the South. The writer or writers would usually be based in the North. The Media Group would in consultation determine the best date for the launch and the main media outlets to be targeted. They would also produce a generic media release that could be 'localized' in individual countries and other background material, photos, etc for journalists. Translations of the report, media releases, etc into Spanish, French and other languages would be done by relevant affiliates. Spokespersons would be nominated in different countries and for different languages. Each affiliate (and Southern country offices if they so choose) would then pre-brief selected journalists in their country, send the report to relevant officials, distribute and follow up the media release, do media interviews, and follow up with officials. Thus the same story with the same message would hopefully appear in many media outlets around the world at the same time, each reinforcing the other.[5] If there were to be media stunts or popular campaigning in some countries around the launch, these would be coordinated and assisted by the Popular Mobilization Group.

Sub-campaign on the garment trade

In 2003, the 'Make Trade Fair' campaign had been running for a year or so, and planning was underway for the sub-campaign on the garment trade. In preparation for this, Oxfam International commissioned research in eight countries on the situation of women workers in the garment industry.[6] This involved interviewing over 1,000 workers, factory owners, managers, importers, union and government officials – and revealed a pattern of abuses of these workers across countries. Wages were very low, often not enough to provide workers with proper nutrition or housing. Workers were being subjected to ever more demanding production targets, and were working very long hours, including excessive amounts of overtime that was often compulsory and unpaid. Employment was precarious with people on short-term or no contracts, and hired and fired at will. Verbal abuse and harassment was common in the workplace. No unions were allowed, nor was collective bargaining. Those who tried to organize their fellow workers or demand better conditions were harassed or lost their jobs.

The potential of employment opportunities in the garment industry to lift people out of poverty, and in particular to give women economic and social independence (for most garment workers are women) was and still is not being realized because of poor working conditions. Southern governments who see cheap and compliant labour as their only comparative advantage in an increasingly competitive trading environment, were failing to enforce laws that are meant to protect workers and their basic rights and, as a result, millions of workers were losing out on their fair share of the potential benefits of a globalized garment trade. A major factor in this is the way the garment industry is structured – with many hundreds of small and large manufacturers of ready-made garments in a variety of Southern countries, but only a relatively small number of buyers and merchandizing companies. Because of this, the large retailers and brand-name companies hold all the negotiating power. As one manufacturer in a Southern country once said: 'You do not tell Walmart the price. Walmart tells you'. Manufacturers who cannot afford to lose Walmart, or Marks and Spencer, or Nike or whoever, as a customer are forced to accept whatever is on offer. They then adjust to the low price offered by squeezing workers' wages. Low wages contribute to long hours as workers compensate for the low rate per hour by working long hours, so that total income per week is enough to live on. The industry is able to push costs and risk down the supply chain and onto suppliers and vulnerable workers who are least able to resist and defend themselves. This is a global business model that thrives when workers are denied the right to organize.

In taking up this issue as part of the 'Make Trade Fair' campaign, Oxfam was keen to focus on women workers in particular, whom it felt were doubly disadvantaged – as workers in these exploitative supply chains, and as a socially disadvantaged group within their own societies. Women are the 'backbone' of the international garment industry. Some 70 per cent of the workforce in Economic Processing Zones (where garment manufacturing mainly happens) are women, usually young, unmarried and from a rural background.

All these issues about the garment industry were summarized in a report released by Oxfam International in February 2004 called 'Trading Away Our Rights. Women Working in Global Supply Chains'. The report called for a number of things: (1) Brand-name companies and retailers should make respect for labour rights integral to their supply-chain business strategies by addressing the impacts of their own sourcing and purchasing practices on the way that producers treat their workers. (2) Producers worldwide should provide decent jobs for their employees, including respect for workers' right to join trade unions and bargain collectively, and eliminating discrimination against women workers.

(3) National governments, South and North, should stop trading away workers' rights in law and in practice, and enforce international labour standards that promote decent employment for poverty reduction, gender equality and development.[7]

Oxfam was keen to run this sub-campaign in alliance with an organization that had an ongoing campaign on garment workers' rights, and which would be able to carry on after the sub-campaign was over and Oxfam had withdrawn. The essence of these sub-campaigns was that they were short term, one of a series of illustrations of the general theme about trade. But the problem with short-term campaigns is that they have to be dropped before anything substantial has been achieved, which is often not very sensible and not generally acceptable to supporters. To overcome this, it was decided that, rather than starting a campaign and then after a few months dropping it, Oxfam would find a long-term ongoing campaign and simply come in and support it for a few months during the sub-campaign to give it a short-term boost. Any supporters that this generated could then continue to work with the ongoing organization and its campaign.

In this Oxfam was lucky enough to find the ideal organization – a European-based group with extensive networks in the South called the Clean Clothes Campaign (CCC) that had been campaigning for many years on the rights of garment workers. Even better was the fact that CCC had a short-term campaign in mind that would be ideally suited to the short-term support that Oxfam envisaged. This was a campaign to use the Olympic Games that were about to be held in Athens in August 2004, and the public interest this was going to attract, to highlight the issues of workers in the sportswear industry. The campaign would contrast the values for which the Olympic Movement stands (fairness, human dignity, etc) with the situation of the women who make the sportswear and uniforms worn at the Games. It was to be called the Olympics Campaign and would run for the months leading up to the Athens Olympics. Its strategy was to focus attention and exert consumer pressure on half-a-dozen or so brand-name sportswear companies – not the major ones like Nike that were the usual targets of such 'sweatshop campaigns' but second-level companies such as Umbro, Asics, Puma, etc that had up till then escaped attention. The campaign would also focus on the international and national Olympics Committees, asking them to put in place measures to ensure that any garment that bore the Olympic logo was made under fair conditions.

In deciding to campaign on an issue of workers' rights, Oxfam also naturally sought and formed an alliance with the union movement, and in particular with the umbrella group, the International Confederation of Free Trade Unions (ICFTU). This involved considerable discussion between the Brussels-based ICFTU and Oxfam over policy and Oxfam's position, but was eventually resolved and an alliance formed. However some aspects of the joint policies positions of the campaign and what could or could not be said – for example on labour rights in China, given that Oxfam had a programme there that could be endangered – continued to be negotiated right up to the last minute. Fortunately CCC already had extensive contacts with the ICFTU, and hence it was a relatively easy matter to form a three-way alliance between Oxfam, CCC and ICFTU to run the Olympics Campaign. The campaign slogan chosen was 'Play Fair at the Olympics. Respect Workers Rights in the Sportswear Industry'. A joint report called 'Play Fair at the Olympics' was released in early March 2004, based on research done by all three agencies into sportswear manufacturers in six countries[8] and under the logos of the three agencies.

So now there were two rival sub-campaigns on garment workers – an Oxfam only one ('Trading Away Our Rights') with its emphasis on purchasing practices, women workers and precarious employment – and a joint one ('Olympics Campaign') with its emphasis on sportswear companies, the Olympic Movement, and basic labour rights such as the right to organize. The former, 'Trading Away Our Rights', was a 'bottom up' or 'supportive' type of campaign that built on and supported a number of national level labour campaigns in a variety of countries – whereas the 'Olympics Campaign' was a 'top down', centrally organized and globally unified, 'directive' campaign and therefore much more in line with the 'Make Trade Fair' model. Because of this and the importance of the alliance, it was the 'Olympics Campaign' that won out and became the focus for Oxfam, while 'Trading Away Our Rights' continued in the background, doing excellent work supporting the national level campaigns with which it had become involved, but a little disconnected from the mainstream campaign.

The Olympics Campaign by the three organizations built up to a peak in the months leading up to the Athens Games in August 2004, and then wound down. What happened during this time, and what it achieved, is described in Chapter 4.

Sub-campaign on agricultural trade

After the Athens Olympics, the emphasis of the 'Make Trade Fair' campaign returned once again to agricultural trade and the WTO negotiations. This was perhaps the most important of the sub-campaigns within the global campaign in that it not only clearly illustrated the central message about trade rules being rigged in favour of the rich and powerful, but also it was an aspect of trade of particular importance to poverty reduction. More than 80 per cent of the world's poor people live in rural areas, and ensuring that agriculture works for them must be at the heart of the international trade agenda.

The drive towards the liberalization of trade[9] by the World Trade Organization and other international bodies was, and still is, putting more and more peasant farmers into direct competition with imports produced by farmers in rich Northern countries who have access to capital, machinery, hi-tech inputs and government subsidies. The result could be millions of poor farmers in the South being unable to compete in their domestic markets and being forced to leave their land for uncertain futures in ever more crowded urban slums. Exacerbating the problem is the dumping of subsidized agricultural products from Europe and the United States onto export markets. The European Union and United States governments heavily subsidize their agricultural producers, and this has led to agricultural surpluses, which have traditionally been disposed of by exporting them – at artificially low prices. This undermines exporters from other countries, including Southern exporters, who do not (or cannot) subsidize their farmers, by lowering world prices and unfairly taking export markets. And because of trade liberalization and the opening up of markets, these subsidized goods are increasingly able to be imported into Southern countries, undermining local farmers who are trying to sell their products on the domestic market. There is a danger of Southern countries being forced to open their markets to agricultural imports before alternative livelihoods have been found for the large populations of vulnerable farmers that will be displaced. The argument that Southern governments are increasingly using is that they should be allowed to retain control over how far and how fast they open their markets to agricultural imports. But they are under considerable pressure from Northern agricultural exporting countries to do the opposite, to give up their protectionist policies and liberalize their agricultural markets as far and as fast as possible.

The rules that governments follow with respect to international trade (on tariffs, quotas, etc) are set via a process of inter-governmental negotiations at the World Trade Organization. Most of these take place at the government official level at the WTO headquarters in Geneva. But every two years or so the politicians become involved when Trade Ministers of the WTO member countries meet together at a Ministerial Conference. It is at these conferences that new agreements are concluded and signed.

There are now around 150 countries that are members of the WTO, the majority of them Southern countries, big and small. But the negotiations tend to be dominated by a few bigger trading nations, which until recently meant the United States, European Union, and a few other Northern countries. However this is now changing as larger Southern countries such as Brazil, India and China begin to exert their influence. At the 2003 Ministerial Conference a significant development took place when a group of Southern countries got together to form what was called the 'Group of Twenty' or G20 and lobbied jointly.[10] This was a group that could to some extent match the influence of the Americans and Europeans, and its appearance changed the balance of negotiating power within the WTO.

In 2004 and 2005, Oxfam's sub-campaign on agriculture was focused on the WTO negotiations of an Agreement on Agriculture, and in particular on the all-important Ministerial Conference that was coming up in December 2005 in Hong Kong. Its main policy calls were for a new WTO Agreement on Agriculture to be signed in Hong Kong that: (1) would not prevent Southern governments from promoting development goals, poverty reduction, food security, and livelihood concerns; (2) allowed Southern countries to cut tariffs in a way that did not undermine their development strategies; (3) allowed full exemption from tariff reductions of food security crops – food that people depend on for their lives (for example rice in Indonesia, corn in Mexico). The campaign's main strategies were to:

a. highlight the 'rigged rules' that allowed the United States and European Union to continue to subsidize their producers and dump agricultural surpluses on export markets, and the hypocrisy of Northern governments that insisted that Southern countries open their markets while resisting the opening of their own;
b. produce and launch in the media a number of briefing papers that documented these abuses;
c. encourage the assertiveness of Southern countries in the WTO by providing them with documented examples of unfair rules and practices by Northern countries and the arguments to counter their negotiating positions;
d. collect millions of signatures in the North and South on the 'Big Noise' petition and present it to world leaders at the Hong Kong ministerial meeting.

How this global campaign by Oxfam manifested itself in India in the lead-up to the Hong Kong ministerial meeting, and what the outcomes were, are described in detail in Chapter 5.

Oxfam in South Asia

Sri Lanka and India both fall within Oxfam's South Asia region. At this stage, there were three Oxfam affiliates operating in that region – Oxfam Great Britain, Novib (later called Oxfam Novib, the Netherlands Oxfam) and Oxfam Australia.[11] Oxfam Great Britain had the largest presence, with programmes in all six countries of the region and a number of offices, staffed mainly by locals, spread throughout them. Novib on the other hand had no offices in the region. It had a large programme in terms of funds dispersed, supporting the work of around 90 organizations, but this was administered from its headquarters in The Hague, assisted by frequent field visits by staff to the region. Oxfam Australia had the smallest programme, focused on northeast India, southeast India and Sri Lanka, with an office in each of these. There was also a new and somewhat embryonic local Oxfam in the region, which was known as the Oxfam India Trust (but has since become Oxfam India). As the name implies, it operates in only one country in the region and is headquartered in New Delhi. The aim is that it will eventually grow and take over the programmes of the 'foreign' Oxfams to become the sole Oxfam in India.

The Regional Strategic Team for South Asia took some time to take up the 'Make Trade Fair' campaign. In 2003, one year after it had been launched, the emphasis of the international campaign was on preparing for the sub-campaign on the garment trade, and this sparked some interest in South Asia. There was already considerable interest in the garment industry and the rights of garment workers amongst the Oxfams in Sri Lanka and Bangladesh, because of the potentially disastrous consequences of recent changes in WTO rules that meant that exports from these two countries were about to lose the preferential access they enjoyed into Northern markets. This meant that they would have to compete for markets on equal terms with the Chinese and others, which could mean massive job losses in the industry. Oxfam Australia's office in Sri Lanka and Oxfam Great Britain's office in Bangladesh were already working with labour organizations to raise awareness of this impending crisis, and to prepare for its consequences. At its meeting in Colombo in July 2003, the Regional Strategic Team decided that it was appropriate to turn this work into a regional campaign (or more precisely a two-country campaign) on the trade in garments and the rights of garment workers. This would be their contribution to the international 'Make Trade Fair' campaign. It would be funded jointly by the three affiliates operating in the region, and managed by a campaign group answerable to the Regional Strategic Team, to be known as the South Asia Labour and Trade (SALT) team. Unlike the international campaign, which had brand-name sportswear companies as its primary target, the campaign in South Asia would focus on governments and on ensuring that they put in place effective measures to protect the rights of their garment workers during the industry restructuring.

Later, in 2004, with the work on garment workers preceding smoothly, the Regional Strategic Team decided to become involved in the sub-campaign on agriculture as well. This was in a sense inevitable given the importance of the role of the Indian Government in the WTO negotiations. Once again it was decided that this sub-campaign would focus on two countries only, India and Bangladesh in this case, and that it would be funded jointly by the three affiliates. Another campaign group answerable to the Regional Strategic Team was formed, called the South Asia Trade and Agriculture group, for which the acronym STAR was somewhat dubiously contrived. The next two chapters describe in some detail how these two Oxfam campaigns – on garment workers in Sri Lanka, and agriculture in India – were run under the guidance of the South Asia Regional Strategic Team as part of the much bigger international 'Make Trade Fair' campaign. They are, in a sense, a microcosm of the type of advocacy that Oxfam and organizations like it carry out on a regular basis in Southern countries around the world.

Notes

1 Oxfam International website www.oxfam.org date accessed 10 December 2008.
2 Oxfam America, Oxfam Australia, Oxfam-in-Belgium, Oxfam Canada, Oxfam France-Agir Ici, Oxfam Germany, Oxfam Great Britain, Oxfam Hong Kong, Oxfam Ireland, Oxfam Novib (Netherlands), Oxfam New Zealand, Oxfam Quebec, Intermon Oxfam (Spain), and more recently Oxfam India.
3 One of the conditions for an organization to be a member of the Oxfam International confederation is that it carries the word Oxfam in its title e.g. Oxfam America, Oxfam Germany. For some, this meant a change of name e.g. Novib became Oxfam Novib.
4 In this chapter the name Oxfam will be used as short-hand for the collection of organizations that make up the Oxfam International confederation, including their various offices in the North and South and the joint Oxfam International offices, and inter-affiliate Oxfam working groups.
5 One of the most annoying aspects of these stories was journalists who described Oxfam International as 'a British charity organization'. Neither of those adjectives is true.
6 Morocco, Kenya, Sri Lanka, Bangladesh, Thailand, China, Honduras, UK.

7 Oxfam International (2004) *Trading Away Our Rights. Women Working in Global Supply Chains*. (Oxford: Oxfam International), p. 8.
8 Bulgaria, Turkey, China, Thailand, Cambodia, Indonesia.
9 That is, the removing of all 'barriers to trade' such as tariffs and quotas, which in the past have been used by governments to protect their local producers.
10 Its membership varies a little from time to time, but basically consists of Argentina, Bolivia, Brazil, Chile, China, Cuba, Egypt, India, Indonesia, Mexico, Nigeria, Pakistan, Paraguay, Philippines, South Africa, Tanzania, Thailand, Venezuela and Zimbabwe.
11 Oxfam Hong Kong and Intermon Oxfam (the Spanish Oxfam) also had very small programmes there, but were not involved in campaigns or advocacy in the region at that time.

4
Case Study: Garment Workers in Sri Lanka

The last two decades have seen the manufacturing of ready-made garments for export become a major industry in Sri Lanka, employing hundreds of thousands of mainly poor rural women and men under conditions that could be classed as exploitative. Hence it was inevitable that when the 'Make Trade Fair' (MTF) campaign began its focus on the trade in garments and the situation of the women workers who made them, it sparked some interest among the Oxfams that operated in that country.

The importance of garment exports in Sri Lanka was the result of a government policy of privatization and investment liberalization that emphasized the attracting of foreign direct investment in the manufacturing of products that benefited from cheap labour. One of the manifestations of this policy was the establishing of areas of concentrated foreign and domestic investment known as Export Processing Zones (EPZs) in which investors could enjoy special benefits. The three main EPZs were established in 1978, 1984, and 1991 respectively – and in 1992 the entire country was declared an Export Processing Zone. Because of its relatively cheap labour, well-educated workforce, and good access into European and American markets via quotas (see below) Sri Lanka became a major centre for the manufacture and supply of ready-made garments to the world market. By 2002 there were an estimated 300,000 workers employed in the industry in Sri Lanka, the overwhelming majority of them being women.[1] While women constitute some 35 per cent of the overall work force in Sri Lanka, in the garment industry they dominate, particularly in the unskilled work categories. The majority of them are young, single rural women who have few other employment opportunities.

The working conditions inside the EPZ factories are not good. Some of the more prominent problems include:

- Long hours of overtime, of up to 60 or 90 hours per month.
- Excessive production targets.
- Poor or non-existent occupational health and safety practices.
- Precarious work with little job security.
- Repression of the right to organize, to form a union or bargain collectively.
- Harassment of women workers in the factory and in the areas where they live.

Health hazards include industrial accidents resulting from inadequate training on how to use protective gear and handle machinery, the removal of safety guards, and defective machines. In addition, ventilation and sanitation systems are often sub-standard. It is not uncommon for managers to limit the number of visits that can be made to the toilet during working hours, and workers in some factories have been banned from drinking water during working hours. Workers can be required to meet unreasonable production targets (60 collars, pockets or hems per hour, when most can only sew 45), and have reported physical punishments for failure to meet these targets. Women often complain of sexual harassment both within the factories and on the streets and public transport on the way to and from work.

Lodgings for workers in boarding houses are generally crowded, unsafe, and unsanitary. In the housing complexes near the Zones, it is not uncommon to have 10 or 12 women sharing one room, and 30 sharing one toilet. They have to wake up early in the mornings to take turns using the single toilet. But despite the poor conditions, accommodation is not cheap for workers. Running boarding houses has become big business for house owners near the Zones.

A major complaint of garment workers is the excessively long hours they have to work for low pay. The low hourly rate means that they must work many hours, including overtime, in order to bring their total weekly income up to a reasonable living wage. If the wage they received for a normal day's work without overtime were enough to live on, which it generally is not, they would be less willing to work long hours. But this would not be in the interests of the factory owner who needs the ability to require people to work into the night when there are rush orders to fill and a short deadline to meet. But this can be a heavy imposition, particularly for women with families who also have

Case Study: Garment Workers in Sri Lanka 69

domestic obligations that they are expected to meet outside working hours. Prior to 2002 the labour laws of Sri Lanka specified that workers were not allowed to work more than 100 hours of overtime per year. Although workers regularly exceeded this limit prior to the amendment, it was voluntary, and they had some means of redress if they were fired for refusing to work the extra hours. But in 2002 this limit was lifted, and replaced by a new limit of 60 hours per month (720 hours per year). The new law does not specify that overtime must be voluntary. Hence workers are unable to refuse overtime, unless they have already worked the maximum 60 hours in that month.

But despite these numerous problems and abuses, the garment industry does provide many thousands of workers with employment and a means of earning an income. Although working conditions need to be improved, it is in nobody's interest to see the industry and the jobs it creates disappear. But this is what appeared to be about to happen in 2002, as a result of a change in the international rules of trade that threatened the access of Sri Lanka's ready-made garments into the all-important United States (US) and European Union (EU).

A few decades ago an arrangement known as the Multi-Fibre Agreement (MFA) was put in place by the US and EU to limit the importation of cheap garments from the South and protect domestic jobs. The limiting was done by allocating quotas to individual producing countries for products made from cotton, wool or synthetic fibres. While this limited access for most countries, in Sri Lanka's case it encouraged growth, for the quotas it was allocated were significantly larger than its then small garment industry produced. The quotas in fact guaranteed an attractive level of access to those important markets, and this was one of the reasons for the industry's growth in Sri Lanka. But the MFA and its quota system did not meet the non-discrimination rules of the World Trade Organization (WTO), and under an agreement reached in 1994, the MFA was to be phased out over a ten-year period from 1995 to 2005. For Sri Lanka this meant it would lose the advantage it had long enjoyed over other garment exporting countries of a generous access into lucrative Northern markets. When the MFA and its quota system were phased out, it would have to compete on equal terms with all other garment exporting countries, some of which were more competitive in terms of labour costs or delivery times. It appeared that Sri Lanka's garment industry, which accounted for more than half of the country's export earnings, was under serious threat, and that up to 100,000 workers could lose their jobs.

While the MFA was supposed to be phased out in stages over the ten-year period, so that countries like Sri Lanka would have time to adjust, in practice the Northern countries procrastinated so that by 2002, eight years into the process, very little had happened. The prospect was that, when the 2005 deadline was reached, there would be a sudden disappearance of the quotas and a sudden and catastrophic loss of orders and jobs. But because nothing much had changed up to that point, the Sri Lankan Government and garment industry was complacent and had done nothing to prepare. There was an urgent need for something to be done, for the government and industry to put in place a plan of action that would minimize job losses by improving the competitiveness of the industry, and measures to ensure that the thousands of workers who did lose their jobs would receive a redundancy package and some assistance to retrain or find another job. But none of this was happening.

In response, Oxfam in Sri Lanka as early as 2002 decided on a campaign to raise awareness of the potential impact of the MFA phase-out and to motivate the government and garment industry to start preparing for it.[2] The strategy initially was to establish a series of dialogues involving the various stakeholders – unions, government and business.[3] In August 2002 the first of these dialogues, a two-day workshop with the unions and labour-oriented NGOs took place in Colombo. As a result, an informal group was established to take the process forward, consisting of the leading figures from the key unions and worker-oriented NGOs. It was referred to by Oxfam as the Core Advisory Group.[4]

While all this was happening in Sri Lanka, at the international level Oxfam was about to embark on the 'Make Trade Fair' sub-campaign on labour rights and the trade in garments, and field offices like those in Colombo were being asked to take part. But there was the question of how this local campaign on the loss of jobs due to the MFA phase-out would fit in with the international campaign with its focus on improving working conditions and workers' rights in the sportswear industry and on the Athens Olympic Games. When this was discussed at the August 2002 workshop in Colombo, the feeling was that they could be integrated. While the work on MFA phase-out would continue to be their main focus, work on working conditions would complement that quite well. They would take part in, and hopefully gain benefits from, being part of the large Oxfam international campaign, but without the focus on sportswear and the Athens Olympic Games.

In the meantime, the process begun in August 2002, of a multi-stakeholder dialogue on the impact of the MFA phase-out continued. The second round of consultation meetings was held in September 2003 over a period of three days – the first day being with manufacturers, the second with government, and the third day with manufacturers, government and buyers together.

Establishing a coalition

When it began this work in Sri Lanka, Oxfam was faced with a group of potential allies with long experience fighting for the rights of garment workers – trade unions, labour NGOs and women's groups – who were disunited and, by their own admission, not operating in a cooperative manner. There were many reasons for this, including capacity differences, turf wars and personality clashes. Also there was an atmosphere of competition, generated by the need that each organization felt to impress the international donor organizations on which it relied to obtain further funding. It was clear that if progress was to be made in protecting the rights of workers in the face of the restructuring, and in a situation in which employer groups were strong and influential and the government was focused on the needs of investors not those of the labour force, there needed to be a group that could act collectively and cohesively and campaign over a long period. The basis of such a group was obviously the organizations that were represented in the Core Advisory Group. Consequently Oxfam invested heavily in turning this Group, who initially only came together when Oxfam asked them to, into an effective coalition that would engage in a long-term coordinated campaign. There had long been a recognition among those in the Group that this level of cooperation and coordination was desirable, even essential, and so they were not unwilling participants in this process. Oxfam was facilitating something that they were keen to do anyway.

In the second half of 2003, the Core Advisory Group was brought together a number of times in order to build a sense of trust and to identify some clear objectives and activities that they could undertake jointly over the coming months – which would then be funded and supported by Oxfam. The participants, after much discussion of rival proposals, eventually identified four issues on which they could work together – only one of which was about the MFA phase-out, the rest being about improving the working and living conditions of garment workers in general. They were:

Compensation. Making sure that the adverse impacts of industry restructuring on workers due to the phase-out of the MFA were mitigated. Ensuring that a comprehensive and adequate compensation package was put in place for workers who lose their jobs. Also lobbying of international buyers and 'brand-name' garment retailers to act responsibly during the phase-out. For this, they looked to Oxfam to provide the necessary international links, and possibly direct campaigning in the North on their behalf.[5]

Living wage. Bringing to the national agenda the concept of a 'living wage', a social wage that recognizes hidden costs and is enough to fulfil basic needs without overtime – and which is recognized by the government and employers as a legitimate basis for setting wage levels.

Living conditions. Ensuring dignified living conditions by creating a healthy and secure environment for women workers.

Freedom of Association. Creating an environment that affirms the internationally recognized right of workers to form unions and bargain collectively.

It took a long while for a sense of trust and working together on joint activities to develop amongst the Group. But it did develop. A significant event was the adoption in December 2003 of a name for the joint Group. What had been the 'Core Advisory Group' for Oxfam took on a public identity of its own as the 'Apparel-industry Labour Rights Movement' or ALaRM for short. In February 2004 ALaRM received its first public exposure at a major media event in Colombo.

As part of the international 'Make Trade Fair' campaign, there was to be a worldwide launch in a number of countries in February 2004 of an Oxfam report on the rights of women garment workers ('Trading Away Our Rights'), and it was suggested by the members of ALaRM that the report be launched in Colombo as well. The question arose of whether it should be an Oxfam event or an ALaRM one. Normally in a situation like this, Oxfam as a foreign-based organization would stay in the background and support its local partners and allies to take the front running. But on this occasion the feeling on the part of ALaRM members was that the event and the issues would attract more attention from the government and industry if it was done in the name of an internationally reputable organization like Oxfam than if it was done by local unions and organizations. And besides the report being launched was an Oxfam one, not an ALaRM one. Hence the event became a dual one – the launch of the Oxfam report in Sri Lanka, and the official launch of ALaRM.

Campaign actions

On 18 February 2004, an official launch and media briefing was held at the World Trade Centre in Colombo to raise awareness and concern about the way garment workers were being exploited. The key message was that, despite being the backbone of the country's economy, the 300,000 workers in the garment industry, 85 per cent of them women, were working under very poor conditions. At a time when the industry was facing major restructuring due to the MFA phase-out, the report attempted to 'set the standard for responsible business practices that respects the rights of women workers'. It aimed to show what needed to change if the benefits of trade were to reach the poor.[6] The launch turned out to be a major event, with around 120 people attending, including representatives from the Labour Department, Board of Investment, garment manufacturers associations, trade unions, foreign embassies, the World Bank and other international donor agencies. Print and electronic journalists from all three languages (Sinhala, Tamil, English) attended and media coverage was extensive. Most of the major newspapers carried the story, and several TV channels featured the event in their evening news. Five radio stations included items in their news bulletins on the day and on succeeding days, including follow-up interviews with Oxfam spokespersons. As a result a number of organizations sought meetings with Oxfam and ALaRM representatives.

A few days after the media launch there was a mass campaign launch for workers organized by ALaRM. The aim of this was to raise awareness among the workers themselves of the potential impact of the MFA phase-out on their jobs, and to introduce ALaRM as a credible and accessible workers' representative. The event was a popular one in that it featured song and dance items and an alternative fashion show demonstrating the hidden talents of the workers. About a thousand workers attended.

As a result of the publicity around the MFA phase-out and pressure from ALaRM and Oxfam, the local representatives of the International Labour Organization (ILO)[7] became interested in the issue. On 21 July 2004, the ILO hosted a multi-stakeholder conference to discuss the potential impacts of the phase-out of quotas. One outcome of this was the formation of a high-powered Task Force under ILO sponsorship, whose members included the Secretary to the Minister of Labour, the Commissioner of Labour, Secretary General of the Joint Apparel Associations Forum (JAAF), the Industrial Relations Officer of the Board of Investment (BOI) and representatives from the Ministry of Finance,

Ministry of Trade and Ministry of Industries. It also included five members of ALaRM, and an Oxfam representative. The presence of the latter and of the NGO members of ALaRM was unusual and was challenged by some members of the Task Force. ILO activities normally only involve representatives of governments, business and unions – not NGOs.

The Task Force met on a regular basis during the rest of the year and at the end produced a comprehensive report with a number of recommendations. However the employers' groups and the Board of Investment were never very keen on the whole process and were certainly not happy with the report's recommendations. According to ALaRM members, they tried to delay and prevent its release.[8] Then on Boxing Day 2004, Sri Lanka was hit by a disastrous tsunami and the Task Force was forgotten for many weeks and months as everyone's attention focused on the disaster. People who belonged to the organizations that made up ALaRM lost family members, and the local branches of those organizations in the affected areas were actively involved in providing immediate disaster relief, as was Oxfam. Some months later, when the worst was over and things had started to return to normal, ALaRM tried to revive interest in the report. But by this time the ILO, in the face of the opposition from the business groups and parts of government, was not willing to push it. The result was that the report was shelved and no action was ever taken.

Earlier in 2004, the Oxfam team in South Asia had made a request to the 'Make Trade Fair' campaign organizers in Europe for assistance. They wanted the Oxfams in Europe to lobby the European Commission for greater market access for Sri Lankan and Bangladesh garments. The issue was the European Union's 'rules of origin'. Some garment exports from Sri Lanka were being excluded on the basis that they could not really be classed as Sri Lankan exports. The issue was – to what extend could ready-made garments coming from Sri Lanka be regarded as Sri Lankan manufactured goods and therefore eligible for entry under that country's low tariffs, when the textiles were manufactured elsewhere (Japan, India, etc) and all that was done in Sri Lanka was cutting and sewing. Most of the value of the product was in the manufacture of the textiles, and the cutting and sewing in Sri Lanka only added a small amount to its value. According to the European Union's 'rules of origin' this meant that they could not be classed as manufactured in Sri Lanka. These rules, it was felt, were unfairly restrictive and needed to be relaxed. Oxfam Great Britain made a submission on this to the European Commission in March 2004, and some lobbying was done in Brussels. But little effort could be devoted to this by the international campaign, as it was an issue for only two countries.

One positive outcome from the Task Force discussions was that the Department of Labour, which is responsible for conditions in Sri Lanka's factories, became interested in the possible effects of the quota phase-out, but realized it had very little information about the number and location of garment producing factories in the country, or how many workers were involved. Hence it decided (with encouragement and assistance from Oxfam) to undertake a large-scale survey of all the garment factories in Sri Lanka using its countrywide network of offices. Oxfam provided the required technical input and financial assistance. One hundred and fifty labour officers were given training on the reason for the survey, research methodology and interviewing techniques, and were then sent out to visit every garment factory in their area of responsibility to fill out a questionnaire (jointly designed by the Department and Oxfam) about each enterprise and its structure, production process, workers, who it manufactured for, etc. As a result, some 745 factories were surveyed in October 2004. The results were analysed and tabulated by Oxfam, and the results handed over to the Department. This meant that the government department responsible for monitoring garment factories now had the basic information it needed to do this. The Assistant Commissioner of Labour later said that this data, which would not otherwise have been available, was of great use to the Department, and had been widely distributed and used.[9]

The process was repeated two years later in 2006 in order to obtain accurate information on what had happened in the intervening period. The final phase-out of the MFA internationally occurred at the end of 2004, and hence data from this survey provided a picture of the actual impact on the industry and workers 18 months after the phase-out. In mid-2006, the Department of Labour reported that some 50 factories had in fact closed down in the post MFA period, and approximately 10,000 workers had been retrenched. While this was far less than expected, the feeling was that the worst was yet to come, that the main impact was being delayed by companies having a hang-over of orders from before the phase-out that was keeping them going – and by the fact that garment exports from China (the Sri Lankan industry's major competitor) were still being restricted. Nevertheless the economic situation in the industry was becoming tighter, particularly for the smaller factories, and wages and working conditions for those workers who remained were deteriorating. Overall the value of Sri Lanka's apparel exports had actually increased, even though the quantity decreased, as there was a trend towards more high-value-added niche market products. It was mainly the larger factories that were equipped to adapt to this market, and hence they were gaining and expanding, while the many smaller factories were struggling to survive and closing.[10] More experienced workers, who were the ones preferred by the larger and more well-established factories, were able to remain in employment, but the younger and less experienced ones were losing their jobs.

Throughout 2005 and 2006, ALaRM continued to campaign for improved conditions and proper treatment for retrenched workers. In 2005 it decided to use May Day (1 May), the traditional day of celebration and demonstration for organized labour around the world, to try to reach the largely unorganized workforce in the EPZs and raise awareness of their rights. Workers in the apparel industry who were members of trade unions normally celebrated May Day with street rallies, carrying banners and shouting slogans, and other union activities. But the majority of the workers were not unionized and would therefore not normally take part in such events, which in any case were seen as very political and therefore a little threatening by the majority of women workers who feared repercussions if they took part. To overcome this, ALaRM members decided to hold a non-traditional event – a procession in the Katunayake EPZ with music and cultural events instead of the usual slogans and banners. The aim was to introduce ALaRM to more workers, to overcome the fear of participating in union events, and to hopefully encourage more participation in future events.

During the months of June and July 2005, one of the ALaRM member organizations, Dabindu Collective, an NGO that ran a centre for workers, undertook a campaign to do something about the poor housing conditions that garment workers were having to put up with. They conducted a survey of about 100 boarding houses in the Katunayake EPZ to gather information and evidence about the bad living conditions there, in order to take it to the local authorities and demand action. Problems experienced by the women ranged from unhygienic conditions in boarding houses to poor street lighting and robberies and sexual harassment returning home at night after working overtime. As a result, several meetings were held with local authorities, police and others to discuss what could be done. The public health authority took some steps to improve conditions in the boarding houses, and the police to improve security on the streets. But the initiative was not followed up and as a result there were no permanent changes.[11]

Other activities that ALaRM undertook during this period included the launch in December 2005 of a research report that set out the impact of the MFA phase-out 12 months after it had come into effect, and called on employers and government to fulfil their responsibility towards workers by putting in place mechanisms to help them face the restructuring. At the press briefing to launch the report, women who had lost their jobs gave personal testimonies. Sunitha Kumudini, a sewing machine operator at a medium-scale garment factory, said that when she went to work one morning, she found the factory gates locked and a notice on the gate saying that the company has been closed until further notice. The company had closed without paying the employees salaries and wages that were owed to them. Another woman, Kumudini, a 40-year old skilled garment worker, said that she is now out of work and cannot find a similar job on account of her age. A mother of two children, she was the only income earner of the family, and since she lost her job the family have been facing severe hardship. Badrika Chandani told a similar story. She was working in a factory in the Katunayake EPZ when the company closed down in May 2004 as it did not get enough quotas. The employees organized and protested but, she said, the management used hired thugs to assault them.[12]

One of the other key issues that ALaRM had decided to work on back in 2003 was to try to improve wages by promoting the idea of a 'living wage' as a basis for determining wage rates in the garment sector, 'a social wage that recognizes hidden costs and is adequate to fulfil the basic needs of a worker from an eight-hour working day'. To determine what constituted a 'living wage' in different circumstances – in rural or urban areas, with and without children to support, etc – it was necessary to survey a representative sample of garment workers to see how much they did actually spend on basic necessities such as food, accommodation and transport, and hence determine what minimum income they needed in order to maintain health and well-being. Staff from ALaRM member organizations and worker activists were trained to go out to boarding houses and interview workers about their expenditure. The survey of some 850 workers was carried out in September and October 2005, but the analysis of the data took nearly a year.

It was not until September 2006 that ALaRM released its report on a 'living wage' for garment workers, at a presentation and media briefing in Colombo. Its basic message was that the average female garment worker needed to earn 10,000 to 12,000 rupees per month if she was to meet basic necessities including proper nutrition, but in practice the average basic wage in the industry was only around 5,000 rupees, which workers could increase to around 7,500 rupees by working long and tiring hours of overtime. The result was widespread poor nutrition and over-work, which was taking a heavy human toll.

The event received extensive media coverage – in ten newspapers, one radio station and two TV channels. The report was released in September in the hope that it would influence the annual Board of Investment increments that occurs every November. But this did not happen. The concept of a 'living wage' was not accepted by the reviewing authorities. However the figures in the report were used by unions in specific wages negotiations; and it did stir up debate in the media and elsewhere. A buyers' representative (from the US supermarket chain Walmart) who was present at the launch was quoted in the media as saying that, in a situation of increased competition from other cheaper labour countries, Sri Lankan manufacturers had to keep production costs as low as possible, and that while employers would like to pay a little more, they were precluded from doing so by cost factors.[13]

In the meantime ALaRM had continued to develop its own internal capacity. Training programmes were initiated for 'second level' activists within its member organizations to build their ability to become active leaders. Several of the ALaRM organizations were built around a single dynamic individual, and the absence of a second level leadership in these organizations was a potentially serious problem. These training courses were in part an attempt to do something about that, to train up promising young people from the ranks, usually workers or former workers, who could eventually take over if and when the leader departed.

By 2007, two NGO members of ALaRM, who had for a period of 12 months or so been running awareness raising programmes with workers, were able to mobilize a group of about 45 workers who had become involved in Workers' Councils in their factories. Workers' Councils are organizations that are promoted by the government and the industry as an alternative to unions, as the official representatives of workers in a particular workplace. Their members are not democratically elected by the workers, but appointed by the employer. This close involvement by NGOs with Workers' Councils was not well received by the trade union members of ALaRM and created some tensions within the coalition. The trade unions' view was that these NGO activities were legitimizing Workers' Councils and undermining the basic right of workers to form unions. The NGOs on the other hand said that, as very few garment factories had unions and this was unlikely to change in the future, surely it was better to have some contact with and ability to raise awareness with workers via a functioning Workers'

Council than none at all. A compromise position was proposed, that in a situation in which workers had no recourse to unions, it was acceptable to use (but not promote) Workers' Councils as an entry point to reach workers.

In the meantime the situation of the garment industry in Sri Lanka and of the workers who rely on it, remained precarious. In 2007, more than two years after the MFA was phased out, the industry was still restructuring – with more adjustment to come as the restrictions that remained in place on China's garment exports were eventually removed. Many factories, mainly smaller ones outside the EPZs, continued to close down, usually without notice to the workers and without the company's statutory payments to the Employees' Provident Fund etc having been made. The economic impact of the phase-out was being used by employers to push for a weakening of worker protections and poorer conditions for those who remained – increased daily production targets, longer hours of overtime, cut back in benefits, suppressed wages and social security payments, delays in the payment of salaries, and ongoing anti-union activities.[14]

The global campaign

Meanwhile at the international level, the sub-campaign on the garment trade reached its peak in the lead up to and during the Athens Olympic Games in August 2004 – and then decreased somewhat when the Games were over. By the time it was over, the campaign had generated an estimated 500 local events in over 35 countries. Hundreds of organizations and many top athletes had supported it, and more than half a million 'Big Noise' signatures had been collected. The European Parliament and the British Parliament had both passed resolutions supporting the campaign's aims; and a bill entitled 'Play Fair at the Olympics' had been introduced in the US Congress (but not passed) that would require the US Olympics Committee to ensure that its garment suppliers met basic labour standards. Many members of several national parliaments also publicly supported the campaign.

The campaign succeeded in bringing seven major transnational sportswear companies around the table with the ILO to discuss a proposed 'programme of work' designed to bring an end to ongoing labour abuses in the sportswear industry. The World Federation of Sporting Goods Industries in July 2004 established a new committee on 'corporate social responsibility', which discussed this proposal. But it did not respond in any meaningful way, and did not give any indication on how it would address the failure of most of its members to follow their own basic codes of practice. Some of the individual companies that were targeted made improvements in their supply chains, and resolution of some ongoing disputes at particular factories were facilitated. But by-and-large there was no real sustainable progress on the ground.[15] Stories of worker abuse and exploitation linked to every sports brand continued to emerge. As the campaign website said of the sportswear companies: 'They've jumped off the starting block, but are nowhere near the finishing line, which they will need to reach if workers lives are to improve by Beijing 2008'.

Many national Olympic Committees supported the campaign's call for an end to abuses and exploitation in the sportswear industry. But the International Olympic Committee (IOC) categorically refused to take any responsibility for workers' rights in their sponsorship and licensing programmes. While making misleading statements in the media about the campaign, the IOC ignored any attempts to move the dialogue forward, and refused to accept the signatures of half-a-million campaign supporters around the world calling for them to act responsibly.

After the Athens Games, Oxfam withdrew from the Olympic Campaign, which then continued in reduced form under the leadership of the Clean Clothes Campaign. But Oxfam did continue to support the national level campaigns, including the one in Sri Lanka, and continued its support for and participation in the ALaRM coalition.

What the campaign achieved

The objectives of this campaign in Sri Lanka were: to minimize the adverse impacts on garment workers of industry restructuring as a result of the MFA phase-out; to promote the concept of a 'living wage' in official deliberations on wage levels; to improve living conditions in the housing areas around the EPZs; and to gain recognition of freedom of association as a basic legal right of the workers. None of these objectives were met to any significant degree. Does this mean that the campaign in Sri Lanka was a failure? Rather it highlights how difficult it is to bring about significant change, particularly in a limited time period, and that there is usually a long road to travel before significant change is reached.

In any campaign there are a number of stages on the way to the eventual objective, smaller changes or sub-goals that need to be achieved before the ultimate goal can be reached. Campaign organizers need to identify such sub-goals or stages, as they are useful for monitoring progress, as 'milestones' against which progress can be measured, but also for keeping activists from giving up in despair. Keck and Sikkink identify five stages in the process of influencing or bringing about change: (1) issue creation and agenda setting, introducing a new issue or perspective into the debate; (2) influence on the discursive positions of states and other advocacy targets; (3) influence on institutional procedures; (4) influence on policy change by the targets; and (5) influence on state behaviour.[16] It can be argued that this campaign in Sri Lanka achieved the first of these stages, and to a limited extent the second, but not the other three. It is probably unrealistic to expect it to have achieved more given the short time period.

In terms of issue creation and agenda setting, the campaign introduced into public discourse in Sri Lanka the issue of the impacts of industry restructuring on workers. In 2004 when ALaRM was launched there was little awareness or discussion in Sri Lanka of the potential impacts of the quota phase-out – and what discussion there was centred on increasing market access for its garment exports by improving the industry's competitiveness or concluding free trade agreements with countries like the United States. Into this situation, first Oxfam (in 2002–2004) and then ALaRM (in 2004–2007) created a public awareness that the implications of the phase-out could be much more serious in terms of job losses, and that it required more attention. This was picked up by the ILO, which established a Task Force and involved the government and industry in serious discussions. This process of introducing new perspectives continued over subsequent years as ALaRM released other reports that received wide publicity, such as a December 2005 report on factory closures, and the 'living wage' report.

The latter in particular aimed to change the terms of debate in that it introduced the idea of wages being determined by what a worker needed to meet basic needs, rather than by what the economy or business could afford or was willing to pay. The concept of a 'living wage' has now become established in Sri Lanka in the sense that the term is now increasingly used by different stakeholders, even if they do not accept it as a practical idea. One of the secondary objectives of the 'living wage' report was to change public attitudes towards women workers, to identify them in the public mind as primary wage earners, and to make the point that the income they receive is not just a supplement to that of the main family income earner, who is presumed to be a male, but in many cases is the primary or sole income of a family – which is why it must be enough to meet basic needs.

What was true of the campaign in Sri Lanka was also true of the 'Make Trade Fair' campaign in general. An overall evaluation of the campaign carried out in 2005 found that: 'The most frequently mentioned outcome of the MTF campaign is that it has "changed the terms of debate". Certainly media coverage and pronouncements by an extremely wide range of public officials indicate that Oxfam helped get both "fairness" and "development" front-and-centre in the debates on trade. The issues Oxfam has prioritised.... significantly raised their profile and coverage indicates that Oxfam analysis is shaping the debate'.[17]

But perhaps the most significant achievement of this campaign, which does not fit neatly into Keck and Sikkink's analysis, was the creation of the ongoing ALaRM coalition, an effective body that could take the campaign for the rights of garment workers forward with greater impact. It is a weakness of Keck and Sikkink's analysis that it does not take into account such organizational capacity building amongst the affected group or those who represent them as a significant stage or sub-goal in a campaign.

The launch in February 2004 and the media coverage it generated brought the coalition to public attention, and subsequent activities including campaigns and the release of other reports reinforced this, and established ALaRM as a recognized and credible voice on issues facing garment workers in Sri Lanka. This is evidenced by its inclusion in the ILO Task Force, and the attention both favourable and unfavourable that its activities generate from the media, government and industry. ALaRM now has the capacity to produce and launch influential reports that present a workers' perspective and are taken note of by the government and industry, even if they do not agree with their recommendation. It is able to organize large-scale joint activities in support of this, such as a signature campaign in 2006. It has also increased its authoritative voice by attracting new members to the coalition, including some of the larger national trade unions. When it was originally formed in 2003–2004 there were six member organizations, but by 2007 this had increased to ten, with two more seeking membership, which would mean a doubling in size within four years. Among the new members are two large national level trade unions that cover many sectors apart from garment workers.

As in any coalition, there are pressures tending to undermine its cohesion, the most obvious being the tensions over Workers' Councils mentioned above, which is probably a manifestation of more serious ongoing tensions – between unions and NGOs, and between individuals. However when asked about the positive achievements of ALaRM, many members said that the fact that it had stayed together for so long, despite the tensions, and was still functioning effectively was a major achievement.[18] The factors tending to split it apart are outweighed by the advantages of staying together, which include: (1) the high profile that members have acquired as ALaRM that most of them did not have as individual organizations; (2) the increased access that they have acquired as ALaRM not just to government but also to the business sector and bodies such as the ILO; (3) the networking and sharing of information that they get when they meet together; and (4) the access that it gives them to Oxfam and its funding, its international networks and its research capacity.

One of the more important factors contributing to ALaRM's success has been its ability to produce well-researched authoritative reports that command attention, set new agendas and change the terms of debate. The involvement of Oxfam and its international networks in this was key. The first of these authoritative reports released in Sri Lanka ('Trading Away Our Rights') was actually an Oxfam one, written and produced in Great Britain on the basis of research done in a dozen different countries by various Oxfam offices. Subsequent locally produced reports were a collaborative effort, with the data being collected by ALaRM members, and the processing and analysis being done by Oxfam in Colombo. It was the combination of the human resources and credibility of ALaRM and the skills and funding of Oxfam that was the key to success.

But producing good documented evidence and reports is by itself not enough. They have to be publicized and popularized so that their messages are heard and taken note of. In this, ALaRM's ability to generate media publicity has been a crucial factor. A range of innovative approaches have been used to do this, including running briefing sessions for journalists, and taking out paid ads in newspapers and on radio. The result was good coverage of its report launches and campaign events in both the print and electronic media and in all three languages. In terms of the different types of tactics identified by Keck and Sikkink, this could be classed as 'information politics', generating politically useful information (local and international research and surveys) and using it where it will have most impact, in this case in the Sri Lankan media.[19] A good example is the press briefing by ALaRM in December 2005 to launch their research report on the impact of the MFA phase-out 12 months after it had come into effect, at which women who had lost their jobs gave personal testimonies to the journalists.

As Keck and Sikkink have noted: 'Information flows in advocacy networks provide not only facts but testimony – stories told by people whose lives have been affected. Moreover, activists interpret facts and testimony, usually framing issues simply, in terms of right and wrong, because their purpose is to persuade people and stimulate them to act'. They go on to say: 'The media is an essential partner in network information politics. To reach a broader audience, networks strive to attract media attention. Sympathetic journalists may become part of the network, but more often network activists cultivate a reputation for credibility with the press, and package their information in a timely and dramatic way to draw press attention'.[20]

Personal stories of workers such as those used at the press launch were extensively used by the international campaign in the North as well as locally. This could also be classed as an example of another of the strategies that Keck and Sikkink identify, namely 'symbolic politics', using symbols, actions or stories to make sense of a situation for an audience that is frequently far away. Such stories bring a large complex situation down to the human level, which is more easily understood and more readily evokes empathy and sympathy for the human victims. The focus on the Olympic Games is an example of the use of a symbol for the same purpose, contrasting the values of fair play that it stands for with the exploitation of those who made the uniform that the officials and athletes wore.

What was not achieved

In terms of the stages identified by Keck and Sikkink, this campaign had only very limited influence on 'the discursive positions' of the government and business sector regarding the MFA phase-out, and no effect on their 'procedures', their policies or their behaviour. ALaRM had the opportunity to exert some influence via the ILO Task Force, but this came to nothing when the report and its recommendations were shelved by the government and ignored by the industry. The government remained unconcerned about the MFA phase-out saying that, in the situation of increased competition without a quota system, Sri Lankan garment exports will still do well. What the basis was for this optimism was not clear. Oxfam had some influence on the Department of Labour, encouraging it to set up Help Desks for retrenched workers – which were then rendered ineffective by denying them resources – and to carry out the two comprehensive factory surveys, supplying the funds and technical expertise to support these. But it was not able to influence the Department in terms of effectively following up on factory closures to make sure workers received their full entitlements.

There is no evidence that the campaign was able to influence the behaviour of owners, managers, and buyers. Nothing improved in terms of the industry's response to the quota phase-out. Factories still closed without proper notice to workers and there continued to be large-scale defaulting on the payments due to workers who lost their jobs. There were a number of reports of sudden overnight closures, of workers turning up on a Monday to find the factory gates locked and the owners gone, leaving them with no way of recovering the wages and other monies owed to them. Employers were successful in shutting out worker representation from various decision-making forums that deal with productivity improvement, image building, de-regulating labour standards etc.

ALaRM is working in a difficult political situation in Sri Lanka, with a government that is more interested in ensuring the country is attractive to investors than in protecting the rights of workers. The garment manufacturers are well organized, strongly opposed to trade unions, and supported in this by a sympathetic government. Many employers are unscrupulous, as evidenced by the number that have closed their factories prematurely and fled without making the payments that they are legally obliged to make to workers and their pension funds. The Labour Department that is supposed to police this is weak and lacks the resources and will to properly enforce labour regulations. The workers themselves are also in a weak position. Their general level of awareness of their rights is low, and their ability to agitate for improvements without being fired is limited.

The unions would say that the only way to change this balance of power in favour of workers is to have them organize and demand their rights on the streets. But on present indications this is a long way off. As in many other developing countries, the workforce is by-and-large unorganized. It is not clear why garment workers in Sri Lanka generally speaking do not join unions. Reasons commonly given are that they are wary of political activities, or scared of being sacked, or too tired after a long day's work to go to meetings, or that they do not identify strongly as workers as they only intend to be in the workforce for a few years before returning to the village. But if it is true that the only way that workers are going to get a fair deal is though organizing and gaining enough negotiating power to force a company to change, then coalitions with NGOs such as ALaRM have only a limited potential. From this unionists' perspective, the ALaRM coalition with NGOs could take some steps along the way, for example by promoting the right to Freedom of Association, but that was all. The rest was up to the unions and the workers.

In this regard, the lack of effort put into the issue of living conditions may be significant. Apart from some limited efforts by one member organization (Dabindu Collective), ALaRM did not take any significant action on this at all. Of the four issues that the coalition agreed in 2003 to be their joint priorities, this is the one that received the least attention – maybe because it was seen as an NGO-type social issue, not a workplace one, and therefore not of interest to the trade unions within ALaRM. It was pushed by the women's organizations within the coalition and some NGOs, but not by the trade unions.

The organizers of this campaign had the perfect opportunity to use a 'boomerang' type strategy, to go around the resistant government and industry and put pressure on Northern bodies that could in turn apply pressure to the government or industry. But this did not happen. Oxfam, with its offices in Europe and the United States where the Northern 'brand-name' companies that source their products from Sri Lanka are based, could have mounted consumer campaigns there to pressure those companies to act responsibly and not move their orders prematurely to cheaper countries, and to have them apply pressure to their suppliers to do the right thing by their workers. But this did not happen to any significant extent. There was also the direct call by the campaign in Sri Lanka for the European-based Oxfams to assist by lobbying the European Commission to modify its 'rules of origin'. But this received little sustained support because it did not fit in well with the priorities and strategies of the international 'Make Trade Fair' campaign, for which market access was not an issue. Also the need for global coherence in the international campaign meant that it had only a limited ability to respond to a call coming from one or two countries only.

This absence of supportive advocacy in the North is even more surprising in light of the fact that, during the campaign, one of the ALaRM member organizations, the Free Trade Zone Workers Union (FTZWU), used this very tactic to get resolution of a situation at a particular garment factory. The management of this factory in Sri Lanka were harassing and threatening workers who were trying to form a union. This was taken up by the FTZWU, which used its international network of contacts in the North to have campaigning pressure put on the brand-name companies that bought from the factory, and on the factory managers and owners directly, by consumers, unions and activists in the North, to have the latter recognize the union in the factory and negotiate with it in good faith. This was largely successful, and the members of ALaRM were aware of this.

The role of an international NGO

In this campaign, Oxfam played a number of different roles at the same time – as facilitator, member of the coalition, funder, and a link to the international level. As facilitator, it was Oxfam that first brought the members of the ALaRM coalition together in 2002, and it was Oxfam staff in Colombo who devoted large amounts of time and energy to nurturing it. It was Oxfam's technical ability to analyse survey data for the various reports that ALaRM launched that contributed to the latter's reputation and credibility. The international reputation of the Oxfam name was used to good effect, particularly in the early stages of the campaign. In 2004 when ALaRM was unknown, the launch of the first report in Oxfam's name appears to have been a major factor in the considerable interest it attracted from the media and a range of stakeholders. Subsequently Oxfam's reputation enabled it to act as intermediary between the trade unions and labour NGOs on the one hand, and the government, industry, ILO, etc on the other. For example the Department of Labour, which has an ambivalent attitude to unions because of past conflicts,[21] was perfectly happy to work with Oxfam (rather than ALaRM) on the two factory surveys and to receive technical and financial assistance from them.

Another key role was that of funder of the campaign. This campaign in Sri Lanka has been funded by Oxfam since 2002 and at the time of writing there were no plans for this to cease. But while Oxfam funding has given ALaRM a certain degree of financial security, it has also left it financially dependent on the international organization, and open to accusations of being foreign influenced. There are no moves afoot to diversify ALaRM's funding sources or to make it in any way less dependent. On the contrary, the tendency has been in the other direction. Some member organizations that suddenly lost their funding from another international donor became dependent on Oxfam funding, not just for ALaRM activities, but for their core programmes – which is an undesirable trend. It could be argued that Oxfam used its role as funder to influence the priorities of the member organizations of ALaRM, for example, by pressuring them to come together and form a coalition and to take up the issues of the MFA phase-out. It is true that they were not unwilling to be brought together, nor to take up the issue, and that as the coalition developed Oxfam took a less pro-active role. But in those initial stages it would be fair to say that Oxfam used its role as funder to drive the campaign in a certain direction.

Another important role that Oxfam played was as a link into international networks. Several members of ALaRM had their own individual links with networks in the North, but Oxfam's was the one most relevant for issues around trade and the effect of the MFA phase-out. It was the organization's particular knowledge of this and of what the United States and European Union were doing that led to the campaign in Sri Lanka in the first place. When the campaign was broadened to include working conditions, Oxfam was once again able to bring an international gendered perspective on what was happening to women workers in the industry worldwide. Potentially at least, Oxfam could have used its international links to greater effect, for example, by providing information about what the international buyers were intending to do once the MFA was phased out, whether they intended moving their orders to China or elsewhere, whether they were going to do this gradually or suddenly, and so on. It could also have put consumer pressure on brand-name companies in the North, and lobbied European governments on their 'rules of origin'. There was an expectation from the international 'Make Trade Fair' campaign that the Sri Lanka campaigners would provide stories, research and evidence that could be used in the North, would host photographers and visiting celebrities, and so on. In return, the Sri Lankans could reasonably have expected more from the Northern-based Oxfams. But this was an international advocacy network in which Northern priorities and strategies dominated.

Legitimacy

As well as acting as a member of the coalition, Oxfam also did things in its own name in Sri Lanka, such as launching its 'Trading Away Our Rights' report and working with the Department of Labour on the factory surveys. This raises the question of legitimacy and mandate. By what right does a foreign-based organization like Oxfam advocate and attempt to influence the domestic policies of a country like Sri Lanka? In normal circumstances, an International Non-Government Organization (INGO) would not campaign or lobby directly or publicly on a domestic issue such as labour rights. Their approach would be to support local NGOs to do that. Oxfam's mandate to act in its own name in this case came from the fact that its allies in the coalition asked it to do so. It was the allies and partners with whom it worked in the ALaRM coalition who gave it its right to speak out.

But what about the legitimacy of ALaRM? Given that only a small percentage of garment workers in Sri Lanka are members of a union, and that labour NGOs have even less mass support, by what right does ALaRM speak for the garment workers of Sri Lanka? While ALaRM speaks from a workers' perspective, it does not represent all garment workers. The unions may be representative, but NGOs and organizations like ALaRM are not. The views it expresses are its own, the views of the coalition, which on the basis of its members having worked with garment workers for so long, it believes are in their interests and represent a defence of their basic rights. As argued in Chapter 2, this gives ALaRM the right to 'a voice, but not a vote'.

Apart from the question of mandate, there are also some practical questions around INGOs doing advocacy in the South in their own name. On the one hand, the use by an organization like Oxfam of its name and international reputation can 'open doors' and be a strength that significantly assists a campaign. On the other hand, because INGOs are generally large, well resourced and well connected, any national level advocacy or campaigning that they do can tend to push aside less-confident local advocacy NGOs. The role of an organization like Oxfam is to encourage and support effective advocacy by local actors, not swamp them or displace them. Hence in most cases it is not appropriate for it to be taking the lead in the South in a public way. However there can be exceptions to this general principle, as happened in the Sri Lanka campaign. Oxfam's official position on this was set down in 2003 by the Executive Directors and Board of Oxfam International:

> Oxfam will seek to support partners and allies in their advocacy and campaigns strategies because they have primary legitimacy in their own countries, and because we believe that this will have most impact in terms of promoting long-term, sustainable change. When we support rather than lead in this way we will subsume our own brand unless there is a justification for not doing so.
>
> Oxfam can also advocate and campaign in the South in its own name where the use of the Oxfam brand significantly increases the impact on poverty, or if it is not safe for partners and allies to do so. We will always determine how and when we use our own voice in consultation with partners, allies, and Oxfam affiliate staff based in the country or region, and will be accountable for such

consultation. We will assess any potential risk to the Oxfam name, and to the credibility of the work, partners and allies of other affiliates, as part of determining how and when we use our own voice. Our assessment will also take into account legal registration of Oxfam Field Offices and potential political, security or legal constraints in the country concerned.[22]

Participation and democracy

A key issue in transnational campaigns like 'Make Trade Fair' is that of participation and democracy within the advocacy network – whether the views and priorities of national level campaigners like ALaRM were heard and taken into account in the international campaign. Clearly in this case they were not. But 'Make Trade Fair' was a global campaign with national level campaigns on the rights of garment workers in a dozen or more countries, each with its own approach and its own priorities and needs, which were not necessarily coherent or consistent with one another. How does a global campaign take account of and respond to all these differing needs and priorities without losing coherence? In fact, the original approach by Oxfam before it joined with the ICFTU and Clean Clothes Campaign was to do just that, to run a 'supportive campaign' at the international level whose primary aim was to provide assistance to the diverse national level campaigns – information, research, financial resources, lobbying in the North when needed, and so on. Global coherence, or saying the same thing to the same targets at the same time, was not considered so important. But the ICFTU and Clean Clothes Campaign wanted a different approach, a 'directive campaign', centrally planned and coordinated, and generating maximum impact by having all participants around the world pressuring the same targets on the same issue at the same time. There are good arguments in favour of such an approach, but what it means for national campaigns is that they have to fit their priorities in with the global agenda and strategy as best they can.

Within INGOs there will always be a tension between these two approaches to global advocacy – between the need to maximize impact by having a coordinated 'directive campaign', and the need to maximize relevance by having a flexible 'supportive campaign' in which Southern-based participants take up issues in their own way, in their own time, and with their own emphasis. In the 'Make Trade Fair' campaign, the setting of strategies and priorities for the sub-campaign was determined by an international overview of what was happening in the garment industry, and was strongly influenced by the advocacy and campaigning opportunities in the North (for example the Athens Olympics) which may or may not be relevant in the South. The best choice of objectives and strategies and targets for a coordinated global campaign is unlikely to be the best choice in all, or even most, of the Southern countries in which it is intended to operate. National level participants therefore have to choose between supporting the global campaign and its approaches (in this case the Olympics Campaign) for the sake of global coherence, or doing their own thing for the sake of local relevance. In this case, the Sri Lanka-based Oxfams and ALaRM chose the latter.

However they still regarded themselves as part of the global 'Make Trade Fair' sub-campaign, and were linked into those people in the Northern-based Oxfams who were still pursuing a 'supportive' approach, despite the dominance of the Olympics Campaign and its 'directive' approach. This had the advantage of giving them access to international research reports and briefing papers, perspectives and information, and the use of the Oxfam name and its resources. On the downside however, the global campaign also made requests of them, to provide local research, information, stories and photos. There is always a danger that those running a global campaign will tend to emphasize the help that the national campaign can offer them, rather than the help that they can offer it. An 'extractive mentality' can develop in which the Southern participants are seen primarily as a source of useful information, evidence, stories etc that can be used in the campaign in the North, as supporting players only in the overall show.

It was not just the global sub-campaign on trade and labour that was seen as being driven by a Northern agenda. The internal evaluation of the overall 'Make Trade Fair' campaign had this to say:

> Although conceptually the campaign was designed to be vertically aligned with strong regional participation and a role for partners, in practice the campaign was experienced as being very 'top down' and Northern focused. Oxfam staff in many regional and country offices felt that they and their partners, rather than being key protagonists in setting the agenda and pressuring for change, were viewed as supporting players, representing the human face of issues....and contributing to awareness raising by participating in global media-related activities. In effect, in the early stages of the campaign regions had to figure out ways to link-up to the campaign, rather

than regions and partners being co-strategists in setting and implementing an agenda.[23]

The evaluation does however also say that the campaign organizers tried to overcome this and adopt a different approach:

> Oxfam made significant progress in moving away from a more centralized, Northern-focused campaigning model, and increasingly took advantage of its assets as a decentralized global organization to innovate, experiment and adjust the campaign in both the North and the South, with promising results on a number of issues in different settings.[24]

But as Jordan and Van Tuijl have stressed, it is not just a question of allowing Southern participants in an advocacy network an equal say in the design and implementation of a campaign. There must also be 'political responsibility' towards those engaged in the campaign and operating in a different political arena. The level of 'political responsibility' in a campaign, they say, can be measured by the compatibility of its different objectives in different arenas, what happens with information within the campaign network, and how strategies, risks and funds are managed.[25] In their terminology (see Chapter 2) this campaign in Sri Lanka would have to be classed as a 'disassociated campaign', as on the second bottom rung of a four-rung ladder. The parallel but different objectives of the campaign in different arenas (national and international) were beginning to clash. The strong push by the international campaign for improved wages and conditions had to be muted somewhat in Sri Lanka as it could have increased the incentive of buyers to take their orders elsewhere. The Sri Lankan objective of improving market access into Europe was not supported, as it did not fit in with the Northern objectives. Campaign strategies were set in the North with little or no input from countries like Sri Lanka. This was a campaign in which the level of 'political responsibility' by Northern participants was quite low.

Notes

1 Central Bank of Sri Lanka (2002) *Annual Report*, p.103. Board of Investment (2002) *Performance Highlights 2002*.
2 In this chapter the name 'Oxfam' is used to refer to any and all of the Oxfam affiliates working on the campaign. In fact most of the work was done by Oxfam Community Aid Abroad, which later became Oxfam Australia. But it

was done in the name of, and with substantial financial support from, two other affiliates, Oxfam Great Britain and Novib (later Oxfam Novib), under the auspices of the Oxfam International Regional Strategic Team for South Asia.
3 M. Burns (2002) *Proposal for a Multi-stakeholder Dialogue in Sri Lanka on the Preparation for and Likely Impact of the Phasing Out of the MFA* (Oxfam).
4 J. Atkinson (2002) *Labour Rights in Sri Lanka. Report for OI Trade Campaign, Labour Wedge Team, of findings of field visit by Jeff Atkinson, 24–28 August 2002* (Melbourne: Oxfam Community Aid Abroad).
5 Oxfam International (2003a) South Asia Labour and Trade Team, Report to RST Meeting, 15–16 December.
6 Oxfam International (2004). Invitation letter to the launch, 10 February.
7 The International Labour Organization (ILO) is the tripartite UN agency that brings together governments, employers and workers of its member states in common action to promote decent work throughout the world.
8 Interviews with ALaRM members, Colombo, July 2007. Gowthaman, Kalani Subasinghe, Palitha Atukorale and Anton Marcus.
9 Interview with Ms. Nadeeka Wataliyadda, Assistant Commissioner of Labour, Colombo, July 2007.
10 Oxfam International (2006) Report by South Asia Labour and Trade Team to South Asia Regional Strategic Team, June.
11 Interview with Dabindu Collective, Katunayake, July 2007.
12 Gamini Warushamana, *Sunday Observer*, Colombo, 18 Dec 2005.
13 Quintus Perera, *Asian Tribune*, 9 October 2006.
14 Oxfam International (2007) Report from South Asia Labour and Trade Team to South Asia Regional Strategic Team, February.
15 J. Merk (2004) *Response of target companies to the Play Fair at the Olympics campaign.* (Amsterdam: Clean Clothes Campaign).
16 M. Keck and K. Sikkink (1998) *Activists Beyond Borders* (Ithaca and London: Cornell University Press) p. 25.
17 L. Roper (2005) *'Make Trade Fair' internal evaluation*. Report to Oxfam International, p. ii.
18 Interviews of members of ALaRM organizations, Colombo, July 2007.
19 Keck and Sikkink (1998) *op cit.*, pp. 18–25.
20 Keck and Sikkink (1998) *op cit.*, pp. 19, 22.
21 Interview with Ms. Nadeeka Wataliyadda, Assistant Commissioner of Labour, Colombo, July 2007.
22 Oxfam International (2003b) Oxfam's Southern campaigning and advocacy – key principles. Communique from Executive Directors and Board Meeting, Dublin, November.
23 L. Roper (2005) *op cit.*, p.11.
24 L. Roper (2005) *op cit.*, p. ix.
25 L. Jordan and P. van Tuijl (2000) 'Political responsibility in transnational NGO advocacy', *World Development*, vol 28, number 12, pp. 2051–65.

5
Case Study: Trade and Agriculture in India

Given the important role that agriculture plays in the economic, social and cultural life of India, it was inevitable that the sub-campaign on agriculture in the international 'Make Trade Fair' campaign would be of interest to the Oxfam offices in India. In 2004 the South Asia Regional Strategic Team (RST), which oversees the operations of all the Oxfam affiliates operating in South Asia, decided to take up this sub-campaign, in particular in India and Bangladesh.

But agriculture and agricultural trade are very broad issues and, in order to determine exactly what they should be focusing on in South Asia, the RST decided to hold a series of consultation workshops with a selection of the local organizations with whom the Oxfams in those countries work, plus other academics and experts.[1] In late 2004 a series of one-day consultation workshops were organized to which were invited representatives from relevant partner organizations, research institutions and farmers' organizations. Four such consultations took place in India (in Bhubaneswar, Lucknow, Bangalore and Ahmadabad), and one in Bangladesh, culminating in a regional conference covering both India and Bangladesh that was held in Dhaka in January 2005.

Each of the consultations involved enthusiastic and often spirited discussion. In India the issues raised tended to be local ones about the policies and practices of state and federal governments and their support (or lack of) for small-scale farmers, rather than about international trade. Because the emphasis in India from the time of Ghandi has been on national self-sufficiency, international trade has not, until recently, received much attention from Indian NGOs. For many of these it was an issue whose relevance to their rural development work was only now becoming evident. While some were well aware of what was happening in the WTO and its relevance, many were not. However some issues did emerge from the consultations that were related to trade, for example: the fall in the world prices for agricultural commodities; the impact of domestic and export subsidies provided by the US and EU to their farmers; proposed regional trade agreements that could have negative impacts on Indian producers; new non-tariff barriers that were emerging in the North, such as quality standards that Indian farmers were unable to meet. One trade-related issue that emerged as a major area of concern was 'contract farming' and the increasing role of transnational corporations in agriculture.[2] 'Contract farming' is a system in which buyers contract to purchase a farmer's crop in advance for a pre-determined price, and in some cases provide the seeds and inputs needed to grow it. It offers several advantages to producers such as no initial outlay for inputs and a guaranteed income from the crop. Provided that the contract and the price offered are fair, it can be an attractive proposition. But unfortunately this is often not the case and farmers are often exploited.

As a result of these consultations, it was decided that the 'Make Trade Fair' sub-campaign in South Asia would focus on 'contract farming' and on the WTO negotiations on agricultural trade. The latter was not so much a reflection of the priorities emerging from the consultations as of the priorities of Oxfam and its international campaign. A need was identified for additional research to support the campaign on particular crops produced in the region, and a research programme was initiated. The Center for Trade and Development (CENTAD), a Delhi-based organization originally established by Oxfam but now independent, commissioned and published a number of relevant working papers, including one on the theory and practice of 'contract farming' in India. Also Oxfam itself commissioned several crop-specific pieces of research in India and Bangladesh.

Pressure from the global campaign

At the international level, the labour rights sub-campaign had now wound down and the 'Make Trade Fair' campaign was focused almost exclusively on influencing the WTO negotiation, and in particular the agreement on trade in agricultural goods. The aim of the international campaign was to have an agreement in the WTO that would force the US and EU to eliminate their agricultural subsidies, and allow Southern governments the power to decide for themselves the extent and pace of opening of their agricultural markets, rather than have it forced on them before they were ready or could adjust. But the US and EU were resisting all of this. Their strategy was to have new categories of subsidies introduced into the WTO agreement that were supposedly not trade-distorting and hence allowable, so that they could on the one hand reduce their non-allowable export subsidies to producers and replace them with other forms of allowable subsidies. The net result would be that heavily subsidized agricultural exports from the US and EU would continue. At the same time these influential countries were maintaining pressure on Southern countries to open up their markets to agricultural imports.

The international campaign was focused on lobbying in the North to pressure the US and EU governments, and in Southern capitals to encourage the assertiveness of Southern governments in the negotiations. As part of this strategy Oxfam was producing a series of briefing papers that set out its case, which were translated into several languages and released to the media worldwide, as well as being made available to Southern negotiators. A typical example that gives the flavour of these briefing papers, and summarizes Oxfam's concerns, is one titled 'From development to naked self-interest: the Doha Development Round has lost its way' released in July 2005. Its central contention was that: 'Instead of promoting the integration of developing countries in the world trading system, the "Development Round" has been turned on its head: the focus has shifted from the development of poor countries to the pursuit by rich countries of their naked self-interest. The EU, the US and other developed countries want a "round for free" for themselves and are expecting developing countries to foot the bill'. In support of this, it sets out a number of examples of the pursuit by the US and EU of their naked self-interest:

> Based on the current negotiating text, neither the EU nor the USA would have to get rid of a single cent of the subsidies that they currently provide to their farmers. In fact, they could actually increase the amount of money spent on subsidies by redefining programs so they fit into legal categories. Oxfam research shows that the EU would be allowed to increase trade distorting agricultural support by \$35 billion, and the USA by \$7.9 billion at the end of the implementation period. At the same time, despite the fact that the total amount of subsidies used by all developing countries is 14 times less than the amount provided by the USA and EU, rich countries are expecting the developing world to reduce its support for farmers by 50 per cent...
>
> In the Doha mandate, all developing countries were promised 'special and differential treatment' (SDT), i.e. additional flexibilities regarding

the depth, scope, and pace of commitments by developing countries, which would take into account their special development needs... Today, the USA and EU talk about 'fair reciprocity' instead, while claiming that special and differential treatment is a barrier to development. They also insist on the exclusion of certain developing countries from SDT under the new Doha agreements, referring to them as 'advanced developing countries' – even though this term has been neither defined nor linked to development indicators. The countries targeted have at least two things in common: (a) they are facing significant development challenges and thus must be permitted to use the flexibilities under WTO rules, and (b) they are perceived as competitors by the rich countries in certain sectors and are therefore targeted for tougher treatment.[3]

India was one of these latter countries, and it was at this stage also playing a vital role in the resistance to the US and EU, as a leader of the key group of Southern countries in the WTO known as the 'Group of 20' (G-20). Hence the organizers of the international campaign were very keen for Oxfam in India to be lobbying the government in Delhi on this WTO agreement because of the key role it was playing in the negotiations. The Indian Government's position was in line with Oxfam's, so all that was required was to encourage it to hold firm and not give in to pressure from the US, EU and others. This would be critical at the forthcoming WTO Ministerial Meeting in Hong Kong in December 2005 where it appeared key decisions were about to be made.

From time to time the Trade Ministers of the G-20 meet together to work out common positions and to strategize and plan – and in March 2005 (two months after the Dhaka regional consultation) one such meeting of the G-20 was held in Delhi, hosted by the Indian Government. This was important enough for the international organizers of the 'Make Trade Fair' campaign to send one of their key Geneva-based lobbyists to Delhi to assist the local team. This was Celine Charveriat, who had overall responsibility for the global campaign's policies and strategy. She also had unique knowledge of the WTO negotiation process through her network of contacts in Geneva, where the WTO is based. Working with her at the G-20 meeting was another key advocate, Delhi-based Dr Samar Verma, head of Oxfam trade advocacy in South Asia. The Indian Government had not provided any facilities or opportunities for civil society groups to interact with the G-20 ministers or their advisors, so Oxfam rented office space in the official venue, the Maurya Sheraton Hotel, so as to facilitate access to the delegations on an informal basis. However there appeared to be a reluctance on the part of the G-20 governments, and especially the Indian Government, to formally acknowledge the NGO presence and interaction. Before the meeting, the Oxfam lobbyists briefed journalists present, many of whom were not well informed on the issues being discussed, which helped establish the organization's credibility with the media. As a result Oxfam and its messages obtained good coverage. Oxfam's response to the Ministerial Statement issued at the end of the meeting also received wide coverage in the local media.

Immediately before the G-20 meeting, Oxfam and another international NGO, Action Aid International, had circulated a joint statement in Delhi urging G-20 ministers to resist the tactics of rich countries of demanding major market access commitments in exchange for insignificant 'concessions' on agricultural subsidies. This statement was then endorsed by 14 civil society organizations and academic institutions from across Bangladesh, India, Nepal and Pakistan. Oxfam and Action Aid were practically the only organizations lobbying and doing media work around the meeting, in spite of the invitations extended to local organizations to participate. The latter's response was generally to ask Oxfam to lead on this, indicating their relative lack of capacity on trade issues.

The Oxfam advocacy staff in India took the opportunity of Charveriat's presence in Delhi to sit down with her and map out a detailed work-plan for the campaign in India over the next nine months up until the Hong Kong Ministerial. Amongst other things she stressed that local staff in India needed to be continuously lobbying the government in Delhi and gathering intelligence from officials and key business groups, in order to inform the international campaigning plans. Also there needed to be at least one major popular campaigning event in India in the run-up to the Ministerial meeting that would capture public attention and generate media attention nationally and hopefully internationally. In May 2005, after her departure, the South Asia team met and took the decision that, because of its importance internationally, they would focus on this short-term WTO agenda leading up to the Hong Kong meeting, and would postpone the longer-term campaigning on issues brought forward by the consultation process, including 'contract farming'. A concrete campaign plan for 2005 was put in place whose aims were to have the Indian Government: (1) support changes to the WTO Agreement on Agriculture that would allow developing countries the power to decide the pace and extent of liberalization of agricultural trade, so as to promote food security, livelihood security and rural livelihoods; (2) maintain the unity and increase the assertiveness of the Group of 20; and (3) lead by example by allowing market access to imports from Least Developed Countries, including its neighbour Bangladesh.[4]

Popular campaigning in India

As well as producing research and lobbying the government, the campaign would have a programme of popular campaigning in India to demonstrate public support for the protection of farmers' livelihoods. This would be branded 'Make Trade Fair', not Oxfam, and its central feature would be 'road-shows' in three different states, that would travel through the countryside explaining the issues around trade liberalization to farmers and rural people and gathering signatures for the 'Big Noise' petition, which would be presented to world leaders at the Hong Kong meeting. There was also to be a photo exhibition on the lives of farmers, to be launched in October along with four case studies on what was happening to the producers of cotton, sugar, oilseed and dairy products. In December, just before the WTO meeting, there would be a 'White Band Day', a special day of action coinciding with an international day in which as many people as possible would wear a white arm band with the slogan 'Make Poverty History'. Some of these plans were however later modified or cancelled.

Because Oxfam in India had no experience of running things like travelling road-shows, it was decided to sub-contract that part of the work to Indian NGOs that had a mass base and experience with this type of popular mobilization. Exploratory discussions were begun with India's largest civil society network, the Voluntary Action Network of India (VANI), but it declined to be involved. One NGO approached also declined because of a fundamental disagreement with Oxfam's reformist views on the WTO. Eventually four agreed to take part: Center for Community Economics and Development Consultants Society (CECOEDECON) based in Rajasthan; Youth for Unity and Voluntary Action (YUVA) a development NGO that works in Maharashtra, Gujarat and Madhya Pradesh; Covenant Centre for Development (CCD) based in Tamil Nadu; and Ekta Parishad, a Ghandian organization that works in eight different states. Oxfam also hired the Delhi-based Centre for Advocacy and Research to do the media work around the road-shows and other events.

In October and November 2005, the road-shows got underway, travelling through parts of Rajasthan, Madhya Pradesh and Tamil Nadu staging theatrical shows, giving talks and collecting signatures. In Rajasthan for example, 60 'Make Trade Fair' campaigners and volunteers from

CECOEDECON travelled through the desert in a procession of camels, visiting villages as they went. As they travelled, they used village level meetings to get the message across to rural people. People took these meetings seriously and the presence of village-level functionaries gave them a certain status. The first few meetings were not well attended – but as the word spread, subsequent meetings attracted larger groups of people, including women.[5] A big attraction for the farmers and their families was the 'Make Trade Fair' street theatre, whose satirical entertainment the audiences enjoyed immensely, as they heard about such things as the difference in subsidies given to farmers in rich countries compared to farmers in India. Although rural people in a drought-prone state like Rajasthan do not necessarily understand issues of global trade, they are very aware of the impact that government policies have on their situation. During the course of the road-show about 6,000 people in Rajasthan signed up to the 'Big Noise' petition calling on governments to make trade fair.[6]

Did 'Big Noise' signatories understand what they were signing? There is no way of knowing. No doubt some did and some did not. According to the internal review of the campaign, staff felt that 'though very few people signed without directly questioning the purpose of the signatures and its implications, there have been cases when women signed up because their husband or peer group is a signatory'. However they also felt that 'from being just a signature drive in its initial phase, 'Big Noise' is now all about informed signatures'. The messages that the campaign hoped to convey during these road-shows were both simple and complex. The simple message was summed up in the 'Make Trade Fair' slogan: farmers should get a fair deal from the sale and trade of their produce. This was easily understood by all and readily taken up. The more complex message, about WTO rules and the need for governments to be allowed to use tariffs and quotas to protect local farmers from cheap imports, was not always readily understood by farmers, and indeed in some cases not understood by staff and volunteers of the partner organizations either. Oxfam was not in a position to control what was being said on placards and elsewhere during the road-shows, and in some cases stray messages crept in, including at times an anti-WTO message, which was not Oxfam's position. In December 2005, just after the road-shows had commenced, a staff member from the Oxfam office in Delhi observed one of the rallies:

> In my recent visit to a rally in Madhya Pradesh I observed that, though the umbrella framework is of course 'Make Trade Fair' and

the spirit behind the slogans and the demand of the farmers is indeed Power to Decide, in letters or popular slogans uniformity seems to be missing. Rather 'Agriculture at Stake' or *Kheti Kisani Khatre Mein* seems to be picking up. We need to be watchful on this and must ensure through research efforts and the popular activities that the essence of Power to Decide remain intact. Also, state rallies suggest as if the campaign is anti-WTO and for trade without the WTO.[7]

The road-shows were essentially a way of reaching a rural audience. For urban audiences particularly young urban dwellers, an open-air concert was used. This was held at the Hamswadhani Theatre in Delhi, and featured celebrity singer Lucky Ali. Organized by Oxfam and the 'Make Trade Fair' campaign in conjunction with a Delhi University college and event organizer Seher, it was originally scheduled for late November 2005 but had to be postponed due to a security scare that led to road closures by the police and the venue becoming inaccessible. After much frantic re-organizing, it was held instead on 10 December. Braving the winter chill, nearly 10,000 eager fans turned up to hear Lucky Ali, filling every available space in the open-air theatre, including the aisles and stairs. The concert was introduced with a 'Make Trade Fair' film, 'On the road to Hong Kong', after which Lucky came on stage and talked about the campaign and the issues, and urged the cheering audience to sign up to the 'Big Noise'. When he started singing one of his hits, the crowd went wild, and for the next two hours, he entertained them with songs and performances, which included inviting people to come up and sign on stage. At the end after an encore, Lucky himself publicly signed the 'Big Noise' petition.[8]

By this stage the publicity and lobbying was clearly having an impact on the Indian Government. At one point just before they left for Hong Kong, the entire trade negotiation section from the Ministry of Commerce spent a full day at a conference organized by Oxfam and CENTAD. This was unprecedented and represented a whole new attitude by government officials towards NGOs and what they had to say.

A few days after the concert, a meeting was organized with Commerce Minister Kamal Nath, the political head of India's trade negotiating team, just before he left for Hong Kong. At the meeting he was presented with the 'Big Noise' petition with over six million signatures on it from all over India, handed over in the form of a placard by Ramakrishna Choudhary, a farmer from Rajasthan. The petition asked the Indian Government to influence decision makers at the WTO to make trade fair for millions of farmers in India who are badly affected by post-liberalization policies, and for millions more people who depend on agriculture worldwide. The Minister in his response assured those present that the interests of small and marginal farmers were of prime importance to the country, and that under no circumstances would they be compromised. He added that he was aware that Indian farmers were not in a position to compete with agricultural producers in the US and EU, who were generously subsidized by their governments.

From 13 to 18 December 2005, trade ministers and officials from 150 countries met in Hong Kong to thrash out a series of agreements on how the trade in various types of goods, including agricultural goods, would be conducted. As well as the official government delegations from these countries there were thousands of people from civil society groups around the world (including a large number from Hong Kong itself) who were busy lobbying, talking to the media, and demonstrating in the streets. Among them was a large delegation of staff from the various Oxfams around the world, including a small number from India. There were also three people from the Indian NGOs Ekta Parishad and CCD, who were involved in the popular campaigning activities in the streets of Hong Kong. The Oxfam International delegation, which included lobbyists, policy experts and media liaison people, worked extensively behind the scenes with a range of Southern governments to strengthen their influence in the negotiations. At the same time it used its media spokespersons (of various nationalities and languages) to try to get its message across to a wide audience – and worked with a broad network of partners and allies to bring civil society pressure on participating governments. At a meeting of 90 Southern governments during the Ministerial Conference, the full 'Big Noise' petition, with 17.8 million signatures from countries all around the world, was presented to Pascal Lamy, the Director General of the WTO.[9]

In the event, the negotiations in Hong Kong failed to deliver much for farmers. Southern countries had to fight simply to keep some of their issues on the table. They found themselves in the difficult position of either accepting a deal that was seriously flawed from their point of view, or being blamed for the failure of the negotiations. Small gains on some aspects of the agreement on agriculture were more than offset by damaging proposals on trade in manufactured goods and services. On agriculture, there was a welcome commitment to allow developing countries the right to protect a small number of products of vital importance to poor farmers (referred to as 'Special Products') and for these to be self-selected by the developing country. There was also a pledge by the US and EU to eliminate their agricultural subsidies by 2013, but this applied to export subsidies only and not to the other more damaging forms. In the EU for example, export subsidies account for only 3 or 4 per cent of overall agricultural supports. The deal did not include any significant cuts to rich countries' domestic subsidies, nor did it propose tightening the disciplines on allowable payments. And there was no guarantee that Southern countries would gain significantly greater access to Northern markets. Of the statement issued by the Ministers at the end of the meeting, an Oxfam spokesperson said: 'This is a profoundly disappointing text and a betrayal of development promises by rich countries whose interests have prevailed yet again'.[10] There was little achieved in Hong Kong that could be classed as a gain, but at least the developing countries, led by Brazil, China and India, held firm and resisted pressure to sign a bad agreement. And they continue to do so. In 2008 the WTO negotiations on agriculture were still at a stalemate.

What the campaign achieved

The central aim of the campaign was to ensure that the Indian Government held firm to its position in Hong Kong and resisted pressure from the US, EU and other Northern countries to prematurely open up its markets to agricultural imports. This was achieved. India and the other developing countries did hold firm and a bad deal was avoided. No agreement on agriculture was signed. There was a commitment that when one is signed, developing countries like India will be able to protect a certain number of self-designated 'Special Products' of vital importance to their farmers – and provided the Indian Government chooses crops that are important to the poor this could be a major 'win'.

But to what extent the Indian Government's resolve in Hong Kong was due to the Oxfam-led campaign, or would have happened anyway, is not clear. Attribution is always difficult in this type of advocacy campaign. Even if a positive effect does occur, as in this case, it is never clear to what extent it is due to the campaign, and to what extent to other factors (perhaps something that happened in Hong Kong?). Governments operate within complex social and political contexts in which they are acted on by a variety of influences internal and external. To isolate the effect of one of these influences (an NGO campaign) from all the others is nearly impossible. All that can be done is to seek the opinions of various stakeholders of the extent of the cause-and-effect relationship between them. In late 2006 as part of the internal review of the campaign, staff members in India were asked whether they thought the campaign had any impact on government decision makers. The Oxfam staff in India had this to say:

> The Commerce Minister has acknowledged the role of Oxfam in awareness generation both in print and electronic media. Moreover, the official language of the Ministry on public forums has changed to include words like fair trade, livelihood security and even the Big Noise signature campaign...The fact that farmers are knowledgeable about issues of importance (to them) and are becoming more assertive in their demands for fair trade and change in policies in their favour has perhaps led the government to at least re-think its stand on these issues. Farmers coming together on such a large scale has made the policy makers sit up and listen. As the Commerce Minister put it in Hong Kong, 'We cannot trade the livelihoods of millions of poor farmers of our country for commerce'.[11]

Oxfam gained some influence with the government on trade issues as a result of the campaign. Its Regional Trade Advisor in India, Palash Kanti Das, who played a key role in the campaign believes that the pressure on the government was such that it felt the need to talk to the NGOs involved, and since then, has been keen to have a government representative invited to any NGO seminar on trade.[12] In the longer term, he believes that Oxfam has gained credibility and influence with both the government and business groups. This view is shared by Dr Samar Verma, the person with overall responsibility for the campaign in South Asia, who added that, as a result of the campaign, Oxfam also began to be consulted by the media as an informed commentator on issues to do with trade and development. It was to Oxfam that journalists increasingly turned for quotes and comments and explanations of technical issues. It became widely and frequently quoted in the media, first on international issues and then on national ones to do with trade and agriculture.[13]

Evidence of Oxfam's reputation with the Commerce Minister, Kamal Nath, came in early 2007 when he invited Oxfam International and another NGO, Consumer Union & Trust Society (CUTS) to be co-organizers with the government of a conference on the future of the WTO negotiations. During the conference, Oxfam policy advisors were given the unprecedented opportunity to meet with and discuss negotiating strategy with the Indian Government's trade negotiators and with the Trade Minister of South Africa, another key Southern government in the negotiations. This is not something that governments normally do with NGOs. Overall the conference was successful, but it did result in Oxfam being seen by some as too close to the Indian Government and too supportive of the WTO.

It was not only Oxfam that gained a new recognition from government. The research organization CENTAD also did. Although established by Oxfam, it became independent some years ago. CENTAD gained a strong reputation with both the government and business groups, who became interested in what it had to say. Its researchers are now often asked by them to give talks and seminars.[14] A seminar in early 2007 organized by CENTAD to launch their South Asia Yearbook was attended by both the current and former chief trade negotiator – and during it, the former chief negotiator remarked that he wished there had been organizations like CENTAD around at the time of the earlier rounds of WTO negotiations, as the outcomes then might have been different.[15]

Other NGOs have also benefited. There appears to have been a general opening up of the space for NGOs in India to dialogue with relevant parts of government on issues related to trade and development. This is the view of Oxfam policy advisor, Dr Samar Verma, who believes that the solid research, analysis and political understanding that this campaign displayed has helped to break down the old view that government held of NGOs as being shallow and ideologically driven. The in-country staff review said: 'The partners felt that local government bodies now sympathize with their cause, but do not openly support due to the nature of their job'.

One of the other achievements claimed for the campaign was that it brought to the development debate in India an analysis of how international trade and development were connected. For many NGOs, the impact of international trade on rural development was a relatively new issue. Das believes that before the campaign most Indian NGOs were more-or-less aware of the WTO and its impact on farmers, but were vague on the details of how that impact was manifested locally. He believes that Oxfam helped bring that perspective into clear focus, which was of considerable interest to them. Many were energized by the simple 'Make Trade Fair' message and the slogan really caught on.[16] This idea that the campaign helped change the views of local NGOs about trade was shared by other Oxfam staff in India, who felt that it moderated an essentially abolitionist view towards the WTO with a reformist one: 'Different sections of civil society are coming together now to talk on trade-related issues. The "reform WTO" angle taken up by Oxfam is an important contribution to civil society stance on trade, which earlier were either pro or anti WTO'.[17] To what extent these changes are significant is however contested. Researcher Shefali Sharma, for example, believes that the complex nature of the issues involved meant that the engagement of Indian civil society with trade issues, and in particular with the WTO Agreement on Agriculture, is always going to be very limited:

> The lack of interest in the global trading body indicates that the main priorities of the political struggle lie elsewhere. Currently, trade advocacy is too removed from the way local people express and view economic policy impacts on their lives. At the same time, the complexities of the trade discourse keeps many from engaging at all. There may be too much emphasis on the WTO as the culprit without adequately addressing national level trade and economic policy decisions that impact on citizen's lives... The research illustrates that trade advocacy work must be grounded appropriately in the broader problems around agrarian displacement and impoverishment, indebtedness and other impacts of structural adjustment in India if citizens are to directly participate in this debate.[18]

It is not possible to say whether the campaign had any significant impact on public opinion and popular awareness of trade issues. It did manage to persuade six million people in India to sign the 'Big Noise' petition to 'Make Trade Fair', but in a country of 1,100 million, this constitutes only a half of 1 per cent of the population. Given the size of the country and its population, it is safe to assume that any effect was small, and confined to the limited geographic areas in which the popular campaigning took place. However, according to the internal staff review, the volunteers from the partner organizations and Oxfam who ran the popular campaigning activities certainly increased their awareness, as did many of the people they talked to:

> The constant flow of information through the campaign was welcomed by all, especially women who were traditionally thought unfit for consumption of information related to issues of policy, matters of agriculture produce (men control the produce in most areas even though women work in all aspects of agriculture), etc. Some of the volunteers and signatories stated that the sense of helplessness regarding the current 'agricultural crisis' is waning as women become more aware as to why they and their

families are facing such competitive markets and government apathy...[19]

The staff also maintained that the campaign generated some extra advocacy by local organizations:

> Farmer leaders are coming out in support of the campaign since it became visible. M.S. Tikait, a leader with extensive following among farmers has asked farmers to join the campaign. Also Rajasthan now boasts of active participation and mobilisation by Kisan Seva Samiti Mahasangh at state level. This organisation gained momentum and strength on issues of agriculture related trade only after the impetus provided by the Big Noise campaign. Earlier they worked for the betterment of farmers but in a disjointed and haphazard manner. Other organisational tie-ups have resulted in taking the campaign to the grass root level in Rajasthan, in the very interiors of the state.

Strategies

If the analysis of Keck and Sikkink of the basic strategies used by advocacy networks were applied to this campaign in India, it could be said that it used two of the four outlined, namely 'information politics' and 'accountability politics'. 'Information politics' involves generating politically useful information and using it where it will have most impact, in this case by providing it to India's WTO trade negotiators.[20] The politically useful information in this case included intelligence from Geneva, Brussels, Washington and elsewhere that Oxfam was able to gather on what the various governments were doing or saying, as well as the briefing papers produced by Oxfam International on the various aspects of the WTO negotiations that critiqued the proposals being put forward in terms of what they mean for developing countries and for the poor. This combination of political intelligence and analysis of negotiation proposals was a powerful combination. Because the positions that Oxfam argued for in these documents were in line with those of the Indian Government, the latter embraced this information with enthusiasm, which led to a close collaborative relationship between the government and Oxfam. The government probably also saw relations with Oxfam as useful, as it was an organization with a popular support base in the countries whose governments were trying to pressure it. It could supposedly influence public opinion in Europe and the United States.[21]

Bringing the benefits of international research and political intelligence to the local situation was a key role that Oxfam played. It was the INGO's knowledge of the WTO negotiation process in Geneva and other Northern capitals, and of the need for India to hold firm in the face of US and EU pressure, that led to the campaign in the first place. When the campaign in India was just getting underway and local NGOs were being consulted on what their priority issues were, and how Oxfam could best help, it was this international perspective that Oxfam could bring that they stressed. What they wanted Oxfam to do, to quote the report from the consultations, was:

- Build the capacity of stakeholders to understand and analyse the impact of globalization on small-scale agriculture.
- Facilitate sharing of information on local, national and global issues relating to trade and agriculture.
- Mobilize stakeholders and carry out advocacy at various levels. Help stakeholders link grassroot realities with international trends.
- Support and carry out research and documentation on the impact of globalization on agriculture.[22]

All four of these points are about Oxfam providing an international perspective to issues of concern. For these partners and allies at least, this is what they saw as the most useful contribution that an INGO could make.

The Oxfam International briefing papers that provided arguments and analysis for Southern negotiators were mainly produced in Europe and were intended for a global audience. They were not specific to India. But similar materials that *were* specific to India, written from a local perspective about local issues, were produced by CENTAD in Delhi. These were also well received by the government and its trade negotiators. The aim of all these reports, local and international, was to change the terms of debate in India around trade and development, to bring into sharp focus the relationship between international trade negotiations and the plight of small-scale farmers. This is a key role that international NGOs like Oxfam can play in a local or national campaign, supplying research and analysis from their international resources, or helping to develop such research and analysis capacity for Southern NGOs, by commissioning academics in the South to produce relevant material, or facilitating the establishment of research organizations such as CENTAD.

The second tactic outlined by Keck and Sikkink, 'accountability politics', means holding powerful actors, in this case the Government of India, to their previously stated policies or principles. Indian officials had stated many times that protecting the livelihoods of the country's farmers was central to their objectives in the WTO. For example in May 2005, the Commerce Secretary, Shri S. N. Menon had said that India's priorities in the WTO negotiations were 'removal of trade distorting subsidies by developing countries, ensuring adequate protection to the livelihood concerns of poor subsistence farmers, and to safeguard food security, livelihood and rural development concerns'.[23] In July 2005, Minister for Commerce and Industry and head of India's negotiating team, Shri Kamal Nath, said: 'The success of the current Doha Round of the World Trade Organisation talks will be judged not by tariffs and formulae but by (a) how many jobs it can create in developing countries; (b) how much the income of farmers in developing countries has risen; and (c) how many poor people have been extricated from poverty'.[24]

It was to hold the government to these commitments that public pressure in the form of the 'Big Noise' petition with its six million Indian signatures was used. Farmer Ramakrishna who was a part of the team that handed over the petition to Commerce Minister Kamal Nath before he left for Hong Kong said he felt that the number of signatures represented the strength of the campaign and that this made the Minister notice the plight of farmers.[25] And as noted earlier, the Minister in his response felt obliged to say that the interests of small and marginal farmers were of prime importance to the country, and that under no circumstances would they be compromised in the negotiations.

What was not achieved

A serious limitation of this campaign was that it was focused on the international negotiations that were happening at the WTO, and not enough serious thought was given to how a 'win' at this level, obtaining a good WTO agreement, would translate into benefits for farmers. Brock and McGee, writing about a similar civil society campaign on trade in Uganda and Kenya, make a point about the difficulties of establishing such a connection:

> [M]any of the CSO actors interviewed reflected on the potential dangers of doing externally focused work without a fully grounded understanding of the implications of trade policy for livelihoods and agriculture... Indeed many discussed the sheer daunting complexity of trying to establish or understand causality between trade

policy and livelihoods. Linking the micro to the macro is a particularly difficult challenge amongst the multiple policies that effect trade outcomes. As such, the majority of those who have downward vertical linkages, particularly with farmers, tend to use them for informing people about the nature of external systems, rather than to gather information about the impact of macro-level changes on micro-level processes.[26]

For an advocacy campaign to produce positive benefits for the poor, many steps are usually needed. In this case, a 'win' at the WTO would need to be accompanied by a number of other sub-goals, including changes of policy and practice by the Indian federal and state governments and Agricultural Ministries, so that farmers were able to gain access to the inputs, credit, information, etc that they needed in order to be able to take advantage of the trading opportunities that were hopefully opened up. The fact that there was no attempt to do this, nor to link the macro with the micro, highlights the fact that this campaign was not built on the need to solve a local problem that was harming farmers, but on the need to support an international campaign around a trade agreement. This was not so much an Indian campaign as the Indian part of a global campaign.

What can probably be said about the campaign however is that, in preventing a WTO agreement that would have prematurely opened India up to subsidized agricultural imports, it prevented the situation for farmers from becoming worse. However there was no clear analysis of this. Nor was there any analysis of the implications of the policies being promoted for other groups in Indian society, for example the urban poor. Subsidized agricultural imports could potentially be beneficial for them in the form of cheaper food, if the lower price of imports were passed on to consumers (something which does not always occur). As often happens in campaigns like this, a choice had to be made between supporting different groups with conflicting interests. In this case the assumption was that preserving the livelihoods of farmers and rural people was a higher priority than potentially cheaper food for urban consumers, as it was poverty in the rural areas and the difficulty of making a living from agriculture that was driving people to the cities in the first place and creating an ever increasing pool of urban poor. But this was never fully analysed nor clearly articulated.

Another shortcoming of the campaign was in the area of alliance building. After getting off to a good start with the regional consultations and building up some interest amongst a number of organizations and individuals, Oxfam then went off on its own with an agenda that had come from elsewhere. This was not good for relations with its partner organizations and potential allies, who would be quite justified in thinking that their time had been wasted and their input and advice discounted. However this was not entirely true. It would be more accurate to say that their experience and advice was taken on board and used, but at a later stage. As in the Sri Lanka case, this was an example of the tensions that can arise between an international campaign and its manifestation at a national level. Global campaigns, especially those aiming to influence an international agreement or process, are by their nature going to be 'directive' with their shape and form determined by an overarching coherent global strategy, usually designed in the North. This means that their relevance to the local national situation in the South is going to be problematic, as in this case.

A major factor limiting the success of the campaign in terms of outreach and generating the level of popular support that was hoped for, was the sheer lack of time. It did not effectively get underway until well into 2005, and it all had to be finished before the Commerce Minister and his team departed for Hong Kong in December of that year. Initially Oxfam had no staff or structures in place to run such a large campaign, even given the sub-contracting. Suitable people had to be recruited and trained at short notice, and new organizational systems put into place to cope with this new set of activities. The result was a frantic effort over a few months that exhausted the staff. A campaign that was serious about building popular support at a grassroots level would have needed much more time. But this was never going to be possible. As Sharma says:

> The pace, timing and strategies for policy advocacy related to the WTO and that of long-term organizing from the grassroots poses limits to effective citizen engagement. Policy change from the bottom up requires mass mobilization that can activate the Indian democratic system. It must be able to motivate politicians to take these issues up and demand accountability from the central government and the Department of Commerce. This requires that grassroots groups and social movements across India take up trade issues in earnest and mobilise at the local, regional and national level. The long-term time horizon that is required to create such a response does not match with the WTO policy process.[27]

Legitimacy

Unlike the Sri Lanka campaign, in which Oxfam's advocacy was mainly carried out as a member of a coalition with local organizations, in this case it ran its own campaign in its own name and only involved local organizations from time to time when it needed assistance. Given this, was it legitimate for Oxfam to be trying to influence Indian Government policy in this way? Did it, as a foreign-based organization, have a right to do what it did?

The first thing to be said is that it was not domestic policy that it was trying to influence. It was the position of the government in an international process of negotiation in the WTO. The position taken by the Indian Government in those negotiations affects farmers in Britain, France, USA, Australia, etc, and millions of peasant farmers and rural communities in other developing countries. Development INGOs like Oxfam would claim to be advocating for the rights of the world's poor rural communities in general, not just those in India. This does not mean that INGOs are claiming to be speaking on behalf of the world's poor. They would say that they are presenting a view that they believe is in the interests of the poor, based on their experience of working with such communities over many decades, but have no mandate to speak as their representatives. Oxfam speaks on behalf of no one but itself, and its views are its own. Its field experience in developing countries may give it a perspective and some credibility, but it does not give it a mandate to speak on behalf of others. It was a case of Oxfam having 'a voice but not a vote'.

Oxfam chose to operate alone in this case, despite the fact that it would have been more legitimate to have worked with local allies, or to have stayed behind the scenes and merely supported local advocates to take the front running. Dr Samar Verma, the overall head of the campaign in India at the time, believes that it had no choice but to run this campaign itself, as there was in 2005 no other organization in the country that could do it, and no alliance that it could join. As evidence of this he tells of the occasion on which the British Foreign Secretary was visiting India and a group of NGO representatives was pulled together to meet with him in Delhi and lobby him on trade and the WTO negotiations. None of these NGOs felt confident enough to make a presentation to the Foreign Secretary on this, and asked Oxfam to do all the talking. A similar thing happened at the time of the G20 meeting in Delhi, when two INGOs ended up doing most of the lobbying of Trade Ministers. It was this lack of local capacity in the area of trade that was one of the chief reasons for Oxfam establishing the Centre for Trade and Development (CENTAD) in Delhi. The international reputation that Oxfam had by then established as an authoritative NGO commentator on the WTO negotiations and their implications for Southern countries, meant that governments were receptive to what it had to say. It had an international reputation that 'opened doors' to government. This was not a case of a foreign organization trying to influence the domestic policies of a Southern country, but of an international organization with an established reputation on trade and development talking to a Southern government about an international trade negotiation process that had global implications. This was the basis of Oxfam's mandate.

Relations with government

The strategy employed by Oxfam was a classic 'insider' one of establishing a relationship with the target and engaging it in dialogue. In this case the dialogue was friendly and supportive, and the relationship that developed between the INGO and government was a cooperative one. For an INGO, such a relationship can be very useful in creating access for lobbying and influencing. But it can also create serious problems. No government is perfect and being associated with one and its failings or abuses may be seen as supporting those abuses. Also some CSOs, domestic or international, will inevitably be opposed to the government on some issue, and being seen as close to an authority that they do not like will have implications for the INGO's relationship with those CSOs. A 2006 survey of policy advocacy in the South by the Overseas Development Institute in London found that: 'There is always a danger that if one CSO is seen to be engaging very closely with policy makers, then the other CSOs perceive it to be a "lackey" of the government. In addition the CSOs themselves feel that if they engage too closely with the government, they run the risk of losing their independence'.[28] In this campaign, Oxfam worked with the Indian Government because of an international strategy of encouraging the assertiveness of Southern governments in the WTO negotiations. India was seen as a key country in that process, one that could lead resistance to US and European pressures, and it was an obvious strategy to support it. But this had implications for the organization's relations with CSOs in India, and with the government of neighbouring Bangladesh, which regards India as a dominant neighbour and a rival in some areas of trade.

A friendly relationship between an INGO and a government over some international negotiation process can also have implications for the INGO's attitude towards it on other issues, including domestic ones. The INGO may not want to upset that important relationship by being oppositional over other issues. On the other hand it could be argued that a good relationship with a government gives the INGO access and the ability to express its concerns over those other policies, where less friendly organizations would not be listened to. This comes down to the 'insider versus outsider' arguments outlined in Chapter 2. It may be possible for an INGO to have a cooperative relationship with a government on one issue and an oppositional one on another, but this would be difficult to manage, and the way in which criticisms were expressed would have to be carefully nuanced.

Participation and democracy

Jordan and van Tuijl make the point that: 'The hallmark of an NGO which fully embraces the concept of political responsibility is its capacity to sustain coherence and consistency between the goals it professes, and the manner in which it pursues them'.[29] In other words an organization that believes in the principles of democracy and participation by the otherwise poor and powerless in things that affect them, should practice these values in the design and implementation of advocacy campaigns that affect them. Was Oxfam therefore true to its values of democracy and participation in the running of this campaign? Although aimed at improving the situation of farmers and rural communities in India, there was little or no involvement by such groups or their representatives in the design of the campaign, or in what was said about them nationally and internationally. The participatory consultation process with (amongst others) organizations that represented rural communities that was initially set up to determine the shape of the campaign was sidelined by an agenda handed down from the international campaign.

But, as argued above, there was a reason for this. The nature of the campaign was such that it had to be 'directive' or determined at an international level and handed down to the country level, because it was part of a global strategy to influence an international agreement. Local relevance was sacrificed for global coherence and impact. But there are dangers in such an approach, particularly if the international campaign loses touch with the grassroots realities, in this case with the real needs and priorities of farmers and rural people and advocates for inappropriate policies at the WTO level. The objectives in different arenas are then beginning to clash. Participation by those whom the campaign is aimed at benefiting or their representative is not only desirable from the point of view of participation and democracy, but also from a practical point of view in terms of keeping the campaign on the right track.

The ideal campaign is one in which there is wide consultation, good communication and common or compatible objectives at different levels – local, national, international – and in which the campaign at each of these levels supports and is supported by the others. This was a campaign in which advocacy in the North and in the South was well coordinated, but instead of a Southern campaign being supported by advocacy in the North, the reverse was the case – the Northern campaign was being supported by advocacy in the South.

Because there was no participation by local NGOs in the final design of this campaign, it was hard to get them involved, as there was little sense of ownership. In terms of the popular campaigning activities, the road-shows and rallies, their participation had to be bought or encouraged by making funding available. But in approaching these organizations and offering money, did Oxfam use its role as funder to distort their organizational priorities? Das's view is that it probably did, but they were interested anyway and excited by the 'Make Trade Fair' message and perspectives, and enthusiastic to take it up. According to him, Oxfam paid them because no matter how interested they might be in the issues and the campaign, without the extra funds they would not be able to do anything. It was seen as a joint effort – Oxfam provided the funds and the ideas, and they provided the people and local expertise to put them into practice.[30] Dr Samar Verma, who led the campaign for Oxfam agrees, suggesting that Oxfam changed their priorities rather than distorted them. The fact that they were willing to take up and support the campaign's messages and objectives indicates that they fitted with their experience. Their involvement was voluntary, although possibly influenced by the funding on offer, and if the message of the campaign had been inconsistent with their grassroots experience they would not have become involved.[31] Indeed some chose not to be, because they did not agree with Oxfam's analysis. Those that did become involved presumably did so on the basis that it fitted with their existing programmes and approaches.

Notes

1 Because this campaign was run jointly by the Oxfam affiliates in South Asia, the name 'Oxfam' has been used to refer to them all jointly. In fact most of the work of this campaign was done by the Delhi-based staff of Oxfam Great Britain, assisted by Oxfam India. But it was done in the name of, and with substantial financial support from, two other affiliates, Oxfam Novib (Netherlands) and Oxfam Australia, under the auspices of the Oxfam Regional Strategic Team for South Asia.

2 Oxfam International (2004) *Small-scale agriculture in the era of globalisation. Sub-national consultations on trade and agriculture. India report.* New Delhi, December.
3 Oxfam International (2005) *From development to naked self-interest: the Doha Development Round has lost its way.* Oxfam Briefing Note, July.
4 J. Atkinson (2005) *'Make Trade Fair' Campaign on Trade and Agriculture in India and Bangladesh* (Melbourne: Oxfam Australia).
5 Oxfam International (2006) Oxfam Big Noise Review. In-country staff interview form completed by Supriya Singh on behalf of the staff, New Delhi.
6 Oxfam International, Make Trade Fair website www.maketradefair.org date accessed July 2007.
7 Kumar Gautam (2005) *The report on the progress and the problems* (New Delhi: Oxfam GB) December.
8 Oxfam International, Make Trade Fair website www.maketradefair.org date accessed July 2007.
9 Of all the countries in which signatures were gathered, India toped the list with over six million signatures.
10 Oxfam International media release, December 2005.
11 Oxfam International (2006) *op cit.*
12 Palash Kanti Das, Regional Trade Advisor, Oxfam GB, New Delhi, interviewed February 2007.
13 Dr Samar Verma, former Oxfam Regional Policy Advisor, South Asia, personal correspondence with the author, 19 September 2007.
14 Palash Kanti Das, Regional Trade Advisor, Oxfam GB, New Delhi, interviewed February 2007.
15 Dr Samar Verma, former Oxfam Regional Policy Advisor, South Asia, interview May 2007.
16 Palash Kanti Das, Regional Trade Advisor, Oxfam GB, New Delhi, interviewed February 2007.
17 Oxfam International (2006) *op cit.*
18 S. Sharma (2007) *India and the Agreement on Agriculture: civil society and citizen's engagement.* Institute of Development Studies, University of Sussex, Working Paper 278, pp. 55–6.
19 Oxfam International (2006) *op cit.*
20 M. Keck and K. Sikkink (1998) *Activists Beyond Borders* (Ithaca and London: Cornell University Press) pp. 18–25.
21 This was certainly the case in Australia where the government's attitude towards Oxfam and its campaign on the WTO Agreement on Agriculture was strongly influenced by the fact that Oxfam could supposedly influence public opinion in the EU and US, whose government Australia wished to convince to eliminate their agricultural subsidies.
22 Oxfam International (2004) *Small-scale agriculture in the era of globalization. Sub-national consultations on trade and agriculture. India Report* (Delhi: Oxfam International).
23 Department of Commerce, Press Release, 24 May 2005, New Delhi. *WTO negotiations entering a crucial phase; workshop for state governments on WTO held.*
24 Department of Commerce, Press Release, 29 July 2005, New Delhi. *WTO stalemate a wake-up call.*

25 Oxfam International (2006) *op cit.*
26 K. Brock and R. McGee (2004) *Mapping trade policy. Understanding the challenge of civil society participation.* IDS Working Paper 225 (Brighton, UK: Institute of Development Studies).
27 S. Sharma (2007) *op cit.*, p. 53.
28 N. Chowdhury, C. Finlay-Notman and I. Hovland (2006) CSO Capacity for Policy Engagement: Lessons Learned from the CSPP Consultations in Africa, Asia and Latin America. Overseas Development Institute, Working Paper 272, p. 8.
29 L. Jordan and P. van Tuijl (2000) 'Political responsibility in transnational NGO advocacy', *World Development*, vol. 28, number 12, pp. 2063–4.
30 Palash Kanti Das, Regional Trade Advisor, Oxfam GB, New Delhi, interviewed February 2007.
31 Dr Samar Verma, former Oxfam Regional Policy Advisor, South Asia, interview May 2007.

6
Oxfam's Global Extractive Industries Campaigning

During the 1990s various Oxfams began supporting the activities of organizations that were defending the rights of local communities affected by extractives activities, principally mining and oil and gas. Thus, Oxfam Australia (then known as Community Aid Abroad) supported communities in Southeast Asia and the South Pacific affected by the activities of mining companies based in Australia. Oxfam Great Britain engaged in dialogues with major oil companies, such as Shell and BP, about human rights violations associated with their activities in Nigeria and Colombia. Oxfam Intermon became involved in discussions around the Chad-Cameroon oil pipeline in West Africa and Oxfam America (OA) gave grants to several organizations in Ecuador in South America working with indigenous peoples in the Amazon to defend their rights in the face of oil exploration and production.

Until the mid-1990s, when Oxfam International (OI) was created, advocacy by individual Oxfam affiliates was largely separate and uncoordinated. With the foundation of Oxfam International, the Oxfams began to exchange information about their programmes and partners in the search for common interests and areas of possible collaboration. Early on, advocacy was identified as an activity where synergies might be most easily generated. Because of the dominant role played by the US Government in international decision making and the presence of important international financial institutions there, in 1996 Oxfam International decided to establish an advocacy office in Washington DC and Oxfam America decided to move its advocacy operations to Washington from Boston so that office facilities could be shared.

Both teams focused on global development issues that increased poverty and inequality, such as debt and World Bank policies, but the agreed-upon division of responsibilities meant that OA was responsible for direct lobbying of the US Government while OI concentrated its efforts on international bodies, such as the World Bank, the International Monetary Fund and the United Nations. There was also a difference in that OA focused both on issues of particular interest to its partners as well as global issues, whereas OI focused exclusively on an international agenda defined by all the Oxfams.

In 1999 OI launched its first global campaign, 'Education Now', aimed at achieving universal access to education for girls and women. This involved campaigning both in Washington DC and other capitals as well as in the regions of the world where the Oxfams had programme activities. However, the degree of involvement of the different Oxfams varied widely, especially in the South, and most of the effort was concentrated at the global level. Meanwhile, in 1998, several Oxfams (Oxfam Australia, Oxfam Great Britain, Oxfam Novib, Intermon Oxfam and Oxfam America) formed an extractive industries working group to exchange information about their activities on this theme and explore possible areas of collaboration. Although the participants in the discussions concerning extractive industries came mainly from the advocacy and campaign units of the Oxfams' head offices, they felt that extractive industries had a greater potential than education for involving and linking partners and programmes in the regions with advocacy in the North in a potential transnational advocacy effort around the role and impacts of extractives, and this was one of the alternatives considered by OI for the follow-up campaign to 'Education Now'.

In the event, OI decided to make international trade the focus of its second global campaign, to give greater priority and resources to advocacy in general, and the campaign in particular, and to ask the regional offices to focus their programme coordination on advocacy. As a result, the Oxfams diverted resources and attention from the emerging work on extractive industries, although without abandoning it entirely. Thus, Oxfam Australia continued a programme centred on its 'mining ombudsman', who investigated and reported on the activities of Australian-based mining companies in Asia and the Pacific, and Oxfam America built its South America-based extractive industries programme into an agency-wide extractive industries team. For its part, the OI extractive industries working group disbanded in 2001.

The OA programme in South America originally covered five countries – Bolivia, Brazil, Colombia, Ecuador and Peru – but by the mid-1990s was reduced to the three central Andean countries of Bolivia, Ecuador and Peru. Furthermore, it focused its attention on working with indigenous peoples in the Andean highlands and the Amazonian basin. In this context, most of its work around extractive industries involved support for NGOs, such as Acción Ecológica and CDES in Ecuador and CEDIA in Peru, and indigenous organizations, such as CONAIE, CONFENIAE and FIPSE in Ecuador and AIDESEP and COMARU in Peru, in their efforts to influence the activities of oil companies engaged in exploration and production in the Amazon. Of particular note was its support for the 'Campaign for Life' which sought a clean-up and restoration of areas affected by the Texaco company's oil operations in the northern jungle of Ecuador. This involved a coalition of Ecuadorian NGOs and indigenous and non-indigenous (settler) organizations with Northern allies. After a class action suit involving these areas was presented in the US, and eventually refiled in Ecuadorian courts, the coalition of actors, since widened and strengthened, continues to be active and receive OA support (as well as support from others).

In OA's South America office in Lima, the support for these activities was seen as part of its overall support to indigenous peoples to strengthen their representative organizations and enable them to defend their lands and territories and sustainably manage their natural resources. They were not conceived of as an advocacy programme as such and the office did not see its role to be directly involved in advocacy on behalf of or in collaboration with its partners, save for occasional efforts to connect them with possible allies in the North. The regional office's role was seen as that of providing financial support to organizations for activities that might include advocacy, but advocacy itself was the task of these partner organizations in the region on regional issues and targets and of the advocacy unit in Washington DC on global issues. At most, the regional office might assist partners wishing to make contacts in Washington or help connect the advocacy unit in Washington with regional partners relevant to global campaigns.

Two elements combined to change this situation. On the one hand, in the second half of the 1990s indigenous leaders and their allies within the region increasingly sought OA's help not only financially but also with information, contacts and training in order to be able to engage effectively with global extractive industries companies that were impinging on their territories. On the other hand, within Oxfam as a whole campaigning and advocacy were receiving greater attention and the regional offices were being asked to include these within their range of activities, in addition to traditional development work.

At first, OA's efforts to develop an extractive industries programme in South America was closely coordinated with Oxfam Great Britain's Peru country office, but, as OI's global campaigning got under way,

Oxfam Great Britain decided to reduce its commitment. In any event, after commissioning several studies, organizing meetings with partners and internal discussions, at the end of 1999 the South America regional office of OA decided to transform the disparate grants in support of extractive industries advocacy into a coordinated and coherent programme.

The problems to be addressed by this programme were seen to be the following: The problem on the *international* level is the absence of enforceable environmental and social standards. The problem on the *national* level is the existence of divided state interests, limited reach and political will, and the lack of inclusion of the sectors most negatively affected by extractive industries. The problem in the *private sector* is that its profit-driven nature does not lend itself to self-regulation, and that it is not on a level playing field with either local communities or governments. And the problem on the *local* level is the lack of capacity to analyse problems and needs, to articulate positions, to make good use of indigenous consultative traditions to build consensus and a unified voice, and to effectively bargain.[1]

In order to remedy these problems, the programme defined three objectives: (1) help the indigenous peoples of the region to assume the fundamental responsibility of the defence of their rights and the sustainable development of their resources and help them negotiate effectively; (2) persuade and pressure governments at every level to protect and defend the rights of indigenous peoples; and (3) persuade the companies dedicated to resource extraction to recognize and respect the rights and needs of indigenous peoples.[2] Finally, the activities to be supported and undertaken were grouped under three key strategies: defence of the right of those affected by extractive industries to be consulted, the strengthening of the organizational and advocacy capacities of affected communities and their representatives and the definition and implementation of appropriate standards by industry and government.

The problems to be tackled were seen as involving traditional programme work (organizational strengthening, capacity building), as well as the 'new' activities of campaigning and advocacy, and as requiring actions reaching from the local through the national and regional to the global and, thus, as requiring a commitment from OA's advocacy unit in Washington and, eventually, the communications and campaign units in Boston. At the same time that the extractive industries programme was formally launched in South America, an extractive industries advocacy officer was hired in the OA policy unit in Washington. Although most programme support by OA to extractive industries advocacy in the region had been focused on oil and gas in the Ecuadorian Amazon, it was decided to give priority to advocacy on mining in the Andean highlands of Peru because of the recent creation of a national organization representing peasant communities in Peru affected by mining in an alliance with a group of national NGOs, the rapid expansion of mining in the country and the greater capacity of the regional office to support and monitor a new programme in the country where its office was located.

At the same time that the interest and initiative for work on extractives was waning within OI in the North, an initiative was gathering force in one of the regional offices. Between 1999 and 2000 OI developed its first five-year global strategic plan. This involved the division of the world into 11 regions, one of them being South America, and the Oxfams active in each region were required to create a Regional Strategic Team and produce a regional strategic plan which would involve joint and coordinated efforts in development, emergency relief and advocacy. Because each Oxfam already had considerable programme investments in support for development activities, progress in consolidating these was expected to be slow and, because Oxfam Great Britain was the only Oxfam with an established capacity for emergency relief in the South, joint efforts on this were expected to focus on capacity building within the Oxfams. Although at the regional level the Oxfams had little experience or capacity in advocacy, all were engaged in advocacy in their home countries and because there were few commitments to existing advocacy campaigns in the regions this was to be given priority for joint activity in the regional strategic plans.

This planning activity coincided with the decision to make international trade the focus for OI's second global campaign, and OI advocacy in the regions was expected to give it priority. However, the scope of the campaign was so vast that OI decided to break it down into a series of sub-campaigns, only some of which (agricultural trade and labour rights) had been defined at that stage. In the course of the planning discussions of the South America Regional Strategic Team it emerged that the OA extractive industries programme was one of the few that was well developed and defined and, since extractive industries was being considered as a possible future sub-campaign for the trade campaign, it was included in OI's regional strategic plan. However, the only Oxfam in the region that expressed interest in being involved was OA, thus inaugurating a period of confusion as to what extent it was an OA or OI campaign or both. This situation required the OA South America staff to coordinate with and answer to both the OI Regional Strategic Team and what eventually became the OA Global Extractive Industries Team.

In early 2000 the recently formed Coordinator (later Confederation) of Peruvian Communities Affected by Mining (CONACAMI) undertook its strategic planning with support from five national NGOs and Oxfam. As a priority for campaigning, they defined the modification of the law governing the virtual expropriation of community lands for mining and a number of cases of conflicts between communities and mining companies that they hoped would be emblematic in promoting wider changes in the policies and practices of the industry. The previous year OA had begun the Advocacy Learning Initiative, a joint project with the Advocacy Institute, which included among its activities workshops for training OA staff and partners. Following on from CONACAMI's strategic planning, a training workshop was held in Lima for OA staff, CONACAMI and its allies, aimed at building advocacy capacities and developing an initial campaign plan. This gave an important boost to the nascent programme in the region.

In July 2000 the Washington-based extractive industries advocacy officer developed a detailed policy paper proposing an advocacy strategy and goals and presenting an analysis of allies, targets and risks. Discussions between staff in the Boston, Washington and Lima offices of OA led to the creation in 2001 of an OA working group on extractive industries which included staff from all three offices and from the programme, policy and communications units, representing 'the first semi-institutionalized programmatic linkage across multiple Oxfam departments and with Southern partners on an advocacy-oriented initiative'.[3] This reflected not only an organizational change but also a change in the conceptualization of advocacy which had been foreshadowed in the 1999 meeting of OI's Extractive Industries Working Group in The Hague which agreed to place more emphasis on getting Southern voices heard in the North and to 'create a "two-front" advocacy campaign with Oxfam agencies implementing extractive industries advocacy campaigns in the North and Southern partners working in the South'.[4] Nevertheless, as an OA staff member at the time observed, 'The challenge of building mutually accountable alliances based on a common vision for change and agreed upon strategies and tactics when money is involved and when there are tremendous physical, cultural and language differences, is daunting'.[5]

From 2000 to 2004 the OA extractive industries working group developed a region-led campaign that included amongst its components the promotion and production of credible research, technical assistance, capacity building and financial support for advocacy by Southern partners linked to Northern-based advocacy and campaigning. These activities aimed at increasing poor peoples' right to be heard and participate in decisions affecting their lives and livelihoods, promoting the equal rights and status of indigenous people in the US and abroad, affecting change in the policies and practices of national governments and changing the terms of the global debate on extractive industries.[6] While the initiative for the campaign had begun in the South America region, by 2004 Oxfam America had extractive industries advocacy campaigns under way in Central America, East Asia, West Africa and the western US. The global extractive industries team was led by the extractives advocacy officer in Washington and the South America regional director acted as sponsor, responsible for relations with OA management.

Traditionally, Oxfam advocacy had been largely directed at governments, public sector agencies and international organizations. However, with the increased power and influence of transnational corporations, especially in the extractives industries, and the diminished weight of national governments, particularly in the South, Oxfam staff were interested in exploring the possibility of developing a campaign directed at changing the policies and practices of industry. To that end, with funding from the Ford Foundation and in collaboration with the Environmental Law Institute, based in Washington, and the Peruvian Environmental Law Society, based in Lima, Oxfam carried out a series of consultations with communities affected by mining activities in Bolivia, Chile, Ecuador and Peru to determine under what conditions they would be willing to consider a certification process for mining companies, how such a certification process might be organized and what standards would be demanded of the companies. Though most communities were sceptical about the possibilities of designing a certification system that would guarantee changes in the policies and practices of companies, this project produced a publication on free, prior and informed consent that was to be a cornerstone for future extractive industries advocacy and a list of 'demands' from the communities that were central to the 'No Dirty Gold' campaign launched in February 2004.

This campaign, which was intended to link advocacy with the gold mining industry in the North with advocacy by Southern partners around gold mining companies in the South, was developed with the Washington-based Mineral Policy Center (later renamed as Earthworks). The objective was to apply public pressure both in the North and South on individual gold mining companies and the industry as a whole by persuading their principal clients in the US, such as jewellery retailers, electronics manufacturers and others, to sign up to a set of demands that they would make on their gold suppliers. Eventually, it was hoped that it would be possible to pressure the industry as a whole (or a core group of key companies) to negotiate a gold certification system with representatives of their clients, NGOs and the communities affected by their activities. Between 2004 and 2007 the campaign gradually signed up an increasing number of gold buyers and obtained expressions of interest by some mining companies so that a process of negotiations about a possible gold certification system got under way in Vancouver in 2006. However, in March 2007 OA decided to reduce its involvement in the 'No Dirty Gold' campaign, leaving the prime responsibility to Earthworks, and announced a new campaign titled 'Right to Know, Right to Decide', allied with the NGO-sponsored 'Publish What You Pay' campaign and linked to the Extractive Industries Transparency Initiative sponsored by governments, the mining industry and national civil societies.

This new campaign focused on two of the principal planks of the 'No Dirty Gold' campaign: gain acceptance by government, industry and public opinion at large of the right of local communities affected by mining to be consulted and exercise free, prior and informed consent and demand transparency by companies and governments about taxes and other payments and the use made of these payments. This campaign allowed OA to focus its efforts on issues that formed an important part of the 'No Dirty Gold' Campaign, thus reducing the dispersion of its energies and resources, and to reduce the level of its involvement in the more technical aspects of the 'No Dirty Gold' campaign and the negotiations about possible certification, matters more within the experience and expertise of Earthworks. Between 2006 and 2007 the US and East Asia regional offices of OA decided to terminate their extractive industries programmes.

In an attempt to achieve a truly global and integrated campaign that would generate synergies between campaigns aimed at targets, and changes, in both the South and the North the team defined the following five objectives:

1. Communities affected by oil, gas and mining projects are *informed, organized and networked* to influence decisions in order to protect their livelihoods and cultures.

2. Companies, governments and individuals who stand to profit from extractive industries *recognize as key stakeholders* the communities that stand to be impacted (environmentally, culturally, economically or otherwise) by operations, and conduct constructive community engagement.
3. Financial institutions, companies and governments recognize and uphold the rights of communities to *free, prior and informed consent* with regards to extractive industry projects that may affect them, and take proactive measures to comply with their obligations in this respect.
4. Extractive industry companies and governments *disclose meaningful information* about potential and actual local impacts, provide appropriate mitigation measures to lessen negative impacts, and compensate communities when damages occur.
5. Governments adopt policies using *transparent processes,* and *enforce laws* that protect communities from the impacts of extractive industries while *ensuring maximum local benefits* from operations.[7]

These were to be achieved through such activities as funding for organizations and networks that worked in multiple ways around the world and whose activities would further Oxfam's programme objectives; advocacy assistance to partners; participation of regional staff in dialogues between extractive companies and governments; support to national, regional and local governments and facilitation of exchanges; and the formation of trans-boundary networks in the South and direct lobbying, strategic research, awareness-raising for change and engagement with extractive corporations and their clients internationally.[8] Subsequently, OA attempted to lay out the theory of change implicit in each of its advocacy campaigns. This meant that, for each campaign, staff members were expected to work with partners and allies in order to make as explicit as possible the underlying assumptions and power analysis, the sequence of activities to be carried out and those responsible for each, the intermediate and final objectives to be aimed for and the expected flow-on from campaign results or outputs to the desired impacts in terms of changes in the lives of the poor.

Extractive industries advocacy in the South America region was an integral component and often the motor of the global campaign, and thus participated in the development of the overall effort. There was a series of experiences that influenced the campaign's evolution and provided lessons for other regions and for the global team as a whole. The OA extractive industries advocacy campaign can perhaps best be summarized through a description of the five emblematic cases in which Oxfam and its partners were involved: Tambogrande, Yanacocha, Tintaya, Camisea and La Oroya.[9]

The first of these, the Tambogrande case, involved a proposal by a 'junior' Canadian company, Manhattan Minerals, to develop an open-cut polymetalic mine in a valley on Peru's north coast. This proposal encountered opposition from the townspeople of Tambogrande and local farmers on an irrigation project developed in the 1950s with World Bank funding. The former were opposed to resettlement and the latter feared that the prospects of the fruit industry would be damaged by contamination. The Tambogrande Defense Front, including urban and rural interests, was created and an alliance formed with a coalition of local and national NGOs with backing from the Catholic Church. After an initial protest got out of hand, leading to the sacking of the company's camp, the Defense Front worked hard to train and to educate its members in non-violent protest, which included the organization of the first local referendum on a mining project, which resulted in an overwhelming vote against the proposal. Because Oxfam funded the referendum the mining industry and national government began a media campaign, which waxed and waned for the next five years and which attempted to portray Oxfam as an environmental organization that supported violence and was opposed to national development.

Nevertheless, the referendum and its outcome generated reverberations throughout the world and the strategic alliance between the Defense Front representing those affected and the coalition of NGOs that provided technical support was an innovation that proved to be effective in other cases. Despite attempts by the company and the Ministry of Energy and Mines to convince the community that the project be accepted, effective local organization and well argued studies largely funded by Oxfam that were critical of the project's environmental impact assessment and of the economic benefits in comparison with alternatives obliged the government to employ a legal pretext to abort the project. In the short run, this was considered by Oxfam and its partners to be a victory because it represented the exercise by an affected community of its right to free, prior and informed consent and of the obligation of companies and governments to respect that right. It also illustrated the need for communities to have access to independent and reliable information in order to enable them to make informed choices. In the long run, however, the lack of a fundamental change in government policies governing community participation in decisions meant that, several years later, communities in an adjacent area were engaged in a similar struggle to have their voice heard about another proposed mining project.

After the end of the country's internal political violence and the emergency measures to introduce neo-liberal economic policies in the early 1990s, the first major mining project to get under way was the Yanacocha gold mine, the second largest in the world and jointly owned by the US-based Newmont Mining Company, the Peruvian Buenaventura Mining Company and the International Finance Corporation (IFC) of the World Bank. During that decade the company generated friction with many elements of the local community over land purchases and contamination, despite the expenditure of large sums of money on community projects. In June 2000 a truck contracted by the company was involved in the largest recorded mercury spill in the town of Choropampa. Both the company and the government reacted in a way that generated considerable distrust and conflict with the town whose unequal battle was recorded in a prize-winning video funded by Oxfam. The conflict over responsibilities and compensation continues without a definitive resolution.

As the company's relations with the city of Cajamarca and the surrounding communities deteriorated, despite attempts by the IFC to establish negotiations, the company announced its intention to expand its activities to Cerro Quilish, a mountain hovering over the city and source of most of its potable water. The city government responded by declaring the area a municipal reserve, an action that was appealed by the company to the country's highest court which, in a Solomon-like judgement, affirmed both the city's right to declare a reserve and the company's right to develop its mining concession provided that it complied with the procedures established by the Ministry of Energy and Mines. In mid-2004, taking advantage of the national Independence Day holidays the company moved its machinery on to Cerro Quilish and began exploratory drilling. This provoked a violent and unified reaction from the usually divided elements of the Cajamarca community, leading to protests and blockades lasting several weeks and mediation by national government authorities until the company felt obliged to relinquish its claim (for the time being). During and after this period OA had been actively involved in conversations with the company through meetings with the top management of Newmont, the majority shareholder, in the US and as advisor to an ethical shareholder group; had provided support to its local partners in Cajamarca, who were the most articulate critics of the company; and had attempted to find ways to generate confidence and encourage a dialogue between the company and the community, but to little avail.

In contrast with its experience with the Yanacocha mine, OA was able to promote a successful negotiation process with BHP Billiton's Tintaya mine in the Cusco region. This mine had originally been developed by a state mining company through the expropriation of land under very unfair conditions from five peasant communities, but had since been sold and was now in the hands of the Australia-based company BHP Billiton. With support from a national NGO, in the late 1990s the affected communities had produced studies indicating abuses in the land acquisition process, contamination and human rights violations and were demanding compensation and an economic contribution to their long-term development. However, they received no response from the company until OA decided to translate the studies into English and send them to Oxfam Australia's mining ombudsman in Melbourne, where the company had its headquarters. The ombudsman informed the company's management in Melbourne that she would undertake an inspection visit to Peru and publish her findings in her annual report in Australia. This threat provoked a response from the company so that at the end of her visit, it agreed to negotiate their grievances with the five communities, their NGO advisor (CooperAcción), the national organization representing affected communities (CONACAMI) and OA, acting as observer on behalf of the mining ombudsman.

This set in motion a four-year negotiation process which resulted in an agreement which provided the communities with compensation in the form of land, created a joint environmental monitoring and early warning process, established compensation for verified human rights abuses and guaranteed company contributions to the communities' sustainable development. Along the way, all participants established minimum levels of mutual trust, developed intercultural understandings and learned much about how to establish and maintain a negotiation process in a context where such negotiations were almost unknown. They did so in the face of criticism of the company by the mining industry in Peru for negotiating in symmetrical terms with the communities and allowing the participation of CONACAMI. For its part, the CONACAMI leadership was criticized by many of its members for agreeing to sit down to negotiate with a mining company and for a time withdrew from the process. However, this experience enabled Oxfam and its partners to demonstrate that under the right conditions it was possible to achieve equitable and positive negotiations between mining companies and surrounding communities, despite failures elsewhere (as in Cajamarca) and the generalized scepticism both within the industry and amongst the communities. The external surveillance by Oxfam Australia and the internal facilitation of OA and CooperAcción played a key role in this successful outcome.

The cases of Camisea and La Oroya are described in greater detail in the following two chapters. The Camisea natural gas project is the country's largest energy project and involved two consortia of private companies: one to extract the gas and the other to transport it to the coast for domestic consumption and export. Concerns were raised by civil society organizations about the possible impacts of the project in the lower Urubamba river valley in the upper Amazon basin, an area of great biodiversity and populated by indigenous peoples in voluntary isolation and initial contacts with the outside world, and in the buffer zone of the Paracas nature reserve on Peru's Pacific coast. In the face of the impermeability of the Peruvian Government and the industry consortia, a coalition of over 20 Peruvian environmental and indigenous rights NGOs, together with representatives of indigenous organizations, developed a common set of proposals and formed an alliance with a coalition of US-based environmental and human rights organizations in order to lobby the US Government, the US Export-Import Bank (Ex-Im Bank) and the Inter-American Development Bank (IDB) to place a series of conditions on proposed loans to the Peruvian Government and the pipeline consortium. Oxfam played a key role in the process by linking the NGOs to the indigenous organizations, through its active membership in both the Southern and Northern coalitions and through its legitimacy as a source of reliable information for US government officials and Bank consultants. Although the Ex-Im Bank decided not to provide funding because of its environmental concerns, the IDB did so, but subject to an unprecedented set of conditions imposed to address the concerns of civil society in both countries.

In the town of La Oroya in the Andean highlands east of Lima a large smelter complex established in the 1920s generated air and gas pollution that seriously affected the townspeople and local farming communities. With the privatization of the state-run company in the late 1990s and its purchase by the US-based Renco Group and in the context of growing awareness in the country of citizens' rights to a healthy environment, local NGOs began to produce and disseminate studies demonstrating the health impacts of the contamination generated by the complex. In the face of constant and, at times, violent opposition from the company and its allies, a coalition of community organizations grouped in the Movement for the Health of La Oroya (MOSAO) in alliance with a technical working group of local and national NGOs undertook a campaign to pressure the Peruvian Government to oblige the company to carry out the environmental management plan agreed to as one of the conditions of purchase and remedy the serious public health situation. The company managed to obtain an extension of the period for the implementation of its environmental programme but one that was modified to include additional investments and involved a detailed programme, frequent reporting requirements and strict government supervision.

Oxfam played a key role in bringing together community organizations and their NGO allies and in helping sustain the alliance over time. Although Oxfam and its allies in the Presbyterian and Catholic churches were relatively unsuccessful in their attempts to obtain changes in the policies and practices of the company through campaigns and lobbying of the parent company in Saint Louis, Missouri, or the Renco Group's sole owner in New York, they did raise awareness in the US about the situation in La Oroya and through their influence in the media played a vital role in shielding the activists in La Oroya from potential harm.

Much of the literature on transnational advocacy explicitly or implicitly portrays these efforts as attempts by Northern advocates to enable their Southern allies to have their voices heard in the North and influence the decisions of Northern institutions – frequently international financial institutions – which have either a direct or an indirect impact in the South (the 'boomerang' strategy).[10] This is illustrated by the Camisea case where an alliance between a broad coalition of civil society actors in Peru and their civil society allies in the US persuaded the IDB to impose conditions on its loan to a pipeline construction consortium. However, even in this case, which illustrates the 'classic' model of transnational advocacy, the Southern actors were anything but passive receivers of Northern assistance. They were able to modify the initial position held by their Northern allies, played a key role in bridging the breach between two coalitions of Northern allies and participated in the lobbying of Northern decision makers during their visits to Peru. Thus, this was far from a situation where relatively passive and powerless Southern civil society actors were being 'saved' by their Northern allies.

The La Oroya case illustrates a reverse situation where the key targets and decision makers were located in the South. Since MOSAO's Northern allies were unable to influence key decision makers in the US, their role became a supportive one that was in some ways more akin to that traditionally played by Southern actors in transnational advocacy coalitions. They provided information and Northern 'faces' in support of the advocacy efforts of their allies in Peru. Above all, they managed to build a protective shield by making actors and decision makers in Peru aware that international news media and public opinion were attentive to the situation in La Oroya and the outcomes.

Transnational advocacy today is no longer simply about achieving changes in the South through influencing decisions in the North. Improvements in the lives of the poor often require changes in the policies and practices of institutions at different levels: local, national and international. They also often require changes in a variety of institutions from the public, private and social sectors. Transnational coalitions need to build the capacity to mobilize their resources to influence decisions in both the North and the South and to implement 'boomerang' strategies that achieve flow-on effects from decisions in the South to situations in the North and to other situations in the South, as well as from the North to the South. These cases alert us to these possibilities.

Notes

1. M. J. Scurrah and C. Ross (2000) 'Resource extraction activities and the local community'. Paper delivered at the meeting of the Latin American Studies Association, Miami, March 16–18, p. 6.
2. Oxfam America. South America Regional Office (1999) *Concept Paper for the South America Regional Program* (Lima: Oxfam America), p. 14.
3. G. Watson (2001) 'From money to movements: Transforming how Northern development agencies support national and transnational advocacy strategies'. Paper delivered at the meeting of the Latin American Studies Association, Washington, DC, September 6–8, p. 12.
4. K. Slack (1999) 'Extractive Industries Working Group meeting in The Hague, 10/18–10/20'. (Boston: Internal Oxfam America Memo), October.
5. G. Watson (2001) 'From money to movements: Transforming how Northern development agencies support national and transnational advocacy strategies', p. 17.
6. Oxfam America (2004) 'Extractive Industries', *Impact @ Oxfam*, Issue No. 2, October, pp. 3–4.
7. Oxfam America (2004) 'Extractive Industries', p. 7.
8. Oxfam America (2004) 'Extractive Industries', pp. 7–8.
9. For more detailed information about these cases see M. Scurrah (ed.) (2008) *Defendiendo Derechos y Promoviendo Cambios: El Estado, las Empresas Extractivas y las Comunidades Locales en el Perú* (Lima: Oxfam Internacional/Instituto del Bien Común/Instituto de Estudios Peruanos).
10. See especially M. E. Keck and K. Sikkink (1998) *Activists Beyond Borders* (Ithaca: Cornell University Press).

7
Case Study: Natural Gas Project in Peru

Catherine Ross

The Camisea Natural Gas Project, Peru's largest energy development project, sparked national hopes and expectations with its promise of economic development and a path toward energy independence. The Project was expected to boost Peru's GDP by nearly a percentage point, and lead to the commercialization of secondary gas products, generating conditions favourable to developing a national petrochemical industry. But the US$1.6 billion Project to exploit Peru's largest gas reserve – 13 trillion cubic feet – carried with it significant potential for damaging impacts. The Project threatened vulnerable communities and ecosystems from the lower Urubamba River valley in the upper Amazon basin, a region of extraordinary biodiversity and home to several indigenous peoples, through the Andes, to the Peruvian coast and the buffer zone of the Paracas National Reserve, Peru's only protected marine area. Finally, the fact that Camisea was intended as the project that would open the Peruvian Amazon to a new era of oil and gas development meant that this Project would set precedents for the management of future projects. Concerns about these issues motivated a broad civil society coalition within Peru and internationally to seek to influence the Project's management by advocating for the resolution of key problems before it could receive financing from the US Export-Import Bank (Ex-Im Bank) and the Inter-American Development Bank (IDB).

The Camisea Project originates in the lower Urubamba River valley of the Department of Cusco in south-eastern Peru, part of the upper Amazon basin that slopes down from the Andes before flattening out in the lower Amazon.

The lower Urubamba and the neighbouring Vilcabamba mountain range, renowned for extremely high levels of biological and cultural diversity, are included in Conservation International's (CI) global list of 25 biodiversity 'hotspots'. The Pongo de Mainique, a steep and dangerous white water river passage that connects the upper and lower Urubamba River valleys, cuts through the only break in the Vilcabamba range and long served as a natural barrier that kept colonists, a risk to degrading fragile rainforest environments, from entering the lower region. A biodiversity survey carried out by the Smithsonian Institution for the Shell oil company in the late 1990s found that the biological communities in the zone were 'in pristine condition' with 'extraordinarily high' levels of endemism and biological diversity. It documented, for example, 51 distinct bat species in one month of fieldwork, compared to 55 species found in Peru's Manu National Park during an intensive five-year study.[1]

The lower Urubamba River valley is home to a population of 10,000, mostly Machiguenga indigenous communities that obtained formal land titles after a long and painstaking process of demarcation and titling, as well as smaller groups of Yine (Piro), Asháninka, Amahuaca, Yaminahua, and about 1,000 mestizo colonists. These groups fish, hunt, and cultivate small family agricultural plots in which manioc (*yuca*) is the principal crop. The presence of the Peruvian state in the area is very limited, with health and education services largely provided by Catholic missions. A number of small indigenous nomadic or semi-nomadic groups remained isolated from contacts with the outside world. In 1990, Peru created the Kugapakori-Nahua State Reserve (the Reserve) to protect these people until they voluntarily came into contact, and to guarantee them the right to the land and natural resources within the reserve.

Shell discovered the Camisea gas fields under an exploration contract in the 1980s. After the election of Alberto Fujimori in 1990, Peru launched efforts to attract foreign investment to the country's energy and mining sectors, including favourable investment conditions such as exoneration of foreign companies from certain taxes, and a waiving of a legal prohibition on oil production in Natural Protected Areas (ANPs). When Shell signed a 40-year exploration and production contract with Peru in 1996, the agreement was hailed as 'the contract of the century'. After controversial human rights and environmental issues had dogged Shell's operations in Nigeria and the North Sea, the company resolved to take on the Camisea Project as a way to both learn and demonstrate how an oil company could do right by the environment and local people. Thus, Shell committed itself to the highest environmental standards, and to creating 'net social benefit' for nearby communities.[2] Its experiment was cut short in 1998, when the Fujimori government modified some aspects of the plan for distribution and commercialization of gas and refused to allow Shell more time to analyse the effect of the changes before making its Final Investment Decision (FID). Shell withdrew after investing over $250 million in the project's initial stages.

In May 1999, the Peruvian Government held a public bidding process for the Camisea gas fields (Lot 88). In contrast to the unified Shell contract, the new operating licenses were divided in two parts: Upstream (production) and Downstream (transportation and distribution). The Upstream component was awarded to a consortium led by Pluspetrol of Argentina, with the participation of Hunt Oil (US), SK Corporation (South Korea), and Tecpetrol of Peru (a subsidiary of the Techint Group, also of Argentina). The Downstream component was given to another consortium, led by TGP, part of the Techint Group, with the participation of Pluspetrol, Hunt Oil, SK Corporation, Sonatrach (Algeria) and Graña y Montero (Peru). The official Camisea Project website cited only one criterion on which the bidding was judged: 'The license was awarded based on the highest offer of royalties presented by the bidders.'[3]

The Upstream component involved seismic exploration; drilling four wells; the construction of an initial processing plant in Malvinas in the Lower Urubamba to separate gas from liquids; the construction of flow lines from the well sites to the Malvinas plant; and the construction of a fractionation plant on the Peruvian coast that would extract from the liquids marketable products, such as propane and butane, as well as condensates, which would be further processed into petrol and diesel. The Downstream component involved the construction and operation of two pipelines – one for natural gas and one for liquids; the construction of pumping stations along the pipeline route; and the distribution of gas in Lima. To carry out the pipeline construction, TGP set up two work camps of between 100 and 500 workers in the Lower Urubamba. The contracts for both components stipulated that construction had to be completed, and the gas on its way to Lima by the first week of August 2004 or fines and penalties would be incurred.

Several concerns were raised by the prospect of exploration, drilling and transportation in such a biologically and culturally sensitive area. Three of four wells were drilled inside the Reserve that protected isolated indigenous peoples, who had little resistance to introduced disease. One researcher claimed that 40 per cent of the Nahua population had died after exposure to Shell workers and loggers after Shell's exploratory work in the 1980s.[4] Isolated groups and titled indigenous communities depended entirely on their natural resources for their diets and livelihoods. An evaluation of the Project's Environmental Impact Assessments (EIAs) carried out by Patricia Caffrey, a former director of World Wildlife Fund's (WWF) Bolivia programme, in early 2002, identified a series of deficiencies in the EIAs' treatment of potential impacts, including damage to aquatic and terrestrial ecosystems and to biological diversity and natural habitats; adverse effects of erosion along the pipeline route; the risk of colonization if the pipeline route was not effectively closed to outsiders; multiple risks involving the new proposed site for a fractionation plant near Paracas Bay; and questions about the level of preparation and institutional capacity on the part of the Peruvian Government to provide adequate supervision and monitoring for a project of Camisea's complexity and size.[5] The report observed that the project violated World Bank Group environmental and social standards, widely considered as best practice and more stringent than those of the IDB.

Additional concerns involved the fact that the companies had not carried out a serious baseline study of biological diversity before beginning the project, and declined to adopt the study or methodology used by Shell in 1997 as a substitute. The division of the project into separate contracts, consortia and EIAs for Upstream and Downstream portions created confusion as to which group would be held responsible for damage caused in overlapping areas. And negotiations the companies carried out with communities for financial compensation were chaotic and characterized by a profound asymmetry of power, preparation and information.[6]

On the coast, the government and Pluspetrol changed the original fractionation plant site to an area within the buffer zone of the Paracas National Marine Reserve. Paracas Bay was a hotspot of marine biodiversity, an important stop on migratory bird routes, and the second most important tourism site in Peru after Macchu Pichu.

Institutional context

The Camisea Project consortia planned to receive loans of $75 million from the IDB and $214 million from the US Ex-Im Bank. Loans would be made directly to the consortia, with the Peruvian Government's guarantee. The Andean Development Corporation (CAF) planned to loan an amount similar to that of the IDB. In anticipation of the project, the IDB in 2002 had approved a loan of $5 million to the Peruvian Government with the aim of strengthening the public sector for the appropriate management, coordination and supervision of the Project. With that loan,

Peru created the Inter-institutional Technical Coordination Group (GTCI), which brought together under one umbrella the more than a dozen government agencies responsible for some aspect of the Camisea Project. The GTCI was meant to coordinate and strengthen supervision, monitoring and accountability mechanisms, and included, among others, the Ministry of Energy and Mines (MEM), which both supervised the group and was a member of it, the Energy Investment Supervisor (OSINERG), responsible for monitoring, and the Camisea Ombudsman's office, newly created to facilitate the conciliation of disputes that arose with respect to the Project.

Oxfam America had a long-term partner relationship with the Machiguenga Council of the Urubamba River (COMARU), a representative indigenous organization uniting over 30 communities in the zone, and with CEDIA, an NGO with years of experience in the Urubamba region. Oxfam supported CEDIA and COMARU in their monitoring of the Project at the time of Shell's contract. These three organizations, together with AIDESEP, a national indigenous organization, and Amazon Watch, a US-based NGO, worked together in 2002 to organize and fund the Caffrey report in response to unease expressed by COMARU's communities that their only information about the Project came from the private consortia. Two other indigenous organizations, CECONAMA and FECONAYY, represented eight communities in the Lower Urubamba and had differed with COMARU on issues related to gas production during the Shell era. Another NGO, Shinai Serjali, had been working in the Urubamba region for two years. Three large international conservation organizations, Conservation International (CI), World Wildlife Fund (WWF), and The Nature Conservancy (TNC), had offices in Peru but generally concentrated their efforts on Natural Protected Areas (ANPs) and so had little experience in the Urubamba region with its patchwork of titled communities.

Shortly after the publication of the Caffrey report, the US offices of CI, WWF and TNC contracted Robert Goodland, a former Senior Advisor to the World Bank for environmental issues, to carry out an in-depth evaluation of the Project that would inform these organizations' recommendations and positions on the Camisea Project.

In addition to the international conservation organizations, another group of environmental and human rights NGOs based in the US began coordinating amongst themselves regarding the Camisea Project. These more activist organizations, including Amazon Watch, Environmental Defense, the Amazon Alliance and the Institute for Policy Studies, maintained contacts with organizations in Peru with whom they had previous relationships. While the large international conservation organizations had experience in negotiating with states and international financing organizations, the smaller groups had strengths in organizing public protests and making use of media for advocacy campaigns.

But in Peru, nine months after the publication of the Caffrey report, no regular coordination existed among organizations concerned about the Project. Individually, representatives of indigenous organizations and NGOs attended public informational meetings convened by the IDB, where they tried to present their concerns. Some had written letters to the companies, the Peruvian Government or the IDB, few of which had received responses. The fragmented nature of these efforts lacked the weight of collective action; precluded effective participation in the meetings convened by the IDB; and prevented a strategic alliance with Northern NGOs willing to help. Oxfam America was particularly concerned about the absence of a clear expression by the affected communities in the Urubamba region regarding their priority issues, concerns and proposals relative to Camisea. Oxfam America believed that the risks presented by the mega-energy project were greater than what individual organizations could hope to confront on their own. It seemed impossible to deal with the challenges of Camisea without addressing the issue of the government's management and supervision of the Project. And it would be unlikely that the indigenous organizations could make headway on these issues without a broad array of allies.

Yet several barriers to collective action existed. The Machiguenga communities of the Urubamba River valley, who would be directly affected by the project, were logically the principal actors. But, while COMARU and some community leaders were concerned about the coming impacts of the project, it was difficult for many in the communities to visualize, anticipate or mobilize against threats they had not yet seen. In addition, many community members hoped for income, through occasional employment with the companies, and for compensation agreements. Thus, the reaction to the Project was mixed. Communications with the Urubamba region were difficult, constituting a challenge for maintaining adequate coordination. The zone is remote and difficult to access[7] and lacked electricity and telephones. Even COMARU's office in Quillabamba had difficulties in communicating fluidly and regularly with the communities.

Another obstacle to wider coordination was the level of distrust that existed among actors. Relationships between indigenous organizations and international conservation groups had been conflictive in the past in the Urubamba region and elsewhere in Peru.[8] Members of several Peruvian organizations believed these institutions might condone faulty management of the Project in return for financial support for their conservation projects through the 'Camisea Fund', a proposed entity that would use government and gas company funding to support conservation and community development in areas affected by the Project.

Distrust existed at many levels: between organizations primarily concerned with environmental issues and those primarily concerned with indigenous rights and community development; between representative organizations and NGOs in general; between North and South; and between organizations that generally preferred a conciliatory approach working within the system and those that questioned the system and tended to adopt more activist strategies. Relations between indigenous organizations and NGOs were also coloured by deeper intercultural issues, as a result of which both sides had difficulty understanding the frameworks, ways of thinking, and priorities of the other. Nor were relations among indigenous organizations free from these dynamics. Neighbours COMARU and CECONAMA had a traditionally thorny relationship and COMARU's priorities sometimes differed from those of AIDESEP, the larger of the two national-level Amazonian indigenous organizations, which it had recently joined as an affiliate.

Forming alliances

Different actors undertook a series of initiatives that led to a partial overcoming of these obstacles and allowed civil society organizations to come together to address the threats of the Camisea Project in a more purposeful and coordinated fashion. In early 2003, Oxfam America hired a professional facilitator to work with COMARU, AIDESEP and CEDIA to help them analyse and articulate their major concerns about the Project. Although these actors did not always agree, this process quickly resulted in the articulation of five main issues of concern (voluntarily isolated peoples; environmental impacts; funding relationships between organizations and companies; government unresponsiveness; and ineffective project monitoring) that they wanted to address through advocacy. This small group then invited additional NGOs to join them in developing strategies. The group became known as the 'jungle group' and, for a time, was convened by AIDESEP, until its president suffered a grave health problem.

In mid-April 2003, the international conservation organizations CI, WWF and TNC published Robert Goodland's report, together with a communiqué of their recommendations to the international lending institutions, the Peruvian Government and the consortia with respect to the Camisea Project. Goodland's report reflected local concerns and the communiqué helped to open the way to broader coordination among Peruvian and international civil society organizations, as it took strong and principled stances that came as a surprise to many Peruvian organizations. The conservation organizations called for best practice environmental standards and an independent monitoring and evaluation plan. They proposed reconsideration of the location of the fractionation plant, citing irregularities and lack of transparency in the selection of the Paracas site; complete closure of the pipeline route to prevent colonization of the Lower Urubamba; the exclusion of all extractive activity from the Reserve; and, after a scathing review of Pluspetrol's biodiversity management plan, recommendations for how it should be improved. Most importantly for opening a path to working together with Peruvian organizations, the conservation organizations declared that they would not accept any financing from the proposed Camisea Fund. On the contrary, they committed themselves to contributing to the Fund, which they recommended should be disbursed to national and local level actors. These positions were well received by Peruvian organizations, and deflated one of the principal sources of distrust that impeded greater collaboration within a broader alliance.

In late May 2003, the Peruvian Environmental Law Society (SPDA) began convening meetings in Lima for all civil society actors interested in the Camisea Project. Many of the large number of organizations that attended might not have appeared without the prior activities undertaken by Oxfam America, the 'jungle group', and the positions taken by the international conservation organizations. The SPDA meetings came at a good time. Many representatives of the organizations present had been attending informational meetings convened by the IDB, the GTCI or the private consortia, and had felt increasingly frustrated that their questions and concerns generally had been dismissed with the message, in the words of the first director of the GTCI, that 'the public should just trust us; there is no reason for you to be concerned'.[9]

A 'consultation meeting' held by the IDB with civil society organizations on 12 May 2003, during a trip to Peru by Bank vice-president Dennis Flannery and seven of 14 directors from the IDB board, was emblematic of these difficulties. The Bank officials had travelled to see the progress of the Project and investigate its alleged problems. Flannery arrived late to the meeting, left early, and although he did not speak Spanish, he did not have a professional translator with him. None of the directors came to the meeting. Flannery announced that after spending four days with the companies and the government, the directors, who would be voting to approve the project in a few months time, had a 'complete understanding and a very well-informed opinion' of the project.[10] The message was clear: for the IDB, the concerns and comments of civil society actors were superfluous and irrelevant. If affected communities and NGOs wanted to be taken seriously, they would have to improve their strategies.

In this context, the SPDA meetings constituted an urgently needed space for civil society organizations. SPDA members took on a facilitating role in the meetings, recognizing the diversity of opinion and perspectives that existed within the group. This meant that participants had to think beyond the issues that directly affected them to understand different aspects and risks of the Project. In one meeting, participants shared prepared analyses of different themes relevant to the Project, and the ensuing discussion permitted an illuminating exchange among those who lived or worked in the Amazon and those who worked on the coast, among indigenous organizations, scientists, environmentalists, lawyers and anthropologists. Those from the Amazon were surprised to learn of the threats to Paracas Bay and coastal scientists learned what was at stake for indigenous communities. One thread linked all the themes: significant limitations in the capacity and political will of state institutions to manage the Project in ways that respected rights and the environment, while generating necessary economic development for the country.

Developing the campaign

The coordinating group had to make strategic decisions regarding its stance toward the Project and its advocacy approach. Participants recognized not only the great expectations raised by Camisea, but also the indisputable importance of the Project for national economic development. COMARU, whose affiliated communities were directly impacted, did not oppose the Project. The group concluded that outright opposition to the Project would run the risk both of being dismissed by the authorities and of undermining the unity of civil society actors. Although some of the Northern NGOs were advocating for the cancellation of the Project, in Peru this stance was seen as neither desirable nor strategically feasible. Rather than opposing the Project, they decided on a strategy of conditioning the Project: demanding that Camisea adhere to social and environmental best practices, respect for human rights and the protection of vulnerable ecosystems and affected communities.

Second, pressuring the Peruvian Government was out of the question as a strategy, given the imperviousness of government agencies to concerns raised. The efforts of civil society organizations even to acquire basic information from the GTCI, MEM, OSINERG and other offices had seldom received a response, and concerns had been waved away with official assurances that the Project was a 'world class' project with no deficiencies. Authorities frequently cast what it called 'environmentalists' in the role of adversaries to the Project and to national development, and declared that such groups would not be listened to as a matter of principle.

Meanwhile, the Project's pursuit of financing through publicly funded entities, like the Ex-Im Bank and the IDB, opened the possibility of seeking strict conditions for project financing. The IDB itself had publicly argued that its participation in the Project would improve its social and environmental standards. Despite the negative attitude of the Bank to that point, it could be challenged to account for the use of public funds and to demonstrate the added value it had promised. The coalition agreed on a strategy of pressuring the banks to condition the loans so as to resolve serious deficiencies before agreeing to financing.

Third, while members of the group agreed with the international conservation organizations' recommendation that the Camisea Fund, financed by the consortia and others, be used to support conservation and community development in areas affected by the project, they were wary of how the promise of financing could distort decision making. Many believed that the promise of funding by Pluspetrol to the municipality of Paracas had improperly influenced the decision to locate the fractionation plant there. The group decided to leave the design of the Camisea Fund off the table until Bank financing decisions had been made.

The group drew up its own platform similar to that of the international conservation organizations, calling for a set of issues to be resolved before financing was approved: a new site selection process for the fractionation plant; specific protections for the rights and health of isolated indigenous peoples; attention to the multiple problems along the pipeline route; transparency of public institutions, including access to information on the Project; biodiversity monitoring; and the design and implementation of an independent, expert monitoring system for the Project. On 2 July 2003, with the signatures of 22 organizations in Peru, it was sent to the IDB, the Ex-Im Bank and the CAF with copies to relevant government authorities and the companies.

This comprehensive letter, signed by 22 organizations in Peru generated an impact in Washington, where conventional wisdom dictated that two or three Peruvian organizations had trouble agreeing on anything, and the IDB sent a high-level consultant to meet with civil society organizations. Northern NGOs now had proposals from Peruvian civil society organizations that lent greater legitimacy and force to their ongoing advocacy efforts with the Banks. The document set out what the Banks, the companies and the Peruvian Government would need to do in order to achieve the acceptance of a large swath of Peruvian civil society groups. With this platform in hand, Peruvian organizations engaged in internal advocacy with their Northern allies. They asked the conservation organizations to suspend work on the details of the Camisea Fund until other issues had been resolved. And they asked Northern NGOs opposed to the Project to suspend their opposition and support the fight for strict conditions in order to speak to the Banks with one unified voice. Almost all the organizations in the US responded positively to these proposals.

The group wrote a new letter, signed by 25 organizations, after reviewing the IDB's Environmental and Social Impact Report (ESIR), a 150-page document in English, which detailed the conditions the Bank intended to require the Peruvian Government and the companies to meet before finalizing its loan. The ESIR was an example of the difficulty civil society organizations had in accessing relevant information; they knew of the ESIR's existence only because the director of the SPDA managed to obtain a copy when he was in Washington for reasons unrelated to the Camisea Project. After the SPDA presented a Spanish language summary for discussion, the group concluded that the draft conditions were far from sufficient, and urged serious attention to address the issues already identified.

At the end of July 2003, AIDESEP informed the group that it had decided to oppose the Project, although its member organization COMARU did not. After a change of leadership due to the withdrawal of AIDESEP's president for health reasons, internal discussions had surfaced of unease both with the decision not to oppose the project, as well as with being part of a large coordinating group where AIDESEP felt its independence was constrained. Members of the coordinating group asked AIDESEP to keep them informed of its activities so that they might support or complement them where possible.

In addition to several letters sent to the financing institutions, members of the coordinating group engaged in a series of activities aimed at making their case before the Banks and attempting to influence broader public opinion in Peru and internationally to support its platform. Immediately after sending its first letter, the group organized a press conference to present its concerns, the growing evidence of environmental damage in the Urubamba region, and its proposals. But, despite a concerted effort to communicate with every major news organization in Peru prior to the press conference, only two journalists showed up, both stringers for US newspapers, and both personal friends of Oxfam's Amazon Program Officer. No articles resulted. Environmental and social concerns about the Camisea Project were not newsworthy in Peru. Three members of the group met with US Embassy personnel in an attempt to influence US officials who might have some sway in conversations with Peruvian authorities and who might report back to Washington, where the US was considering Ex-Im Bank funding and its vote within the IDB. The group also reached out to possible opinion-shapers, including newspaper columnists, the ex-Minister of Energy and Mines, who had signed the original contract and disagreed with the site change to Paracas, and the national Ombudsman's office.

NGOs working in the Paracas region detailed with data, studies, maps and scientific arguments the threats the fractionation plant posed to the zone's exceptional biodiversity and the aquatic life of the Bay. NGOs and indigenous organizations concerned with the Kugapakori-Nahua Reserve brought together evidence of contacts made by company employees with isolated people, drew up elements to be included in the draft legislation for the administration of the Reserve, and commented on a report commissioned by Pluspetrol regarding its protocol for workers inside the Reserve. The NGO Shinai Serjali monitored health concerns related to the Reserve and to indigenous communities and commented on the deficiencies of a public health study commissioned by Pluspetrol.

Within their capacities, organizations monitored ecological damage occurring along the pipeline route, reporting it publicly and to the relevant companies and government agencies. In the Urubamba region, communities reported significant erosion and turbidity in the rivers and an alarming drop in the presence of fish, the chief source of protein for the inhabitants of the zone. Two communities reported that construction activities along mountain ridges had caused earth to collapse into the springs that provided them with fresh drinking water; previously crystalline springs now ran muddy. CEDIA and COMARU documented areas in which the TGP consortium had deviated from the pipeline route that had been planned and coordinated with communities, in one case crossing into a natural protected area it was legally obliged to avoid. This information eventually led OSINERG to fine TGP $1 million.[11]

These reports and fragmented initiatives to monitor and bring attention to the impacts of the Project reinforced civil society organizations'

Case Study: Natural Gas Project in Peru   145

call for an independent monitoring programme that would incorporate mechanisms to ensure that identified problems were addressed rather than ignored. Grave problems with erosion had been reported in mid-2002 by the consulting firm contracted by TGP to monitor its work in pipeline construction. The firm, Knight Piesold, repeatedly had drawn attention to erosion problems in its monthly reports, warning that, without proper erosion controls, such unstable areas could turn disastrous in the rainy season. Knight Piesold finally took the unusual step of calling for pipeline construction to be halted until erosion control could be addressed.[12] TGP apparently ignored the warnings, as did OSINERG.

Northern NGO Environmental Defense hired US-based Global Village Engineers (GVE) to send an expert in engineering and environmental management to walk 60 km of the pipeline route, documenting construction practices. The resultant July 2003 technical report warned that 'significant and possibly irreversible adverse ecological impacts' could result from TGP's practice of clearing vegetation and soils from the entire route before the pipeline's installation. Basic erosion controls and other routine protections had been bypassed. River crossings were carried out with 'no consideration for protecting the aquatic environment'. In certain segments, more than two vertical meters of exposed soil had been eroded, ending in rivers and streams, with a loss of approximately 100 tons of soil and vegetation per meter of pipeline.[13] Amazon Watch and the US offices of Oxfam America and WWF posted electronic alerts on their websites, asking readers to write to the IDB demanding a response to the concerns of civil society organizations before any financing was approved. Oxfam America's alert generated more than 4,000 emails sent to the US director on the IDB board.

One key strategic initiative for influencing the Banks involved Environmental Defense and other NGOs in Washington who worked to link the Camisea Project to an ongoing process within Export Credit Agencies (ECAs), including the Ex-Im Bank. ECAs – government financial institutions whose objective is to promote and strengthen their country's exports by offering government-guaranteed credit and political risk insurance to exporting companies – had been targets of severe criticism during the 1990s for the absence of environmental criteria in their decision making and for their lack of accountability for notorious environmental problems caused by projects that they supported. In response, the US Ex-Im Bank had begun to lead an initiative among ECAs to improve and strengthen environmental standards. This process was slated to culminate in an upcoming meeting of global ECAs in which the Ex-Im Bank and carefully cultivated allies would propose a new environmental code to be adopted by all. Would the Ex-Im Bank risk losing the credibility it had gained throughout this long process, months before presenting its proposal, by financing a project whose environmental deficiencies were widely known? Northern NGOs that had previously been involved in pressuring ECAs used the information coming out of Peru to make the case that it should not.

A delegation headed by a senior advisor within the US Treasury Department, the agency that advises both the Ex-Im Bank and the US director of the IDB on investment decisions, came to Peru in July 2003 to investigate the concerns. The trip was unusual; the Treasury Department generally conducts its due diligence without field visits. In a meeting with Oxfam America, members of the delegation were surprised to learn that civil society groups did not oppose the project, but rather sought to resolve important issues before the project could go forward. This information seemed to imply a changed dynamic for the advisors; rather than a fight between 'yes' and 'no,' the question was 'under what conditions?' The US delegation expressed openness to hearing concerns that were predicated on shared principles of transparency, good governance, indigenous peoples' rights, and environmental sustainability, but wanted to see evidence and data that supported the concerns.

Oxfam America played a key role in this process, working to bring actors together initially, and serving as a link between indigenous communities and organizations in the Urubamba region and NGOs in Lima, sometimes struggling to make sure information was shared among these groups as the complexity of advocacy activities deepened and the pace quickened. Oxfam also served as a source of reliable information and analysis for US government officials and Bank consultants who sought a greater understanding of civil society organizations' concerns.

Lead-up to Banks' financing decisions

With Bank decisions on financing fast approaching, NGOs in the US and Peru urged the US Government to pressure the IDB to postpone its financing vote for six months to give Bank directors time to analyse the relevant information and adopt the necessary changes. They urged the US Government to pressure Peru to postpone the deadline date for gas to be delivered to Lima, because this obliged the companies to operate in haste and forgo proper controls in construction.

The Peruvian Government moved to address conditions it had agreed to over a year before in a formal letter of intent to the IDB, an indication that pressure tied to funding from international institutions could be an effective incentive. Titles were issued for the Megantoni Sanctuary, the Otishi National Park, and Machiguenga and Asháninka communal reserves – new Natural Protected Areas in the zone of influence of the Project, whose titling processes had long languished without government action. OSINERG saw an increase in the number of its personnel and, in late July, Peru promulgated an executive decree that sought to comply with a condition that required raising the level of protection of indigenous peoples in the Reserve.

Through a US Freedom of Information Act request, two Northern NGOs obtained an evaluation of the Upstream component carried out by consulting company URS for the Ex-Im Bank and IDB. The IDB in May had promised to share the evaluation with civil society organizations, but then reneged, fuelling speculation that only those documents that were not critical of the Project were made public. The evaluation, which Northern NGOs photocopied and sent by courier to Peru, warned in clear terms that the Paracas Bay site for the fractionation plant was troublesome; that one maritime transit accident would be sufficient to wipe out entire populations of endangered species, such as the Humboldt Penguin, and that Pluspetrol's level of preparation for such an emergency was 'woefully inadequate'.

The IDB announced at the end of July that it would postpone its vote on Camisea financing for one week. Shortly after that, the Ex-Im Bank also postponed its decision. Peru's president Toledo blamed NGOs for the delay and publicly vowed that, despite the obstacles civil society groups tried to place in the way, Camisea gas would flow to Lima by the immovable deadline of 4 August 2004. A few days later, the IDB communicated a second postponement of its decision, this time for one month. The IDB's new date meant that the Ex-Im Bank would be making its decision before that of the IDB, contrary to the order of decisions in the original schedule. Both banks dispatched delegations to Peru again, an unprecedented level of involvement for the US Treasury in vetting an Ex-Im Bank investment. The Treasury Department's mission had the explicit mandate of investigating the implications of the plant's location in Paracas. While most of its time in Peru was spent with the government and companies, the delegation held a separate meeting with NGOs outside of its official schedule. The meeting lasted over two hours, during which the delegation probed deeply on a series of issues and NGOs provided data and evidence that backed their concerns.

In the final days before the Bank decisions, indications appeared of a shift in public opinion through articles in several national and international newspapers. On 28 July, *The Washington Post* published a front-page article that detailed the controversial and unresolved aspects of the Camisea Project. The article, translated and reprinted the following day in major Peruvian dailies, helped to achieve what civil society organizations had not: Camisea was suddenly news in Peru. The signals of doubt from financing institutions received more balanced treatment than had previous news about the Camisea Project. Some articles, even in media sources that had previously presented only the government's version of the Project, began striking a more reflective note. The editorial page of *Expreso* asked, 'Does the Camisea Project comply or not with international environmental impact requirements and the protection of Amazonian tribes...in the jungle as well as in Paracas?' If financing should be blocked, it continued, 'the principal responsibility will be the government's, for not having been rigorous in requiring a technically well-structured EIA. We hope that has not occurred'.[14]

Certain themes ran through the government discourse with respect to the Project. First, the government rejected in principle the existence of any problem associated with the Project. Rather than showing willingness to investigate, confirm the validity of and resolve alleged problems, it accused any critic of being opposed to national development. President Toledo said that civil society groups were 'putting stones in the path' that his government was determined to push aside.[15] Second, IDB financing was presented as the ultimate 'green seal of approval' for the Project. If the IDB, with its public financing and environmental safeguards, approved the Project, it would constitute indisputable proof that environmental and social protections were adequate. Third, its discourse suggested that the government saw the ability of the Project to meet the August 2004 deadline as the exclusive indicator of its success. Although the US delegation recommended that the deadlines be relaxed to permit better attention to environmental issues,[16] the government held firm. Finally, the government discourse demonstrated closeness to the companies, with little indication that it conceived of a role for itself in supervising the companies or being vigilant for the appropriate management of the Project. This attitude served to deepen the concern of civil society organizations regarding governance and the lack of policies, practices and mechanisms to assure that the Project would represent a step toward sustainable and strategic development for Peru.

The Banks' decisions

On 28 August 2003, news of the Ex-Im Bank's decision exploded across the front pages of Peru's newspapers. The Bank's board voted against the long-planned loan to Pluspetrol of $214 million for the Upstream component of the Camisea Project. A spokesman said simply, 'The Project was rejected because it did not comply completely with the Ex-Im Bank's environmental requirements.'[17]

A flurry of interview requests, for which the coordinating group was unprepared, followed, giving civil society groups a media platform to make their own perspectives heard as a counterpoint to the government message. The group quickly developed a set of talking points to emphasize in interviews. There were neither official spokespersons nor any significant level of coordination. Those interviewed emphasized that at no time had the group ever called for the rejection of financing, but that they had asked that minimum conditions be achieved and problems resolved before moving forward with the Project. This message pointed to the government's responsibility to exercise adequate supervision and ensure high standards, and questioned the government's tendency to blame NGOs for documenting and bringing to light the reality of what was happening during the construction phase of the project, and for seeking resolution of the problems.

The government tried to mitigate the image of a setback caused by the rejection. Jaime Quijandría, the newly-named Minister of Energy and Mines, dismissed the rejection of the Ex-Im Bank as a 'pyrrhic victory' of environmentalists, continuing with the idea that NGOs had sought to paralyse the Project. He said that there were substitutes for Ex-Im financing, and that the government would guarantee financing through the use of national pension funds in the absence of other options. Other voices began to weigh in, giving credence to the civil society organizations' views. A columnist in the daily *Correo* wrote:

> What causes most concern is the obstinacy of the Peruvian authorities in trying to block out the sun with one finger, attempting to minimize the problem to a mere question of financing... But to ignore the rejection of the Ex-Im Bank as if it were just another credit window can be fatal, because for the authorities in Washington, the Camisea Project is disqualified at birth in its environmental management.... The rejection of Washington... is

only a warning signal to the government and the consortium, who should redesign their strategy.[18]

On 10 September 2003, the IDB voted to approve a loan of $75 million, adding $60 million in guarantees. The US Director abstained from voting. The Bank attached a series of conditions to the financing that were far more stringent than what had been proposed a month earlier. The IDB also took the unusual step to include a list of conditions that the Ex-Im Bank had drawn up which Pluspetrol would have to comply with, although the IDB loan was to the TGP consortium.

The decision-making process had no precedent in the history of the IDB. The Bank had never before engaged in such lengthy discussion and consultation with stakeholders before an investment decision. The conditions applied not only to the consortia and the government, but also to the IDB itself. Through the conditions, the Bank formally committed itself to ensure an unprecedented degree of supervision, project control and public transparency. It committed itself to make public all studies, evaluations and inspections in order to permit a thorough knowledge of the Project's social and environmental impacts. The conditions also obliged the Bank to establish a system of independent monitoring designed in consultation with civil society actors.

The government of Peru interpreted the decision as an indication of the Bank's complete satisfaction with the Project's human rights and environmental protections, the sought-after 'green seal'. But a reading of the strict conditions attached to the loan, some to be complied with before financial closing of the loan and others before disbursement, belied this view. If the IDB followed these commitments, the government and the consortia would have to substantially improve their policies and practices related to vulnerable people and ecosystems affected by the Camisea Project and the Bank would have to implement an independent monitoring system that provided regular reports to assure that the commitments were being followed.

No one among the civil society groups felt victorious. The organizations had deployed their maximum efforts on a strategy they had recognized at the outset as limited and risky. Although the conditions were certainly an improvement, they did not guarantee the adequate management of the Project. The Bank had not required a reconsideration of the fractionation plant site in Paracas Bay, only the monitoring of the impacts that might occur there. It had not required the immediate repair of ecological damage along the pipeline route. Members of the coordinating group were sceptical as to whether the Bank had the capacity, the political will or the institutional mechanisms to ensure compliance with its conditions. Personnel from the IDB had demonstrated camaraderie and loyalty with government authorities and the companies; would they withhold disbursement from their partners if conditions were not met? Beyond the Project already underway, two adjacent hydrocarbon concessions (Lots 56 and 57) were about to be licensed; there was little time to reverse bad management precedents before the area affected by oil and gas projects expanded in the Amazon. It was unclear whether the fight to condition the Camisea Project would be remembered simply as a memorable battle in a lost war.

New challenges faced the coordinating group. Monitoring compliance with numerous and detailed Bank conditions required concrete and specific work along the pipeline route, around the Reserve, and in Paracas Bay. The design of the Camisea Fund needed attention. Some groups wanted to follow up the promise of an independent monitoring scheme. Most of the organizations involved in the coalition did not have Camisea advocacy in their annual work plans, and many had dedicated early mornings, late nights, and taken away time from other projects to do what Camisea required; they felt pressure to return to the projects for which their NGOs had received funding. While a large coordinating group of 25 organizations was useful and necessary to advocate for financing decisions, it was not clear what its role would be going forward. For these and other reasons, and without any particular plan, the coordinating group split off into smaller affinity groups.

Civil society organizations found that they had limited capacity to monitor the degree of compliance with loan conditions, many of them technical. The group did manage to carry out a review of compliance, by patching together input from different organizations, before the IDB Annual Meeting in March 2004, held in Lima. This would have been an ideal time for the IDB, the Peruvian Government and the companies to celebrate financial closure, but the IDB, while more optimistic about the degree of compliance than Peruvian organizations, pushed back the closure until May. It was clear that civil society groups would not be able to closely monitor the conditions, and the Bank disbursed the loan some months later without further comment from the coordinating group.

During the IDB Annual Meeting, civil society groups met with vice-president Flannery as well as with some Bank country directors. When they asked for clarification on the process within the Bank of confirming compliance with loan conditions, they were surprised to learn that, after the vote, the Directors had no further role in ensuring that the conditions they had approved would be met. Neither did there exist an internal audit to verify compliance. Rather, the power to consider whether or not the conditions were met rested exclusively in the hands of the head of the private sector division, who did not have to justify his decision before any other level of management. To civil society groups, this seemed an indication of weak institutional controls, given the financial and environmental risks inherent in a Project as complex as Camisea. Civil society organizations also pressed Bank executives and directors for progress on the plans for independent monitoring and an independent evaluation of the impacts that had already taken place. With new gas projects starting up in the Urubamba region, groups were also concerned as to how cumulative impacts on the entire region would be evaluated and addressed, as individual EIAs developed for particular oil blocks would not capture them.

Independent monitoring was a priority, as distrust in the existing official monitoring programmes rose as a result of continued discrepancies between the content of official monitoring reports and the testimonies from the communities, the lack of response to those problems identified, and occasions when alarming results of project monitoring or evaluation had not been made public. One such occasion involved a memo leaked to civil society organizations in early 2004. It revealed that monitors from GTCI, OSINERG and MEM who travelled to the Urubamba region just before the IDB's vote on financing had reported on a disastrous situation of erosion, instability of slopes, and streams filled in by large amounts of eroded soil. The memo had urgently recommended immediate remedial action and, in the strongest terms, requested that OSINERG prevent TGP from shutting down its work camps in the zone until great swaths of unstable earth could be secured and streams restored. Not long after the date on the memo, more large landslides occurred in the region. The memo had never become public, similar content had never appeared in official monitoring reports, and even the IDB was unaware of it until civil society organizations shared it.

Yet the Bank had not acted on its commitment to develop an independent monitoring mechanism. At the Annual Meeting, the head of the private sector division claimed that the existing monitoring carried out by the Bank was independent, as it was not carried out by the consortia. But vice-president Flannery appeared to renew a commitment by the Bank to work with civil society groups on a design for

Case Study: Natural Gas Project in Peru   153

independent monitoring. In subsequent months, an IDB representative met with a core group of organizations to develop an independent monitoring proposal. Peruvian and Northern organizations spent considerable time clarifying principles and mechanisms for such a system, coordinating it with the IDB, and getting input and agreement from members of the larger coordinating group and from AIDESEP. These meetings dragged on inconclusively and stalled when it became apparent that the Bank was willing to continue to meet but had no intention of funding the independent monitoring function.[19]

The experience of attempting to hold the Bank accountable to conditions of compliance and independent monitoring revealed the weak capacity of civil society organizations to monitor the complex project in the absence of any political will on the part of the government or international institutions, especially when these organizations were doing essentially voluntary work without specific funding. The larger coordinating group disbanded and did not come together again to reconsider new strategies until early 2006, when it reconstituted itself with the name of Camisea Citizen Action (ACC), and obtained external funding.

Camisea's operational phase

Camisea began fulfilling economic expectations immediately. From 2004 through 2006, according to an IDB report, Camisea generated net payments of over $500 million to the Peruvian Government in royalties and taxes; from 2007 through 2033, it was expected to increase Peru's GDP by 0.8 per cent, adding over $15 billion to national output.[20]

But, after being inaugurated with fanfare on 5 August 2004, its initial operational phase was marred by a series of accidents. The first liquid spill took place only five months after the gas and liquids began to flow. Five additional spills took place within the Project's first two years, including a pipeline explosion and a spill of over 6,000 barrels of liquid within the Machiguenga Communal Reserve that was the second largest spill in the history of the Peruvian Amazon. The spills galvanized action on the part of Amazonian communities. COMARU and CECONAMA, working together for the first time, visited the Minister of Energy and Mines in Lima, delivering a letter that asked that all residues of the spill be cleaned up and the communities be given guarantees that similar spills would not occur before the communities engaged in public hearings on future projects in the zone. Five months later, after having received no response, the communities refused to engage in public hearings for Lot 57. As spills continued to occur, the level of resistance and organization grew in the Amazon. After the fourth spill in November 2005, in an unprecedented display of coordination and cooperation, COMARU, CECONAMA, FECONAYY and a small group of colonists organized a blockade of the river to prevent the transit of company boats that lasted for five days with the participation of over 2,000 people. Although the large coordinating group no longer met regularly, it mobilized to support the Urubamba communities and their calls for an independent audit of Project impacts and a strategic environmental assessment of the region.

Implementation of the loan conditions was spotty at best and civil society monitoring insufficient to credibly hold the larger actors' feet to the fire. IDB officials seemed eager to accommodate lenient interpretations of the conditions and return to the relationship of cosy camaraderie to which they were accustomed with the Peruvian Government. A December 2004 law passed by the Peruvian Congress created the Camisea Fund. The law not only ignored the proposal a working group led by an IDB consultant had developed that contained criteria designed to assure transparency and effective use of funds, but also contravened the official letter of commitment from the Peruvian Government to the IDB. The IDB declined to protest or mention it.

After Peru finally agreed in December 2005 to conduct a technical evaluation of the pipeline, the study was plagued by irregularities, including a last minute revision of the terms of reference which removed elements that would have provided a comprehensive understanding of why the pipeline failed, and a delay of nearly two years in producing the report. The IDB hired a consulting firm to carry out an environmental and social audit of Project impacts. However, the July 2007 report commented only on management and administration systems – which it found to be adequate – rather than on impacts. This report gave the IDB the green light to continue developing a loan for the second stage of the Camisea Project, called Peru/LNG, without ever resolving or even recognizing the impacts of the first stage.

In early 2006, the Peruvian Ombudsman's office issued a report that was strongly critical of the Project from a human rights and governance standpoint. Around the same time, a report by US-based E-Tech International in anticipation of a February 2006 IDB Camisea consultation meeting presented evidence that, in the rush to meet the government deadline, TGP had used second-hand and corroded pipes in its construction. Spectacularly, one of the stretches of the pipeline E-Tech identified as the most dangerous, exploded shortly thereafter, generating media attention in Peru and the US.

Peru did not wait long to make good on its promise that the Camisea Project would be the cornerstone that opened the Amazon to new and intensive oil and gas production. From 2006 to 2008, Peru approved licenses for exploration and production of oil and gas projects in over 50 separate blocks in lowland regions. A Ministry of Energy and Mines map shows hydrocarbon blocks covering approximately 80 per cent of the Peruvian Amazon. The second phase of the Camisea Project, called Peru/LNG, includes increased production in the Amazon, the construction of an additional pipeline, the expansion of the fractionation plant near Paracas Bay and an LNG plant to prepare the gas for export. The IDB and the IFC agreed in early 2008 to finance the Project with a combined amount of $700 million. Civil society groups in Peru and the US worked with limited success to ensure that the social and environmental problems that plagued the first Camisea Project would be both addressed and avoided in the second.

The US Government sent some promising signals during the consideration of funding for this Project, issuing position statements regarding both IFC and IDB funding that cited as yet unresolved issues around Camisea, urged the Banks to be more transparent and forthcoming with problems that should arise, than the IDB was in the Camisea Project, and warned that it intended to stay involved long beyond the financing decision and throughout the Project. Notably, the US Government has required the IDB to provide quarterly reports to its Board of Directors to detail the progress, or lack thereof, made on a series of environmental, social and governance concerns.

Camisea Citizen Action (ACC) has served as the coordinating hub for Peruvian and international organizations for advocacy on the Peru/LNG Project and has contributed to public debate more broadly by generating information and analysis on issues related to Camisea, indigenous peoples' issues, and hydrocarbon development through a newsletter, as well as in-depth analyses and reports. One ACC report analyses compliance with the original Camisea loan conditions and another analyses the absence of a coherent hydrocarbon strategy in Peru and makes recommendations.

What the campaign achieved

This case study describes the process by which civil society actors in Peru and the US brought about a new level of scrutiny of the social and environmental aspects of the Camisea Project, and of hydrocarbon development in general in Peru, and how these issues became part of a public agenda after the Project previously had been conceived of only in macroeconomic terms. It also explains how disparate social actors and NGOs initially distrustful of each other came together with the aim of influencing the Project. Finally, it attempts to demonstrate how international financing institutions became convinced that there were grave problems in the design and implementation of the Camisea Project and took this into account in financing decisions.

One major achievement of the campaign was the recognition by international lenders of the Project's flaws, formalized in the rejection of financing by the Ex-Im Bank and the strongest environmental and social conditions ever placed on a project by the IDB. On the way to achieving this, the coordinating group leveraged an extraordinarily high degree of public engagement with the process on the part of the Banks. Civil society groups exposed poor institutional and governance structures and mechanisms within the Peruvian Government and within the IDB, both of which are currently the subject of greater scrutiny from the US Government within the Peru/LNG Project. The Camisea campaign transformed a routine request for international financing for a gas project critical to Peru's economic development into a national and international debate on the seriousness of the claims made by the government, private companies and international lenders that they respected indigenous peoples' rights, environmental sustainability, transparency and good governance.

Another achievement of the campaign was (eventually) successfully challenging the general government domination of public discourse on national economic issues. National public opinion, as indicated by news reports in television, radio and print media, moved from strong support for the Project on entirely macroeconomic grounds to scepticism regarding the capacities and sense of responsibility of the companies and the government. This contributed in part to the national Ombudsman's office taking an interest in extractive industries and assuming an important role in investigating issues relating to extractive projects, governance and human rights. During the media boom after the Ex-Im Bank decision, capable civil society spokespeople were able to counteract many of the claims made about the groups when the government and companies were the only actors heard in the public discourse. The fact that the organizations were taken seriously by major institutions outside of Peru was an important factor here, as news organizations waited to see whether international bodies would give critics any credence before vetting their claims themselves.

Recognition of the problems and threats posed by the Project changed a general public view that, as the Project was vital for economic development, collateral damage simply would have to be accepted, to a questioning of whether such damage could be avoided by reasonable measures, higher standards, and stricter supervision. The denial of the Ex-Im Bank loan was a key factor in this, as it gave a high-level answer to the question as to whether such carelessness and environmental risk was really necessary.

An internal achievement of the campaign was the construction of relationships and trust among actors that had little to do with each other previously. The experience might encourage those sceptical about whether indigenous peoples' organizations and environmental groups are able to work together. Coordinating group members did not entirely overcome distrust and lack of affinity, but enough to serve as conscientious and reliable allies. This gave indigenous communities in the Urubamba region greater confidence that they had potential supporters outside of the region, and led to the formation of a strategic new entity, the ACC, concerned with indigenous rights, environmental integrity and hydrocarbon policy in Peru.

Factors contributing to change

Several factors can be identified that allowed the coordinating group to achieve what it did. First, long-term partnerships in the Urubamba region between COMARU and its communities and Oxfam and some Peruvian NGOs laid the groundwork for relationships of trust that made the coordination possible. When the Project began, the Urubamba region was flooded with newcomers – company personnel, contractors, consultants, government authorities, and representatives of the IDB. This caused significant unease in the communities. If NGOs had tried to enter at the same time to form relationships, they would likely have been treated as unwelcome outsiders pushing yet another agenda.

Second, the working relationship developed between indigenous communities and NGOs, through Oxfam and Peruvian NGOs known to them, was crucial as it provided NGOs with access to current information about what was happening in the zone that could be used in political arenas in Lima and Washington and lent credibility and legitimacy to the entire alliance. Also, the nature of the coordinating group, unlike in some campaigns, united community groups and NGOs, and allowed both NGOs and indigenous views to be presented together and in coordination, rather than one subordinated to the other.

Third, the ability of both Peruvian and Northern civil society organizations to move beyond their differences and come to agreement on an unusual strategy – not outright opposition to the Project, but approval only after satisfying strict conditions – and to develop a common platform of issues allowed them to eventually influence financing decisions.

Fourth, civil society organizations engaged in consistent and effective lobbying. Most had been following the Project in their own areas of concern for some time and their knowledge and analysis of it and its impacts allowed them to speak authoritatively about the complex issues surrounding the Project, rather than in small 'sound bites'. Additionally, the platform developed provided a framework for coordinated lobbying of different actors without the need to constantly check in with one another before every action.

Fifth, when the opportunity finally came for civil society organizations to be heard in the Peruvian news media, they responded magnificently. A number of articulate, knowledgeable, and engaging people without prior experience in media interviews lent credibility to the campaign and made viewers, listeners and readers comfortable with the reasonableness of their arguments. The campaign's multiple faces and voices underlined the diversity and breadth of the campaign.

Finally, outcomes might have been different if the US Government delegation had not been led by an astute, principled and analytic senior advisor who insisted on digging beneath the platitudes of the government and companies to identify the Project's shortcomings.

While the campaign developed organically and without reference to transnational advocacy literature or theory, all four strategies Keck and Sikkink identify were used in the campaign.[21] The strategic use of information, or 'information politics', was an essential element and included information from frequent communications to the Urubamba region, the Caffrey report, the Global Village Engineers report, and E-Tech's investigative report on the pipeline. Each of these documents came at the right time to give the coordinating group reliable and documented information that could not be easily dismissed. Unearthing documents the government or the Bank had tried to hide became part of this strategy as well. 'Leverage politics' was the central strategy, seeking to influence international institutions that could in turn influence actors and policies in Peru. And 'accountability' politics figured in the strategy of calling the IDB to make good on its promise of providing added value to the Project and on the government and companies to live up to their claim that the Project adhered to the highest international standards.

In terms of 'symbolic politics', the group capitalized on international interest in Amazonian biodiversity and indigenous peoples' rights, themes that made headlines in international media, but did not hold as much symbolic power in Peru. Peru's mainstream media often presents biodiversity as an abstract concept and indigenous Amazonians as an exotic 'other' in Peruvian society. One of the reasons given in the final report on Peru's Truth and Reconciliation Commission for how it was possible that the real number of victims killed in the era of political violence in Peru turned out to be double the number perennially cited until then – 70,000 rather than 35,000 – was that the vast majority of them were indigenous people who were not seen as part of the 'in-group' (in sociological terms) by those that traditionally defined Peruvian identity. It is possible, but unlikely, that the Camisea campaign helped to overcome this bias. Several interviews were conducted later in the campaign with Walter Kategari, then chief of COMARU. Kategari also gave an eloquent, sophisticated and moving speech at the inauguration of the pipeline in Malvinas in August 2004, which was broadcast live on national television.

Within Peru, on the other hand, Paracas Bay as a symbol of Peruvian patrimony held greater power and was accessible to a greater number of Peruvians. Paracas was the site of General San Martín´s landing during the War of Independence. A large percentage of Peruvians, especially from the capital city of Lima, have visited Paracas and could feel diminished if harm were to come to the area. When a famous rock formation on the Paracas peninsula was destroyed in an earthquake in 2007, the loss was widely lamented. As Paracas is easier and less expensive to get to from Lima than the Lower Urubamba, it was logical that Peruvian press would focus on threats to Paracas over the Amazon. For this reason, it was crucial for Amazonian actors to ally with those working on the coast in order to project their concerns on a larger national stage.

Limitations of the campaign

The capacities and strategies of civil society actors were far from adequate to meet the coordinating group's original goals. Despite the loan denial by the Ex-Im Bank to Pluspetrol on environmental grounds, the fractionation plant went ahead in the buffer zone of the Paracas reserve. Civil society strategies were insufficient to prevent serious environmental damage to the Urubamba River valley through uncontrolled erosion, possibly irreversible damage to fragile aquatic and terrestrial ecosystems, and brusque changes to the way of life of indigenous communities. The impact on the region's extraordinary biological diversity may never be known, given the absence of a serious baseline study and inadequate monitoring. The coordinating group's capacity was weak for monitoring loan conditions set down by and for much more powerful actors lacking the political will to comply with them. The attempt to develop an independent monitoring system was a failure. And the Peruvian Government, with a wink and a nod from the IDB, attempted to subvert the original aims of the Camisea Fund. In sum, the government and the companies successfully externalized the costs of producing gas onto vulnerable communities and ecosystems.

Internally, full communication between NGOs in the field and Lima was not always fluid, not only because of logistics and distance, but also because the leaders of COMARU were greatly overstretched, facing numerous demands. Also, while NGOs were accustomed to exchanging information over the phone on a transactional basis, this was not always culturally easy for Machiguenga community leaders. The absence of a concrete action plan impeded greater involvement of the communities.

In terms of the five campaign stages proposed by Keck and Sikkink, The coordinating group successfully *created issues and set agendas*, and certainly *influenced discursive positions of states and international organizations* who defended themselves against civil society groups' criticism by referring to environmental and indigenous peoples' rights issues. The degree of *influence on institutional procedures* is less clear, but the fact that the IDB reviewed and modified its environmental and indigenous rights standards after the Camisea loan was granted may have been influenced by the campaign. In this sense, the campaign also benefited from others that went before it. The campaign to influence Export Credit Agencies to develop and implement robust environmental standards for their financing activities was likely a key factor in the denial of the Ex-Im Bank loan. *Influence on policy change of target actors* also may have been achieved indirectly; that is, not as a particular objective of the Camisea coordinating group, but as an indirect result. The US Government has promised to play a more active and long-term role in overseeing international financial institutions' loans to the Peru/LNG Project. *Influence on state behaviour* is the stage most difficult to draw direct lines to from the Camisea campaign. Certainly, Peru complied with many of the loan conditions, titling new Natural Protected Areas in the Urubamba region, for example. And the US Government's position papers regarding the Peru/LNG Project refer to improvements in the Peruvian Government's capacity to manage projects. However, it seems unlikely that the experience of Camisea set positive precedents for the high number of new hydrocarbon projects being initiated in Peru today.

Issues raised

Is a campaign with a complex message doomed to fail? Most media outlets that covered the coordinating group's positions erroneously reported that members opposed the Project. The confusion was difficult to clear up. Oxfam America's Lima office had to carefully edit the draft wording for its electronic alert to ensure that it asked members to impose conditions rather than to reject the loan. The US Treasury delegation was surprised to learn that the organizations in Peru did not oppose the Project, as it had been informed by media and the Peruvian Government. It was unclear whether the government's accusations were a product of blindness imposed by its own frameworks or whether it was a politically calculated strategy to present the public with a story of heroes and villains, with civil society groups cast in the latter role.

Yet, while its complex message was not easy to get out to the public, the group's decision not to oppose the Project had advantages in terms of legitimacy. Advocacy based on principles, such as human rights, environmental integrity and transparency, opened avenues to relationships with key allies and allowed the group to demonstrate commonality with institutions, which, at least publicly, espoused these same principles. Civil society organizations tried to use empirical evidence of problems and deficiencies in project management to establish why they and their advocacy targets shared a common problem. The group proposed possible ways to address the problems identified, but was not closed to other suggestions, which left room for substantive discussions on the ways in which principles could be achieved.

Another factor that aided the coordinating group in its claim to legitimacy was the unity, diversity and breadth of organizations in the alliance, showing that a wide array of disparate actors were in agreement on a fundamental set of issues. With the exception of AIDESEP in the final months before financing decisions, no major voice within civil society aired discrepant views, and even AIDESEP backed the coordinating group's proposals. This broad representation and unity of civil society groups made it difficult for the IDB to turn elsewhere for the legitimacy it needed as an institution which was seen to engage in good faith with the public. The Peruvian Government attempted to deflect civil society organizations' criticisms by claiming their untrustworthy motives and ignorance of the Project, and by trying to control information that might justify questioning of the Project. The government questioned the legitimacy of the Peruvian and international groups in the press and even in a meeting between civil society organizations, the IDB, and government agencies when government representatives claimed that, as appointees of democratically elected leaders, *they* were the *real* civil society.

The campaign made extensive use of a 'boomerang strategy' by using influential institutions in the North to pressure a reluctant Southern target. But one weakness in this case was that, by the time financing decisions actually came up for a vote, the construction phase of the Project was so far along that the influence financing institutions might have through their conditions was already limited. Despite the large number of conditions applied to the IDB loan, the Ex-Im Bank's decision to deny the loan may have been a more powerful influence in changing the course of the Project. The strictest and most strategically written conditions came from the Ex-Im Bank, rather than from the IDB, and the US government was open to civil society concerns and shared its critique of IDB culture and institutional weaknesses. The campaign erred in assuming that the conditions applied to the IDB loan had been internalized in the Bank, rather than seeing that they resulted from US government pressure. Despite generalized and historic mistrust among Peruvian civil society organizations with regard to the US government, reinforced by a widespread rejection throughout Latin America of the Bush administration's foreign policy initiatives at that time, the US government proved to be the coordinating group's most effective ally in its 'boomerang strategy'.

Did the IDB fulfil its promise to add value to environmental and social aspects of the Project? Certainly, the IDB engaged with civil society actors on an unprecedented level, continues to hold consultation meetings, albeit poorly designed, and created pressure through loan conditions that contributed to many positive measures being taken by the government. However, the IDB also demonstrated institutional deficiencies in supervising a project of Camisea's magnitude and sensitivity. Aside from placing full power in the hands of one person to sign off on compliance with conditions and declining to react publicly when Peru created a Camisea Fund that violated formal agreements, administrative units overseeing environmental and indigenous peoples' issues are notoriously marginalized in the Bank compared to the Private Sector Division. How persuasive could the IDB be, therefore, through its Private Sector personnel, in persuading the Peruvian government to give high priority to environmental and indigenous rights protections in the Project? The IDB's lack of seriousness in negotiating an independent monitoring programme, after having formally committed itself to doing so, as well as its distortion of the social and environmental audit to serve its purposes of justifying its participation in a new project without resolving or coming to terms with the problems of the first has created a level of distrust that will be difficult to overcome. While the IDB claims to promote democratic governance, transparency and effective management, evidence from the Camisea Project undermines these claims.

Regarding the nature of participation within the campaign, it is notable that while much of the literature on transnational advocacy portrays Northern organizations as controlling and directing campaigns, in this case, Southern organizations exerted control by convincing Northern groups opposed to the Project to modify their positions and to suspend their opposition in order to support the unified position of the Peruvian organizations. Within Peru, the diversity of the coordinating group for the Camisea Project and its initial low level of initial trust meant that leading through facilitation worked better than an aggressive style of leadership. A facilitative style in meetings allowed participants to be comfortable that they would be heard, rather than railroaded or manipulated into following another's agenda. In some moments, when the leadership was more directive than facilitative, the alliance lost some of its convening power. Regarding roles inside the coordinating group, there was a broad recognition that communities organizing in defense of their rights were the most important pillars of the coalition's advocacy, and that the group was 'at the service of the organizations and communities who are suffering impacts because of the Project activity'.[22] Yet the diversity of participation meant that all voices within the group were valid; NGO opinions were not subordinated to those of indigenous communities, nor *vice versa*. Peruvian NGOs had an important role in demanding accountability of their own government, something international NGOs could not easily do. International NGOs assumed an important role in creating spaces for common analysis and joint advocacy that might not have taken place without them.

When Shell posited that oil and gas companies would increasingly have to prove themselves by demonstrating a high level of environmental and social responsibility, it assumed that national governments were logically interested in ensuring best practice, high standards, and net benefit for their citizens. But the experience of Camisea suggests that other motives and concerns may interfere or prevent a national government from assuming the role Shell envisioned. Transnational advocacy networks face particular challenges when working in a democratic state whose government attempts to close off avenues for public input, comment and criticism. The Peruvian government tended to see the Project only in macroeconomic terms and seemed unwilling to assume its role of enforcing standards and watching out for the national interest of sustainable development over the long term. Project management lacked an integrated long-term vision; the legal framework did not require a strategic analysis that included indirect, secondary and cumulative impacts. One of the most important contributions of civil society organizing around the Camisea Project was to reveal the bankruptcy of the government refrain of 'just trust us', and to demonstrate that problems and deficiencies in individual projects are not likely to be solved without addressing the broader issue of the state's model of social and environmental management.

Notes

1 F. Dallmeier and A. Alonso (1997) *Biodiversity Assessment and Long-Term Monitoring, Lower Urubamba Region, Peru* (Washington DC: Smithsonian Institution), pp. iii–iv.
2 For more on Shell's experience in Camisea in the 1990s, see P. May et al. (1999) *Corporate Roles and Rewards in Promoting Sustainable Development: Lessons Learned from Camisea*, (Berkeley: Energy and Resources Group, University of California).
3 http://www.camisea.com.pe, date accessed November 2006.
4 Glenn Shepard, who carried out his doctoral research in the zone, and was fluent in the Nahua language, reported in his PhD dissertation that 42 per cent of the population had died after having contacts with outsiders. The figure is disputed by the head of the Dominican Mission in the zone at the time.
5 P. Caffrey (2002) 'An independent Environmental and Social Assessment of the Camisea Gas Project', Available at http://www.bicusa.org/en/Project.Resources.5.aspx. Accessed in November 2008.
6 S. Tegel (2003) 'The price of development: impacts of the Camisea Gas Project on the Matsigenka people of the Peruvian Amazon', unpublished paper.
7 From Lima, the trip requires a flight to Cusco followed by an eight-hour bus ride to Quillabamba, a seven-hour ride in a bus or truck until the road ends, then a canoe ride through the treacherous Pongo de Mainique. Company personnel travelled directly by plane to Malvinas.
8 For more on this issue, see M. Chapin (2004) 'A challenge to conservationists', *World Watch*, November/December, pp. 17–31.
9 Personal notes from GTCI meeting, late April 2003.
10 Personal notes from the meeting.
11 The fine had not been paid as of late 2007.

12 TGP Monitoring Reports, June 2002 and July 2002, Knight Piesold. No longer available on the Camisea website. See also J. Grimaldi, 'Texas firms line up US aid in Peru', *The Washington Post*, 20 November, 2002.
13 J. Maughan (2003) *Camisea Natural Gas Project Environmental Evaluation* (Washington DC: Global Village Engineers).
14 'Camisea: indispensable aclaración del gobierno', *Expreso*, 8 August 2003.
15 'Camisea: indispensable aclaración del gobierno', *Expreso*, 8 August 2003, and Speech by Alejandro Toledo, 15 August 2003.
16 Personal communication from a member of the US delegation.
17 'Ex-Im Bank rechaza financiamiento para proyecto de gas en Perú', *Reuters*, 28 August 2003.
18 *Correo*, 29 August 2003.
19 The Bank subsequently hired a consulting team to investigate the reasons for its failure to implement independent monitoring. Before the end of the contract term, the consultants withdrew because of lack of cooperation from IDB personnel.
20 Apoyo Consultoria (2007) *Proyecto Camisea: El impacto sobre el mercado de gas natural y estimación de los beneficios económicos. Documento elaborado para el Banco Interamericano de Desarrollo*, pp. 7, 65–6. Available at http://idbdocs.IDB.org, date accessed 30 November 2008.
21 M. Keck and K. Sikkink (1998) *Activists Beyond Borders* (Ithaca and London: Cornell University Press) pp. 22–5.
22 Interview, A. Bernales, Grupo Peruano de Resolución de Conflictos, 7 January 2005.

8
Case Study: Jobs and Health in Peru

Martin Scurrah, Jeannet Lingán and Rosa Pizarro

At the end of the 1990s, local groups in the city of La Oroya, Peru, struggled to draw attention to a problem that everybody was aware of but nobody had yet addressed: the high levels of pollution affecting its population living near a minerals smelter operation. The city of La Oroya had a long and complex relationship with the metallurgical facilities, a powerful local stakeholder, crucial to the region's development. This was a difficult context for groups trying to address the consequences of decades of environmental neglect, as local authorities' support leaned towards Doe Run Perú (DRP), a company reluctant to invest in modernizing its facilities and lowering pollution emissions. Although the presence of air pollution was evident, nobody had an idea how serious the problem really was. Local NGOs conducted a series of studies to assess the impact of pollution on the local population's health. The results were shocking, showing that the population, and especially the children, had blood lead levels that far exceeded the maximum acceptable limits set by the World Health Organization. That was the beginning of an uphill battle to make the state and the company take action to protect people's health. This case has become emblematic as it reversed the usual model of international advocacy: southern organizations providing information to campaign efforts in the North to influence decisions in the North. In this case, the efforts focused on a campaign with international support that with time legitimized and strengthened efforts at national and local levels.

La Oroya is the capital of Yauli province, located 182 kilometres east of the city of Lima at the intersection of major roads that connect the Peruvian capital with the regions and cities of the Andean highlands and the central Amazonian basin. The city is located 3,700 meters above sea level, in the upper part of the Mantaro River basin.[1] Because of the geological characteristics of the area, the province is rich in mineral resources, which form the basis of its economy. Other economic activities include farming and livestock, but they are eclipsed in importance by mining. The province is home to significant large- and medium-scale mining operations, among which the La Oroya metallurgical complex stands out. Located in La Oroya since the 1920s, it is the largest smelter in the country and directly or indirectly is the area's largest employer and main economic activity.

In 1901, a new mining code allowed companies to acquire an unlimited number of long-term mining concessions and operate them as they pleased.[2] In this context, the Cerro de Pasco Copper Corporation, a company founded in 1902 in the US state of Delaware, acquired about 80 per cent of the mines in the central highlands which enabled it to wield hegemonic control over the regional economy for more than seven decades. With the expansion of its production in Peru and the idea of integrating its operations, in 1917 Cerro de Pasco established a smelter in La Oroya. When the operation went on line in 1922, it not only led to the closing of all other smelters in the central highlands, but it also prompted the company to supply the smelter from its own mines, making Cerro de Pasco a monopoly in relation to the other mining companies in the region. It also made it a very influential stakeholder in Peruvian politics and economics as the company controlled approximately 32 per cent of the country's exports.

In 1973 a reformist and nationalist military government expropriated the Cerro de Pasco Corporation, which brought to an end more than half a century of history for the US company in Peru. The new state-run company, Centromin Peru, introduced changes to link the mining sector with the rest of the regional and national economy. There was continuity, however, in the way the company treated its workers and the environmental damage that its operations caused in its area of influence. Just as Cerro de Pasco had done, Centromin Peru managed health, education, housing and recreational services and even the sale of its products to its workers, which '… created a clear social distinction between the families that benefited from the company's services and those who were independent'.[3]

This city-camp model, which had characterized mining since the early 20th century, gradually began to change with the arrival of a new kind of mining in the 1990s, with social and economic consequences for the cities and regions, such as La Oroya, that had grown up around mining operations. In the 1990s, the hyperinflation crisis and internal conflict inherited from the previous decade provided a context conducive to the new Peruvian government's implementation of neo-liberal policies. An aggressive policy of privatization and support for private investment was implemented that would free the productive sector from state intervention. In the mining sector, these measures established advantageous conditions for future investors and buyers in order to stimulate private and foreign investment. Generous tax concessions were offered and the conditions for repatriating capital and profits were loosened. Meanwhile, the government took measures to restructure state-owned companies, including reducing personnel and clearing up financial and legal encumbrances.

At another level, there was also a growing sensitivity towards environmental issues leading to an emphasis on sustainable development discourses. This drew attention to economic activities that were eminently extractive, such as mining, which was also a source of pollution. Amid these concerns, mining in Peru, which was considered a strategic economic sector, had to adjust. The Peruvian government implemented a regulatory and institutional framework aimed at conserving the environment and for the first time passed an Environment Code in 1990. The code '... introduced important environmental principles and management tools, such as the principle of prevention, the principle that the polluter pays, guidelines for environmental policy, environmental impact evaluations, and others'.[4] This early regulation suffered later modifications pushed by interest groups prioritizing private investment. Each ministry was made responsible for promoting investments and managing its own environmental agenda, acting as both defendant and prosecutor on environmental issues and hampering effective oversight.

In the case of mining, the Office of Environmental Affairs (DGAA) was established as part of the Ministry of Energy and Mines (MEM) in 1992 to promote and supervise environmental matters in the sector. In 1993, regulations for environmental protection in mining and metallurgy were issued, establishing three tools for environmental regulation and management in the sector: 1) environmental management and adjustment programmes (PAMAs), which had to be presented for projects that were under way when the regulations were issued; 2) environmental impact assessments (EIAs) for new projects; and 3) environmental audits for monitoring compliance with the PAMAs and EIAs. As a complementary measure, maximum allowable limits were set in 1996 for atmospheric emissions and liquid effluents from mining and metallurgical operations. With all of these changes in the state structure, the stage was supposedly set for encouraging development combined with environmental awareness, as well as for taking action to resolve long-standing environmental problems like that of La Oroya.

In this context, the restructuring of Centromín Peru began and, in 1994, 100 per cent of the company's assets were put up for sale; but the sale failed for lack of bidders. One of the serious problems facing the state-run company was its environmental 'liabilities' – environmental problems that had accumulated over decades which made the investment unattractive. In 1996, therefore, the decision was made to break up the company and sell it in parts. In early 1997, so that the La Oroya metallurgical complex could be put up for sale separately, the complex's assets were transferred to Metaloroya S.A., a subsidiary of Centromín Peru. A public bidding process ensued, which was won by the Mexican company, Industrias Peñoles S.A. With no explanation from the privatization commission, however, the concession was subsequently awarded to Doe Run Perú, a subsidiary of the US-based Doe Run Resources Corporation, which was, in turn, part of the Renco Group, owned and controlled by Ira Leon Rennert.

Government environmental policy guidelines required a PAMA for any mining project already in operation which had to state what policies and investments the company was committing to within a maximum ten-year time period in order to bring its operations into line with current environmental legislation. The Centromín PAMA was approved in January 1997, before the sale of the complex, and was restructured in August of the same year. With these environmental commitments already assumed by the state-run company, in October the operation of the smelter was transferred to DRP. At that time, the PAMA was modified again, with the US company committing to a lower investment than the amount indicated in the original agreement. Since in neither case the PAMA was sufficient to mitigate the smelter's environmental impacts, this started a series of modifications in the company's environmental commitments, as well as of successive postponements of completion dates. In 2003, with 60 per cent of the time elapsed for the PAMA's completion, the company had made only 23 per cent of the environmental investments to which it had agreed.[5]

The campaign

Although pollution has affected the soil, air and water of La Oroya since the metallurgical complex opened in the 1920s, until the late 1990s little or nothing had been done about the situation. The lack of interest in the issue on the part of all stakeholders (grassroots organizations, the central, regional and local governments, the company,

NGOs, and so on) can be explained by the lack of overall awareness of environmental issues, which took a back seat to labour and economic matters that were considered more urgent and important. There was also a collective reluctance to investigate or confirm their fears because people suspected that it would not be easy to find solutions that would combine health and environmental conservation with the defence of economic activities and employment.

Because of this, it was difficult for those who wanted to draw attention to the pollution and its effects on the residents' health to get a hearing on the local scene. By the 1990s, the urgency and importance of environmental issues had gained legitimacy, especially among NGOs and international cooperation agencies. These groups therefore did not need an excuse to take an interest in problems in a traditional mining area, such as La Oroya. In 1997, the UNES Consortium, a coalition of three local NGOs formed by CooperAcción, Filomena Tomaira Pacsi and Eco-Andes, was born with the goal of working on a comprehensive development plan for the province of Yauli-La Oroya. The three institutions knew each other as they were working on labour rights in La Oroya, when the topic drew the attention of Christian Aid, which was interested in addressing the pollution problem in the area and gave initial support to the consortium.

One component of the project was environmental recovery. Work began with the population in both urban and rural areas on environmental planning workshops to develop and validate an environmental recovery plan. The workshops awakened in the participants a desire to protect the environment and the community members involved decided to form an Association of Environmental Delegates (ADA). On its own initiative, ADA organized an exhibition of animals that were sick or deformed, allegedly because of pollution. In response, the company launched a dissuasive campaign that weakened the grassroots groups' commitment to the new association:

> ... the company started using strategies to keep these people from continuing. They went to the communities. They offered the president's assistance, personal assistance, community assistance .... For example, they started giving them medicines for their animals. They went from community to community to give them medicine, saying that their animals were in that condition not because of the pollution or the smoke, but mainly because they didn't know how to care for their animals .... They minimized the people's concerns; they mistreated them; they did whatever they could. We still have a

small group of delegates, but many got scared; they were frightened because their families didn't want to support them either....[6]

Meanwhile, as part of the programme, environmental monitoring and health studies were begun. In 1999, the consortium started the first environmental monitoring of water, air and soil, finding significant levels of lead particles. Months later, the consortium did a health study of pregnant women and children under age three, which coincided with a similar study by the Ministry of Health's Office of Environmental Health (DIGESA). Both studies found that the people of La Oroya, especially the children, had extremely high blood lead levels, which directly affected their health because of the serious effects of prolonged exposure to heavy metals on the respiratory and nervous systems. Although these were not the first studies done in the area, these new studies were the first to offer scientifically irrefutable evidence. Subsequent studies would repeatedly confirm the high levels of pollution to which the population of La Oroya and its surroundings was exposed.

The consortium's study, however, was the one that caused the greatest commotion and friction on the local scene. Because of a smear campaign against the consortium's work that had already been launched by the company and its allies, it was not easy for the promoters to do the study openly. When the results of the study were made public, criticism was not long in coming. The company and its allies tried to discredit the consortium, alleging methodological errors; when the results of the company's own study were made public, however, they were similar to those of the consortium and DIGESA.[7]

The company then changed its strategy, trying to shift the blame for the pollution problem onto others. It claimed that the main source of pollution was traffic on the central highway running through the city, along which hundreds of vehicles pass every day. It also argued that the health problems stemmed from environmental pollution dating back over the smelter's 80-year history and from the population's poor hygiene and the lack of public cleanliness, so that the solution therefore lay in changing people's habits and behaviours. In the city, the company launched personal hygiene campaigns, painted public buildings, built public toilets and sinks and started 'educational programmes' in the media, stressing that preventive measures depended solely on individuals and their habits. With these efforts, it attempted to silence those who were pointing to the company as the main source of pollution in the area, a strategy that collapsed in 2002, when a study by the Peruvian

Environmental Law Society (SPDA) and the Interamerican Association for Environmental Defense (AIDA) demonstrated that the pollution was mainly due to the increased concentration of toxic pollutants after the complex was privatized and, therefore, to pollution from the smelter.[8]

Between 1996 and 2002, therefore, a series of studies by civil society groups, public agencies and the company itself scientifically confirmed what had been an open secret in La Oroya for 80 years: that the metallurgical complex's operations continued to pollute the city, especially La Oroya Antigua (the oldest part of the city). This demonstrated that the pollution did exist, that it was harmful to human health, especially for children and pregnant women, and that the source and cause of the pollution was the company's plant. By late 2002, the environmental problem and its harmful effects were public knowledge in La Oroya and an environmental movement began to emerge.

Establishing a coalition

Efforts by the UNES consortium, church workers and local leaders to address the environmental problem had laid the groundwork for the most committed people to begin discussing the possibility of forming a movement to defend the health of the residents of La Oroya.

In 2001, Oxfam America organized a workshop gathering around 30 La Oroya community leaders in which they discussed the possibility of creating a movement composed of individuals and grassroots organizations' representatives. The group was called Movement for the Health of La Oroya (Movimiento por la Salud de la Oroya, MOSAO) and was formalized in April 2002. Behind these individuals were grassroots organizations, such as the Association of Environmental Delegates (ADA), the La Oroya Antigua Defense Committee, the Popular Assembly of La Oroya, the Committee of Neighbourhood Boards of La Oroya, the Human Rights Committee of the Parish of La Oroya and the La Oroya Chamber of Commerce. The grassroots organizations were joined by NGOs working in the area, such as Labor, CooperAcción, Filomena Tomaira (the UNES consortium) and Eco-Andes; soon afterward, the Joining Hands against Poverty Network, a coalition of Peruvian NGOs and projects funded by the Presbyterian Church of the US, would join them.

Since the NGOs in MOSAO tended to overshadow the grassroots organizations and leaders, the decision was made to separate MOSAO from the NGOs, which formed a technical working group to support MOSAO. The major challenge for the movement and its allies was to raise awareness about the pollution and the responsibility of the government and the company in the area's environmental and health problems. The health studies by the consortium and DIGESA, and later the report by Cederstav and Barandiarán[9], provided a basis for publicizing the problems. It was also important to lobby so that the necessary measures would be taken at the national and international levels to mitigate the problems caused by the pollution.

In 2002, an international campaign was launched in the United States with the collaboration of Oxfam America, the Joining Hands against Poverty Network and other organizations allied with MOSAO and the technical working group. A first inquiry about the company revealed that Doe Run Resources (DRR) had a similar problem to that at La Oroya with its smelter in Herculaneum, Missouri. The inclusion of the Joining Hands against Poverty Network in the movement then proved to be crucial; members of the Presbyterian Church in Herculaneum had already started to put pressure on local, state and national authorities to address the problems generated by the lead smelter there. The network made it possible to establish communication between residents of the two cities so they could share experiences and strategies in order to build capacities and cohesion within the groups.

At the same time, contact was made with US media to publicize the problem internationally and put pressure on Doe Run Perú's home office. In October, the *St. Louis Post-Dispatch* published an editorial about the situation in La Oroya, harshly criticizing Doe Run. The editorial prompted a reply from Jeffrey L. Zelms, vice-president of Doe Run Perú, in which he highlighted the improvements the company had made in its five years of operations in La Oroya, as well as its investment in upgrading schools and health services in the city. Later, in December 2002, Craig Cheatham, a journalist from the *St. Louis Post-Dispatch*, produced a hard-hitting documentary for television station KMOV in St. Louis, *La Oroya, City of Lead*, which not only revealed the serious pollution problem to the world, but also won him various international prizes. Cheatham's visit to Peru was coordinated and sponsored by Oxfam, which had been interested in the issue since a 2001 visit to La Oroya by Chet Atkins, a member of the Oxfam America board of directors. Atkins, a former congressman, was in Peru on US State Department business and took advantage of the opportunity to visit La Oroya and see the situation. Struck by the conditions he found, he later sent a friend, documentary producer Steve Atlas, who did a rough cut of a documentary, with interviews and footage from the area. Cheatham's documentary included some of the footage shot earlier by Atlas.

The partnership of MOSAO and the technical working group with Oxfam and the Joining Hands Network made them the target of criticism by the company's allies, who tried to discredit the local residents' struggle. This, however, was just the beginning of an international campaign that would create more and more controversy over the US corporation's environmental policies, repeatedly charging it with a lack of ethics and scant commitment to the community where it worked, as well as the owner's strategy of getting rich no matter what the cost. In July 2003, an article published by Michael Schnayerson in the American magazine *Vanity Fair*, exposed Ira Rennert, owner of the Renco Group, of which DRP was part. It described Rennert's questionable business moves and companies enjoying poor environmental records. Among other things, it claimed that Rennert was building a 100 million dollars mansion in the Hamptons on Long Island, New York, even though people living nearby his smelters were suffering serious health problems due to toxic emissions. This article started a campaign of direct pressure on the owner of Doe Run, but he proved difficult to target and the campaign brought no major results.

The campaign initially had the greatest activity and impact outside Peru (especially in the US) because Peruvian national media had not yet become interested in La Oroya's environmental problems. Furthermore, it was decided not to target Doe Run Perú directly as there were difficulties organizing a local campaign due to the company's powerful position in the region and the sensitivity towards the topic in the area: local groups were keen to support the company as there were rumours that NGOs wanted to close the smelter, and local leaders faced threats and harassment. As a consequence, efforts focused on promoting debate and raising awareness of the pollution problem through seminars and workshops at the local level. Another important step was to file a law suit against the state to oblige it to declare a health emergency in La Oroya, so that the Health Ministry would have to take immediate measures to provide health care to people suffering high blood lead levels.

Thus, at the beginning of 2002, MOSAO and the technical working group had established some important alliances at the national level. To raise awareness and launch a local and national health campaign, two significant events were held. The first was a local public forum on comprehensive health care and management in La Oroya and the second, at the national level, was held in the National Congress where Congressman Hildebrando Tapia announced draft legislation that would declare a health emergency in La Oroya. That initiative did not bear fruit, however, because some months later an emergency was declared in the entire Mantaro River valley, involving four regions and overshadowing the problem of La Oroya.

The two events constituted the local and national launch of the campaign sponsored by MOSAO and its partners, leading the company to start a fierce counter-campaign against MOSAO, including intimidation of its members. The company and its allies constantly accused MOSAO of being just another NGO whose real intention was to close the company and create conflict, because its income from international cooperation agencies depended on that, an argument that swayed local public opinion in a place marked by distrust and high dependence on the company.

While local people closed ranks against MOSAO, setting the stage for major confrontations, at the national level the company appeared to be open to dialogue. One of the first meetings between the company and MOSAO came toward the middle of the year, when the issue was discussed in the Mining Dialogue Group, an informal but influential group of persons from mining companies, NGOs, government agencies and communities that met in Lima on a monthly basis. These early dialogues were halted by MEM's rejection of DRP's request for a PAMA extension in November 2003. Claiming financial problems, the company had already filed three earlier requests to reschedule or postpone the most important PAMA projects until the end of the PAMA period. Despite the denial, in February 2004 Doe Run again announced that it would ask MEM to extend its PAMA deadline until 2011 and launched a campaign to gain support, attacking possible enemies and acquiring some strong, unconditional allies.

In fact, by 2002, MEM had already found that its oversight of PAMA projects was not based on sound technical information. Confronted with scientific evidence of environmental damage, most of which was caused by the smelter, MEM had no choice but to order the company to take complementary action to mitigate the environmental problems.[10] Because Congress had begun to pressure MEM on oversight of mining companies, the Office of Mining in MEM decided not to grant the extension and to impose sanctions on the company. In 2004 and 2005, a tension that had been brewing for years intensified after DRP asked MEM to extend the deadline for compliance with its PAMA to 2011. The media and the public awaited the ministry's response, amid an atmosphere that helped create important partnerships for MOSAO and the technical working group. This scenario was also facilitated by the work these groups had done over several years, especially at the international level. The issue gained increased legitimacy and visibility, and the company's constant postponement of investments required by its PAMA was exposed as major media, such as the Lima daily newspaper *El Comercio*, started publishing reports about the health problems in La Oroya.

The company established two key alliances, one with the local municipality and the other with the trade union. By including these two stakeholders, the company tried to show that it had grassroots support for its request. In March 2004, the Provincial Government of Yauli-La Oroya agreed at a council meeting to support DRP's request for an extension. Months later, the company's union signed on to that request. By then, people were alarmed because rumours were circulating that the smelter would close if the extension were not granted.

Locally, people were increasingly divided and the situation was becoming more and more violent. In April 2004, members of MOSAO and the technical working group were physically attacked by people associated with the company while leaving a meeting at the Congress. MOSAO filed a request for guarantees with the Interamerican Human Rights Commission. Meanwhile, the provincial mayor and the union began to call strikes and marches in the city to pressure the authorities to approve the extension request, which the company had not yet formally filed. In December, these pressure tactics became more violent with a 48-hour strike in the city and roadblocks on the central highway, coinciding with the publication of MEM's draft text of Supreme Decree 046, by which the company and its allies, using various pressure tactics, laid the groundwork for formalizing the request for an extension in late 2005.

Although aggression against MOSAO and the technical working group increased, the movement gained some new allies in key sectors, such as Congress and MEM, and continued to raise awareness nationwide about the problems in La Oroya. In April 2005, after Doe Run made a presentation in Congress on progress with the implementation of its PAMA, the ministry, MOSAO and the working group took two important steps. The first was to form a multi-sector government committee to assess the problems in La Oroya and the second was to re-establish a forum for dialogue between the company and the movement within the framework of the Mining Dialogue Group. In the interim, MOSAO and the technical working group won a sympathetic hearing at MEM from the director general of mining, who began to open channels for including MOSAO's views in the ministry's analysis of the problems in La Oroya. The company's power would become clear when she was forced to resign after opposing the approval of Supreme Decree 046 (see below the section 'Factors contributing to success'). She later revealed that the company had more than one unconditional ally in the ministry: '... every time DR got into trouble, it would go to the MEM Office of Environmental Affairs and get them to modify the deadlines, modifications that obviously had irregularities. That's how they avoided fines and left everything until the end ...'.[11]

Campaign over the deadline extension

The day before 2004 ended, Supreme Decree 046 was published. This law allowed mining companies to request an *exceptional extension of deadlines* for finishing environmental projects included in their PAMAs.[12] This measure obviously benefited Doe Run directly, since it was the only mining company that had publicly expressed its intention to request an extension to its PAMA deadline and, in fact, DRP was the only company that took advantage of the supreme decree; in late 2005 it submitted a formal request for an extension of the deadline for completing the sulphuric acid plant that was part of its PAMA, thus demonstrating that Doe Run had powerful influence in the Ministry.

In late 2004, the Environmental Health Office (DIGESA) announced that it would undertake a 'haematic census' of children and pregnant women in La Oroya. The results were presented at a press conference in March 2005 and, according to a press release from Doe Run in St. Louis, showed an *improvement in blood lead levels*. The study was carried out under an agreement between DIGESA and DRP, signed in July 2003, with the goal of implementing the 'Comprehensive Plan for Control of Lead Poisoning in Children and Pregnant Women in La Oroya Antigua: 2004–2010'. As a result, five children were referred to Lima for further tests and later sent to the hospital in the city of Tarma for treatment. A group of 66 children was also taken temporarily to 'pollution-free' areas, such as Casaracra and Paccha, in an adjacent valley.

Meanwhile, MOSAO and the technical working group were discussing the possibility of a new health study, which was to be coordinated with St. Louis University in Missouri with the help of the Joining Hands Network. These efforts coincided with the appearance in the regional spotlight of Huancayo Archbishop Pedro Barreto, who publicly expressed concern about health in La Oroya and the environmental situation in the Mantaro River valley. He was asked to take charge of coordinating the new health study. In December 2004, a communiqué from the Archdiocese of Huancayo, inviting the parties to the conflict to talks that could lead to a comprehensive solution, coincided with the announcement of a new health study in La Oroya.

Amid the announcement of the positive results of the haematic census, the company's unconditional supporters stirred up anger against the Catholic Church and Archbishop Barreto. Opposition to an independent study that would give greater legitimacy to the environmental movement's claims led to violence, including physical and verbal aggression. In August, when the St. Louis University School of Public Health's study of contamination in households in La Oroya and Concepción and its effects on the health of residents began, members of the research team were accosted by local residents who were angry about the study. Despite fierce opposition from some sectors of the population, which made the study's organizers worry that they might not be able to obtain the necessary samples, a few days later the team had exceeded its technical targets. In December, when the preliminary results of the study were released, the high blood lead levels in children in La Oroya were confirmed. Fernando Serrano, the lead researcher, said: 'From a public health standpoint, the levels of lead, antimony, cadmium and other metals found in La Oroya are extremely high'. This allowed for comparison of the two studies, which in fact produced similar results. The people who were fighting for approval of the Doe Run PAMA extension, however, tried to interpret them tendentiously.

The study by the US university and its coordination by Archbishop Barreto put the issue in the international spotlight again, as the study was covered by international media such as Reuters, UPI, *The New York Times*, *The Miami Herald* and other North American outlets; this also led to new exchanges with St. Louis, with the Archbishop's mediation. These events brought MOSAO and the health problems to national and international attention again, positioning the organization as a stakeholder with solid arguments that were seen as credible by the media. Meanwhile, with the formation of a 'dialogue round table' for talks in Huancayo as part of the quest for a comprehensive solution to the region's environmental problems, the conflict moved out of the local arena, where there was hostility toward the movement, and into a regional scenario, winning sympathizers and support.

The campaign for a deadline extension for the Doe Run PAMA had not stopped. On the contrary, in 2005 the company had managed to meet the requirements outlined in Supreme Decree 046 for justifying its request to MEM's Office of Environmental Affairs, including the 'social licence' for the request. To do this, the company held four informative workshops and three public hearings in August and October to present the results of the health risk study and answer participants' questions. But the study reports were not released, and the workshops and public hearings were stacked with the company's supporters and held in an atmosphere of intimidation that did not allow questions or opinions other than those expressed by the company. Nevertheless, the company formally submitted the minutes of those meetings to justify its claim that it had obtained the required 'social licence'.

On 20 December 2005, the company formally submitted to MEM its '... request for an exceptional deadline extension for completing the sulphuric acid plant' called for in the PAMA for the La Oroya metallurgical complex, seeking an extension until the end of 2010 to finish the project. The next six months, until MEM publicly announced its final decision, saw an unprecedented whirlwind of campaigning for and against the PAMA extension. It was clear that two groups were facing off in the city of La Oroya. One national newspaper described it this way:

> La Oroya, a city divided ... the people are split into two groups. Some defend the US company and others reject its presence and its lack of commitment to the population's health .... The first group calls itself the Multi-Sector Committee of the Province of La Oroya and consists of homemakers and workers who claim they are independent and receive no money from the company, although they cannot explain where they get the money to cover the cost of their trips to Lima to lobby for the company ....[13]

The claims of both groups could be heard in Lima. The group now known as the Multi-Sector Committee for the Economic and Historical Relevance of La Oroya, led by a La Oroya councilwoman, marched in Lima in support of the company's request and delivered a petition with 25,000 signatures to MEM on the eve of its first announcement, a pressure tactic that was repeated several times before the ministry announced its final decision.

Similar strategies were used by MOSAO, which tried to pressure MEM with letters, marches and vigils both in Lima and by its allies abroad. Immediately after Doe Run filed its request, the NGOs that were part of MOSAO's technical working group tried to convince the National Mining, Petroleum and Energy Society (SNMPE) to impose a public moral sanction on DRP, an SNMPE member, for failing to honour its commitments. In response, the SNMPE issued a statement saying that its '... member Doe Run Perú, in accordance with the commitment it made to the country by signing the SNMPE Code of Conduct, is obligated and committed to allocating and guaranteeing all economic resources for acquiring, installing and operating the necessary plants and equipment to enable it to implement and comply with all of the obligations outlined in its PAMA'.[14] Although the position was mainly one of wait and see, it was the first time the industry group had publicly distanced itself from an important associate. In fact, in the face of national and international criticism and scrutiny, during the course of the campaign the national mining society changed its strategy from an initial closed defence of the industry to one of promoting corporate social responsibility. This was promoted initially by a group of multinational companies through the Mining, Minerals and Sustainable Development initiative whose concern was to demonstrate that mining is sustainable, even though it involves the extraction of non-renewable resources. As the number of mining conflicts in Peru increased, some of these companies felt obliged to become more actively involved in changing the national mining society's posture from uncompromising defence of the industry to the promotion of ethical codes and standards. With this new approach, companies like DRP represented an embarrassment and a liability for the industry as a whole, leading to behind-the-scenes pressure on the company.

This tarnished the images of the company and the ministry, with the latter being seen as being lax and aligned with company interests. To try to bolster confidence in the strictness of its procedures, the ministry called in experts from the World Bank to evaluate the health risk study and from a local Business School (Universidad ESAN) to evaluate the financial information provided by the company. Based on that information, on 17 February MEM issued a 90-point commentary on Doe Run's extension application, gave the company 30 days to respond to its requests for clarification and required a new time-line of no more than three years for completing the PAMA projects. In general, the points raised by MEM demanded stricter and more precise standards than those proposed by Doe Run. The company was also required to provide more detail about the actions it would take to study human health risks and implement the recommendations of the study that had already been done, as well as do more detailed socio-economic studies and expand and extend the agreement signed with the Ministry of Health to provide health care to the population. The company also had to reformulate the escrow fund contract and agree not to make payments or transfers to third parties or any entity connected with the company that could affect its ability to comply with the PAMA. Finally, the company had to agree to fulfil the commitments it had made at the public hearings.

While the announcement did not paint the best picture for MOSAO and the technical working group, since it indicated that MEM was likely to accede to the company's request for a deadline extension, the unprecedented strictness required by the ministry reflected the pressure that had been brought to bear. Meanwhile, news about the conflict, as well as the health problems and pollution in La Oroya, received prominent play in the national media, which not only provided information, but also took editorial stands on the issue. Several of the country's leading news publications ran stories and publicized the arguments offered by MOSAO and the technical working group.

This was followed again by a counter-campaign favouring the company and attacking some media and NGOs. In addition, the company launched a costly campaign to publicize its technical and business achievements and its 'social responsibility' activities. MOSAO also launched its first paid publicity campaign, with low-cost communications strategies to influence public opinion, such as sandwich boards on Lima's beaches, door-to-door distribution of a mock 'credit card' with a slogan about Doe Run's lack of credibility, and technical information that was shared with the country's more serious media. Amid this atmosphere of tension, the company responded to the points MEM had raised, and the conflict entered the home stretch.

In the days before MEM's final announcement, the political climate in La Oroya grew increasingly violent. Members of the so-called Multi-Sector Committee held another protest march in the streets of Lima to call on the ministry to rule in the company's favour; it then called a provincial strike in La Oroya with the same demand. A group of residents of La Oroya reported that they and family members had received death threats because of their opposition to pollution from the smelter, accusing the mayor of being behind the threats, an accusation he denied.

Finally, on 29 May 2006, MEM approved the extension:

The minister of energy and mines stated that, after the corresponding technical evaluation, a three-year extension had been granted for the company to complete its investment in mitigating the environmental impact of its activities. He explained that the concession was granted on the condition that DRP sign an escrow contract and a letter of guarantee. Other commitments included the construction of three sulphuric acid plants, the reduction of stack and fugitive emissions, meeting air and water quality standards, soil monitoring, health care for children and pregnant women, and the cleanup of houses, streets and critical areas.[15]

Although this response was more or less expected, it was rejected by those who had been involved for a long time in environmental defence. Eliana Ames, coordinator of the MOSAO technical working group, criticized the ministry's decision, saying that it rewarded a company for not having fulfilled its commitments.[16] Days later, MOSAO and the technical working group issued a formal statement against the extension granted by the ministry, saying it was condemning the people of La Oroya to more months of pollution with impunity. Various national and international media headlined their reports, 'Pollution with impunity'. The pressure brought to bear by civil society had an effect, since the ministry had to apply stricter criteria that would have been unthinkable before. MOSAO and the technical working group were aware of this. However, they pressured for the non-extension of the PAMA and, as a last resort, MOSAO and the technical working group presented a petition to overturn the ministerial resolution, knowing that it was unlikely to bear fruit.

Implementation of the decision

Once the decision had been made to extend the environmental management plan under new conditions and with some variations, the issue arose as to its implementation, in view of MEM's track record of lax supervision and steady support for the company. On 28 June, in response to a legal action presented by the Peruvian Environmental Law Society (SPDA) in 2002, the Constitutional Tribunal, roughly equivalent to a Supreme Court, issued a judgement giving the Ministry of Health (MINSA) 30 days to declare a health emergency in La Oroya and implement an emergency health plan based on national air quality standards which would give special attention to children and pregnant mothers. It also called on DRP to reduce its levels of contamination and safeguard the health of the La Oroya population.[17]

On 31 August, in response to a case presented the previous year by the SPDA and two US NGOs the Interamerican Association for Environmental Defense (AIDA) and Earthjustice, and an Argentine NGO, Centre for Human Rights and the Environment, in light of the fact that the State had not heeded the Constitutional Tribunal's sentence requiring protection measures, the Interamerican Human Rights Commission (CIDH) in Washington DC issued a judgement. This called on the Peruvian State to implement urgent precautionary measures to protect the health, integrity and lives of the La Oroya population in general and, in particular, of the 65 claimants, who included more than 30 children and older people suffering from serious respiratory problems.[18]

Despite the signing of an agreement between DRP, MINSA and the regional government of Junín (whose jurisdiction encompassed provincial governments, such as that of La Oroya-Yauli) to undertake a programme to carry out the courts' decisions, on World Environment Day in June 2008, MOSAO announced the results of a study by a local doctor which showed that a large number of babies were being born in La Oroya with 'alarming' levels of lead already in their blood[19] and claimed that 97 per cent of the children of La Oroya suffered from physical and mental disabilities. In response, DRP issued a statement that the level of lead in children's blood in La Oroya had declined 50 per cent between 2004 and 2007, from 32 micrograms per decilitre to 17, a level still above World Health Organization (WHO) allowable limits.[20] For his part, on 3 August the Minister of Health met with the Archbishop of Huancayo to communicate his ministry's commitment to reduce the impact of lead contamination on the children of La Oroya and to announce that MINSA had extended health monitoring of children to those between six months and 16 years. He also declared that he was exploring the possibility of negotiating inspections by foreign lead poisoning and exposure experts.[21]

Nevertheless, the public debate about the effectiveness of the implementation by the State of the Constitutional Tribunal and CIDH rulings and the level of protection and remediation of the health problems continued. The agreement signed between DRP, MINSA and the Junín regional government required that each year the level of lead in a sample of children less than six years old be measured. On 15 October, in a presentation to the Working Group on Clean Production of the National Congress, DRP representatives claimed that in 2004 there were 35 mg of lead in the children of La Oroya and that these had been reduced to 26 mg. However, according to the technical working group and MOSAO, the baseline study made in 2004 was of 100 per cent of the children in La Oroya Antigua, the most contaminated part of the city, whereas the studies in 2005, 2006 and 2008 were based on a sample from five sectors of the city, including several with lower levels of contamination, so that the levels of 31.76, 29.24 and 22.72, respectively, could be explained by sample differences as much as by any real declining trend in blood lead levels.[22]

In August 2006 the National Environmental Council (CONAM) approved an action plan to improve the quality of the air in La Oroya.[23] This plan had been under development since 2002 and involved consultations with various grassroots organizations in La Oroya, including MOSAO; but faced opposition from the company and its allies and enjoyed only limited cooperation from MEM. It called for the design and implementation of an environmental early warning system when air pollution levels exceeded maximum allowable levels.[24] However, when CONAM attempted to install the Air Quality Technical Committee in La Oroya it was prevented from doing so by violent protests by townspeople belonging to an organization that defended the interests of DRP.[25] Environmental journalist Milagros Salazar explained this reaction as follows: 'Amongst the people there is a fear that the use of masks (covering the nose and mouth) during the hours when the contamination is greatest will end up placing the city in quarantine, frighten away visitors and, as a result, affect commercial activity.'[26]

On 11 September, over a thousand people attended a public hearing organized by CONAM as part of the consultation process about a proposed set of measures to protect the population at times of especially acute contamination. A contingency plan had been developed which would involve three levels of alert and generate constant information about the levels of concentration of gases in the air and enable the population to take measures to protect themselves.[27] However, because of both public and covert opposition the contingency plan was not implemented, despite the fact that an official from DIGESA revealed that 'if the contingency plan had been approved, La Oroya would have had to be declared in a state of emergency as many as 11 times in October alone and 15 times in November, owing to the large quantity of sulphur dioxide emissions'.[28] A report by the Air Quality Technical Committee in early 2008 concluded that the metallurgical complex had not met annual emissions standards for lead (50 mg per cubic meter of air) during 2007, even though these standards were well below international levels. The report also concluded that DRP had done little to reduce the risk of exposure of the population to contamination. Nevertheless, the monitoring of air quality had improved because DIGESA had established four air quality-monitoring stations.[29]

In June 2008 MOSAO sent a letter to the Minister of Health requesting that a state of alert be declared in La Oroya by DIGESA due to the environmental contamination, offering that the social organizations of La Oroya would work with the mayor to sensitize the population in favour of the implementation of the contingency plan.[30] At the same time, CONAM publicly requested MINSA to declare a state of alert in La Oroya; the Regional Government of Junín to assign specialists in environmental education to La Oroya; the Municipality of La Oroya to implement the measures contained in the contingency plan; and DRP to meet its environmental commitments.[31] Furthermore, in a meeting organized by the Archbishop of Huancayo, the regional executive secretary of CONAM revealed that during June and July there had been 106 moments when contamination levels exceeded the trigger point for issuing alerts to the population, all of which had been ignored by MINSA. He said that there was an urgent need to implement the contingency plan that had been approved in October of the previous year.[32]

During states of alert the population is urged to shut the windows of their houses and people affected by lung problems or pregnant women to remain indoors.[33] Contamination standards in Peru are based on monthly averages, not the number or level of peak events. Thus, any particular month might be considered to meet acceptable standards, even though there may have been days with high levels of contamination.[34] The mean annual concentration levels of sulphur dioxide emissions exceed WHO acceptable levels by a factor of two or three.[35]

On 13 August record sulphur dioxide contamination levels were registered in La Oroya at the Sindicato monitoring station, the closest to the smelter, where levels exceeded 27,000 mg per cubic meter of air. DIGESA declared a state of emergency from 9.15am to 12.45pm and asked the president of the La Oroya Provincial Civil Defense Committee and the head of the National Civil Defense Institute in Junín to implement the actions required by the contingency plan. Since Peruvian air quality standards permit up to 364 mg per cubic meter, this level was 74 times above the allowable maximum. Previously, on 4 August the same monitoring station had reached 22,000 mg per cubic meter and on 21 July 17,000 mg. During the first fortnight of August, 63 alerts were issued: a state of emergency was declared on 12 occasions; contamination was declared to be at dangerous levels on 31 occasions; and on 20 occasions caution was advised. States of alert had only been declared since the beginning of the month.[36]

For its part, DRP claimed that particle emissions had been reduced by 74 per cent, lead in the air by 61.7 per cent and effluents in the Mantaro River by 89 per cent since 1997.[37] They also claimed to be reinvesting all their profits in environmental measures and that since 1999 they had been carrying out a programme of voluntary plant shutdowns at the moments when the climatic conditions impeded the gases' rapid dispersion.[38] In September DIGESA changed its methodology for measuring the air quality at its four monitoring stations to hourly averages, which, as the natural resources manager in the Junín regional government pointed out, meant that DIGESA's equipment would not reveal the peak levels reached during each day.[39] On 30 September DRP inaugurated a new sulphuric acid plant, it's second, at a cost of $50 million. A third and final sulphuric acid plant was scheduled for October 2009, by which time DRP said that they would have invested $245 million in measures to reduce contamination, versus the $107.5 million agreed upon when they bought the plant in 1997, and sulphur dioxide emission levels would have been reduced to acceptable levels.[40]

Along the way DRP was involved in several skirmishes with the international environmental community. In August 2006 DRP was granted ISO 14001 certification by TUV CERT (TÜV Rheinland Industrie Service GmbH). This certified that the environmental management system complied with the norms of ISO 14001 which supposedly provided the company with the necessary elements to control the impacts of its activities.[41] The company described the attainment of ISO 14001 certification as 'an important milestone with reference to our compliance with our commitments with our communities, our employees and the environment' and a 'recognized symbol of a company's dedication to superior quality, client satisfaction and continuous improvements'.[42] However, on 11 March 2008, the evaluators of the German firm TÜV Rheinland withdrew DRP's ISO 14001 certification.[43] This was apparently due to pressure from some international environmental organizations: representatives from the environmental organizations AIDA and Earthjustice stated that TÜV Rheinland was acting responsibly by taking this action.[44]

In September 2006, the Blacksmith Institute included La Oroya on a list of the ten most contaminated places on earth and included it again on its 2007 list.[45] However, in May 2008 the Institute issued a report on the situation in La Oroya that indicated that no more measures were needed than those already being implemented by the company in order to reduce contamination to acceptable levels. Anna Cederstav of AIDA argued that the report's authors had based their conclusions on conversations with company and government officials only: 'The Blacksmith report is a summary of information presented by DRP that does not evaluate the accuracy of the company's claims, ignores government and company monitoring data that show DRP's failure to comply with air quality standards nor does it discuss the relevance of the numerous recommendations contained in resolutions and previous studies by organizations and authorities other than the company'.[46] Nonetheless, despite its own report, in September the Blacksmith Institute included La Oroya in its list once again and was joined by Graffiti, which considered La Oroya to be amongst the five most contaminated places on earth, and the Green Cross in Switzerland, which considered it to be amongst the ten most contaminated.[47]

Over this same period, MOSAO and its allies undertook three campaigns around the situation in La Oroya. In June 2007 an inter-faith religious delegation led by Mons. Pedro Barreto, SJ, Archbishop of Huancayo, and including a prominent member of the Jewish community, travelled to the US to seek a meeting with Ira Rennert, owner of the Renco Group, chairman of the Fifth Avenue Synagogue in Manhattan and described by Elie Wiesel as 'a deeply, deeply religious man' and by Hillary Clinton as 'the biggest polluter in America'.[48] However, when the religious delegation met with DRP in Lima on 8 June, they learned that DRP was no longer owned by Doe Run Resources and were refused meetings with the former mother company in Missouri and with Ira Rennert in New York.[49]

In October 2007 two US nuns initiated a lawsuit in St. Louis, Missouri, against the Renco Group on behalf of 137 Peruvian children for negligence in not controlling the emissions of toxic substances from its smelter in La Oroya. The Renco Group managed to have the venue changed on two occasions to the federal court, where procedures are much slower, but on 6 August 2008, the federal judge in St. Louis approved the plaintiff's request to withdraw the case from the federal court and resubmit it to a local court in the State of Missouri where it is still under consideration.[50]

On World Environment Day in June 2008, a US organization called Legacy 13 launched the 'Save La Oroya' campaign. This involved the dissemination of three short documentaries, a photo exhibition and the distribution of posters and bookmarks. The campaign was undertaken in Peru and the US and was focused on Ira Rennert, the sole owner of the Renco Group, emphasizing that, as the 57th richest person in the US and the 307th richest person on the planet with a net worth of \$6 billion and as the recent purchaser of two condominiums on Park Avenue, New York, for more than \$60 million, he could well afford to invest in measures to resolve the health and environmental problems in La Oroya.[51]

All three campaigns focused their activities in the US because of the lack of leverage over possible targets in Peru and the weaknesses that had developed in MOSAO and the technical working group. During the months after MEM's decision to extend the dates for the completion of DRP's PAMA, the level of activities of both MOSAO and the technical working group declined. In early 2007 the coordinator and two key members of the working group left to work as advisors to a member of Congress. The SPDA participant ceased to attend meetings as other issues assumed priority in his organization and then the Joining Hands Network's coordinator was reassigned to the US. A new parish priest in La Oroya decided to withdraw the Catholic Church's support from MOSAO and, as a result, the Catholic Church's social action committee also withdrew from the working group and the Church's activism became focused on the activities of the Revive Mantaro Project based in Huancayo. This meant that during 2007 some of the working group's most experienced and active participants left. They were replaced by relatively inexperienced persons who had not participated in the PAMA extension campaign, and were thus less knowledgeable and motivated. This was particularly the case with the coordinators from the NGO Labor, which received funding from Oxfam for this purpose. The frequency of meetings, the participation at the meetings and the quality of the discussions all declined. Conflicts also occurred between the Joining Hands Network's information officer and other members of the working group in the second half of 2007, as the former became impatient with the latter's lack of initiative and the latter with the former's lack of coordination and consultation. This ended with the termination of his contract with Joining Hands Network and the latter's distancing from the working group.[52]

At the same time, a parallel process was occurring in MOSAO. MOSAO was not included in the list of organizations designated as members of the municipality's environmental monitoring commission, which was the main channel for community supervision and control over the implementation of the activities included in the PAMA extension decision, although a person linked to MOSAO was eventually incorporated.[53] Without the support and orientation from a weakened working group the level of activities of MOSAO also fell. The institutions involved in both the working group and MOSAO diverted their attention to other priorities and key allies, such as Red Muqui, the national network of NGOs working on mining issues, and the Catholic Church's CEAS, lowered the level of their interest and support.[54]

These weaknesses were evidenced in two main areas. The opportunities for civil society monitoring of the implementation of the PAMA extension decision were centred in the municipal environmental commission. However, the civil society participants had no training or experience with the technical aspects of environmental monitoring and received little support from the technical working group which itself was in need of reinforcement from environmental specialists. In the face of civil society's lack of effective participation in the commission, the representatives from the local state university and the regional government also became less involved and the state participants were content to uncritically accept the information and reports submitted by the company.[55]

In their relations with their international allies the working group and MOSAO lacked clarity of vision about the role and objectives of possible campaigns after the PAMA extension decision. After the relative failure of the visit of the delegation of religious leaders to the US, which had been organized by the Archbishop of Huancayo and the Joining Hands Network's coordinator, neither MOSAO nor the working group had the capacity to take advantage of the network of allies in the US built up in previous years. It is significant that both the lawsuit against the Renco Group in St. Louis and the 'Save La Oroya' campaign aimed at Ira Rennert were initiatives taken by Northern allies who experienced frustration at the lack of direction and guidance from MOSAO or the working group. For its part, Oxfam directed its attention to other priorities and reduced the frequency of its meetings with the working group. At a meeting of the Oxfam America global extractive industries team leader with the working group early in 2008 to define the support that Oxfam could provide in the North, the lack of ideas and initiatives was evident. Nevertheless, it was hoped that the level of initiative and activity of both MOSAO and the working group – and their respective member organizations – would increase in the course of 2009 as the PAMA completion date approached.[56]

What the campaign achieved

Through this case study we attempt to explain how the impacts of contamination by DRP on the health of the inhabitants of La Oroya became part of the agenda of public discussion after being ignored for five decades and what caused the Peruvian Government to approve a final extension to the company's environmental management plan subject to unprecedented stringent conditions after acceding to DRP's previous requests for delays and modifications and exercising only moderate supervision.

The campaign succeeded in achieving public recognition and acceptance of the fact that a major health problem existed in La Oroya and that it was caused by the accumulated and ongoing pollution from DRP's refining and smelter complex. Although the city's inhabitants had suspected that the fumes from the complex were affecting their health there was almost a taboo on public discussion because it was not clear whether the problem could be addressed without forcing the closure of the plant with the subsequent loss of jobs and incomes. For its part, the company was also reluctant to accept the existence of a health issue and attempted to attribute it to other causes. Thus, the recognition of the problem and its causes was a victory in itself.

At the same time, the campaign managed to achieve a change in national and international public opinion from support and/or neutrality towards a company initially perceived as socially responsible (in comparison with the previous owners) to scepticism and/or criticism as the activities of the Renco Group and its owner in the US became more widely known and experience was gained with the company's response to criticism in Peru. The general public tends to give the benefit of the doubt to major actors in the community and to be suspicious of activists' criticisms unless they are well supported and argued and the target of criticism behaves in ways that confirm the accusations. However, in La Oroya the task was more difficult because of the dependence on the company as a source of jobs and income, its local alliances and its control over the local media. Nevertheless, after the Ministry's decision on the PAMA extension and the demonstration that the company could afford the investments called for by MOSAO to reduce contamination, support for the company waned, though this did not translate into increased support for or recognition of MOSAO.

A more tangible achievement was the Government's decision to extend the period for the implementation of the environmental management plan for a lesser period than that requested and subject to conditions of unprecedented strictness and with the likely result that pollution would be reduced to legally permissible levels. Although this was an important achievement, the campaign had publicly advocated for the denial of the extension and, hence, this was not necessarily perceived as a victory for MOSAO and its allies.

Other tangible achievements were the decisions of the Peruvian Constitutional Tribunal and the Interamerican Human Rights Commission to demand that the Ministry of Health undertake specific measures to address the health impacts of DRP's contamination in La Oroya. This involved additional sectors of the State – the Ministry of Health, the environmental agency CONAM (now the Ministry of the Environment) and the Junín regional government – that were less closely aligned with the company in remedying the situation in the city.

Subsequent achievements attributed to the campaign include the decision of the Peruvian State Ombudswoman appointed by Congress in 2006 to become more involved in mining issues and their impacts on citizens' rights; the creation by CONAM of an early warning system and emergency action plan when air pollution exceeds acceptable limits; changes in the location of the air quality monitoring stations; and a series of changes in the policies and practices of the regional government, MEM and MINSA.[57] For MOSAO's national and international allies these 'flow-on' effects were significant because an important reason for their involvement in La Oroya was to use this as an emblematic case demonstrating the consequences of low environmental standards and lax enforcement and the need to change government and industry policies and practices. There was always an underlying tension between MOSAO, which was focused entirely on resolving the problems in La Oroya, and its allies who sought broader changes applicable to a much larger number of cases and circumstances.

Factors contributing to success

One factor in the campaign's success was the production and dissemination of studies demonstrating the existence of a public health crisis and its source in the contamination generated by DRP's metallurgical complex. While the early studies by the UNES Consortium were criticized, their results were rapidly confirmed by studies carried out by others, especially international institutions, such as the Center for Disease Control, AIDA and the School of Public Health at the University of St. Louis. These not only undermined the arguments of the company and the ministry but also stimulated national and international interest and concern. Similarly, the results of studies undertaken by the campaign, which demonstrated the company's financial capacity to undertake the investments needed to reduce pollution, were corroborated by those commissioned by the ministry, and also served to undermine the company's argument that it would be forced to cease operations if it were obliged to make the investments being asked of it.

Another reason for success was the creation of MOSAO, a coalition of community organizations in La Oroya representing local interests and working to have the environmental plan fully implemented, and the technical working group of local and national NGOs providing advice and support. The strategic alliance between these two institutions was vital for counteracting the company's claim that the 'community' (supposedly represented by the municipality and the trade union) was unified in its support for the request for an extension and its argument that the NGOs were meddling in community matters and could not speak in the name of its citizens. Though often muted, MOSAO represented a legitimate community voice throughout the campaign. On the other hand, MOSAO's technical and advocacy capacities were severely limited. It could not have commissioned, undertaken or distributed the studies without the technical working group's support; it could not have organized an effective campaign on its own; it could not have lobbied the ministry and national media without the technical working group's accompaniment; and the technical working group was crucial for developing and maintaining the international alliances.

In a company-dominated town, where intimidation was a frequently used tactic, the campaign could not have survived or flourished without the support of international allies, such as Oxfam and the Catholic and Presbyterian Churches, that not only provided financial support but also connections to solidarity groups in the company's home town in the US and elsewhere and to the international media. These contacts not only served to put the company on the defensive in its home base but also generated an important 'echo' in the media in Peru, legitimizing the campaign and its claims.

Given that the company exercised an important influence in MEM through former company employees working in the ministry and former government functionaries working in the company, as mentioned (see the section 'Establishing a coalition'), another factor in the campaign's success was the ability of the technical working group to develop informal alliances with the Director of Mining, who did not form part of the DRP clique, and with key members of congress. This enabled them to transmit the information, conclusions and recommendations of their studies to key decision makers and provide them with credible, alternative proposals to those of the company and its allies. This encouraged ministry officials to persist in their efforts to craft a PAMA extension proposal that would oblige the company to honour its commitments.

Lawsuits against the Ministry of Health, channelled both through the country's cumbersome legal system and the Inter-American Human Rights Court, were successful both in a legal sense and also in legitimizing the campaign's claims that a health problem existed. In a country with a long tradition of passing laws and regulations that are never implemented, decisions by both the nation's highest court and the CIDH requiring the Ministry of Health, in collaboration with the company and other sectors of the state, to undertake and report on specific measures were significant achievements. They required well-documented research, skilled and dedicated local lawyers (such as those in the SPDA) and international human rights allies (such as CIEL and Earth Justice) experienced in developing and presenting cases to the CIDH.

There were also contextual factors that contributed to the campaign's success. In the 1990s communities in the Andes had begun to react to the aggressive expansion of mining activities on their lands and territories, leading to the creation of a national organization (CONACAMI), whose mobilizations and protests helped place the issue of mining and its social and environmental impacts on the agenda of public debate. In the early years of the La Oroya campaign, CONACAMI was active in stimulating the creation of the Environmental Delegates Association (ADA) and involving surrounding peasant communities in the campaign and some of the key NGOs in the campaign had also supported the foundation of CONACAMI (SPDA, CooperAcción, Labor, ECO-ANDES and Oxfam). CONACAMI was always a point of reference for MOSAO, even though there was no formal alliance between them, and for the relatively small group of national NGOs working on mining issues that considered the DRP case to be emblematic.

The campaign also coincided with the final years of President Fujimori's authoritarian government. Levels of political violence were declining and with the transitional government of President Paniagua and the democratically-elected Toledo Government at the beginning of the century there was suddenly greater political space for organization and expression, encouraging the creation of social movements around issues of political, social and economic injustice. Thus, even in a town as dominated by fear as La Oroya, there was a new sense of freedom and that ancient wrongs could finally be addressed.

This period was also one of increasing concern about environmental issues in the world at large and in Peru in particular. The country's first environmental code had been passed in 1990 and, though subsequently weakened, expressed and encouraged concerns about environmental issues. The country's environmental movement began to emerge in the 1990s as new NGOs were formed and international environmental NGOs opened offices and programmes in the country and established alliances with local organizations and activists. The private sector also started to endorse a corporate social responsibility discourse that, in the case of mining, was led by a group of multinationals through the Mining, Minerals and Sustainable Development initiative. Some companies in Peru were actively involved in the promotion of business ethics and better standards in the industry, placing pressure on DRP from within the industry.

Finally, in a national context of conflicts between mining companies and communities, campaigns about particular cases and public debates about the role of mining in society, public opinion gradually shifted from resigned inevitability that Peru would always be dependent on mining for its economic growth and development and that mining's social and environmental impacts were unavoidable to a more critical appraisal of the industry's standards and behaviour and of the State's responsibilities and actions in defence of the public interest. This shift opened up spaces for MOSAO and its allies to have their voices heard in the media, required the company and its allies to defend and justify their positions and began to create a climate of opinion more favourable towards government regulation and control.

In terms of the four strategies that, according to Keck and Sikkink, are employed in transnational advocacy (information politics, symbolic politics, leverage politics and accountability politics),[58] the campaign used *information politics* to skilfully generate and employ information about the health impacts of the smelter in order to place the issue on the public agenda and pressure MEM to supervise the company's implementation of its environmental programme, as well as information about the company's financial situation so that MEM could feel justified in requiring additional investments and financial guarantees.

At least two media allies, one based in the US and the other in Argentina, received awards for their moving accounts of the situation of children and families in La Oroya. Photos and videos of deformed animals and disabled children, stories of sickness and deaths at an early age and accounts of burning eyes and hacking coughs were all employed as forms of *symbolic politics* to draw attention to the situation in the city and influence national and international public opinion.

Likewise, *leverage politics* were employed to involve powerful external actors, like the Catholic and Presbyterian Churches, the international media and national and international courts, in the defence of the rights of a beleaguered MOSAO and an intimidated local population. However, the use of *accountability politics* to require the sole owner of DRP in the US to apply in La Oroya the ethical principles espoused as Chair of New York's leading orthodox synagogue and funder of a centre for the study of ethics were unsuccessful.

What was not achieved

When the La Oroya smelter complex was sold to DRP, an environmental management plan, which was intended to reduce ongoing contamination by the plant to acceptable levels, was negotiated by MEM with the new owners. During almost ten years, however, the levels of contamination actually *increased*, as DRP intensified production and delayed the investments aimed at reducing pollution. The responsibility for cleaning up the accumulated contamination resulting from some 80 years of operation prior to privatization was assumed by the state company Centromin and subsequently transferred to another state company, Activos Mineros, which delayed taking action with the argument that it would not make sense to start cleaning up contamination accumulated from the past until DRP had ongoing contamination under control. Since this is not expected to occur until the end of 2009 there will still be ongoing impacts on the health of the population from accumulated heavy metals and the respective responsibilities of DRP and Activos Mineros will need to be defined. Some of those involved in the campaign have also expressed doubts that the quality of the air in La Oroya will reach minimum international standards even after DRP has completed its environmental management plan because of what they perceive as high official permissible limits for contamination in Peru.[59]

In the course of the research sponsored by the campaign it became clear that contamination is not confined to the city of La Oroya and its immediate environment. The study carried out by the University of St. Louis selected the city of Concepción in the Mantaro River valley as a control group on the assumption that it was far enough away to have what could be considered 'normal' levels of contamination and thus serve as a point of comparison. However, to their surprise the researchers discovered that levels of contamination were not significantly lower in Concepción, thus indicating that the fumes from the plant were generating impacts over a much wider area than originally believed.[60] Furthermore, subsequent studies sponsored by the Revive Mantaro Project, have recorded high levels of contamination in the region's rivers, suggesting that, even if air pollution is eventually brought under control in La Oroya, there will be ongoing and accumulated contamination of water in most of the Mantaro River basin, with its associated health impacts, from past and currently active mining operations throughout the region.[61]

Although steps are now being taken to remedy the health problems in La Oroya resulting from contamination, especially from high lead levels in the blood of children, this has been only in response to legal decisions, which have their own limitations. It is claimed that the Ministry of Health is not fully carrying out the measures required by the Constitutional Tribunal and that, while it is responding more fully to those of the Interamerican Human Rights Commission, these only apply to the 65 claimants in the suit. The measures thus far are confined to children from 0 to 6 years of age and do not address the health problems of those with high lead blood levels from other age groups.[62] This may reflect a reluctance of the ministry to devote the necessary resources in the face of competing priorities, the weakness of the Judiciary relative to the Executive within the Peruvian state and the need for monitoring and vigilance to ensure that decisions are actually carried out.

A number of those interviewed stressed the lack of training and technical expertise within civil society and even within the ministry. Those participating in the environmental monitoring mechanisms are dependent on the information and interpretations provided by company representatives and lack the technical capacity and access to independent expertise needed to enable them to form their own judgements. This is related to the perception that, since the end of the campaign, there has been a sharp fall-off in the level of activity of the advocacy coalition.[63] This is not an uncommon experience in advocacy campaigns. The most exciting and glamorous periods of such campaigns are those prior to the making of key decisions by campaign targets, after which activity levels fall. However, if new campaigns and targets are not defined or mechanisms established for monitoring the carrying-out of the decisions made, the campaign coalition may gradually decline and unravel and the apparent gains made may be lost through weak or no implementation. This seems to be a danger in La Oroya.

Civil society organizations need to be prepared for the consequences of long and intense campaigns which can lead to organizational over extension and individual 'burn out'. The skills learned and the experiences gained during the PAMA extension campaign were not capitalized by the organizations participating in the technical working group and were inadequately transferred to MOSAO and its member organizations, so that when staff left a vacuum was generated and capacities weakened.

In terms of Keck and Sikkink's five stages in transnational advocacy campaigns,[64] the campaign in La Oroya certainly managed to place health issues, DRP's failure to comply with its environmental management plan and lax government supervision on the national political agenda; the mining industry no longer claims that its activities automatically produce development and it has felt obliged to assume a corporate social responsibility discourse; the campaign certainly achieved changes in State procedures for modifying and supervising PAMAs, including the restructuring of OSINERGMIN as an independent monitor of DRP's compliance, and new regulations governing citizen participation and consultation on mining matters, including environmental monitoring; it achieved changes not only in policies directly affecting the situation in La Oroya but also in the general environmental law, requiring financial guarantees and environmental standards; but few changes in the overall behaviour of the company or the State, especially MEM.

Legitimacy

Whether latent or explicit, in transnational advocacy campaigns there is always the issue of the legitimacy of those involved in the campaign alliance to be advocating for change in specific contexts. In reaction to Oxfam's support for CONACAMI and a local referendum in the town of Tambogrande on Peru's north coast, in which the inhabitants voted overwhelmingly against a proposed open pit mine, the government and mining industry undertook a media campaign aimed at discrediting Oxfam by claiming that it was supporting violence, was anti-mining and was opposed to the country's development. This campaign questioned Oxfam's right to 'interfere' in the country's internal affairs and engage in 'politics', when its supposed mandate was to reduce poverty and provide humanitarian aid, and was particularly virulent in La Oroya, where the local media continuously questioned the agency's legitimacy and motives in an evident attempt to persuade Oxfam to withdraw its support for the technical working group and MOSAO and for these to distance themselves from Oxfam. While this attempt to question the agency's legitimacy probably had some effect in local and national public opinion it had little impact on the campaign alliance. However when Mons. Barreto was appointed Archbishop of Huancayo (with jurisdiction over La Oroya) for some months he maintained his distance from both Oxfam and the technical working group because of the company's media campaign. It was only after he had the opportunity to get to know Oxfam on a visit to the US that he revised his view of its role and legitimacy.

Within La Oroya itself, the formation of MOSAO and its separation from the technical working group was an important step towards legitimizing the campaign. MOSAO was a coalition of local community organizations and thus could legitimately pretend to represent the interests and concerns of wide segments of the community and speak in their name. The technical working group did not present itself as representing the local community but as a group of advisory and support organizations. Through the alliance between MOSAO and the technical working group the latter could claim that it had been invited to help and advise local institutions and therefore had a legitimate presence in the town. The continuous and active involvement of MOSAO as a full member of the alliance gave the campaign legitimacy and a local face and voice. The involvement of the Catholic and Presbyterian Churches, especially during the final year of the campaign leading up to the ministry's decision on the extension of the PAMA, allowed Oxfam to reduce its visibility and the campaign to acquire some of the legitimacy attached to religious organizations. This was reinforced by the presence of both churches in the city of St. Louis and the town of Herculaneum, where DRP had its headquarters and where the local community had suffered similar impacts to those in La Oroya. In this way, both international and local members of the alliance contributed legitimacy to the campaign as a whole and to each other. The international actors could legitimately be involved because they were supporting genuine representatives of the La Oroya community. For their part, the latter found their legitimacy as representatives reinforced by the recognition received from respected international organizations.

Participation and democracy

The extremely hostile atmosphere in La Oroya meant that the activists in MOSAO were constantly subjected to threats and intimidation and attempts to create divisions or separate them from their advisors in the technical working group or their international allies. Nevertheless, the very fact that MOSAO was a relatively weak and embattled organization meant that it was very dependent upon its advisors and allies who, in turn, were well aware of the dangers and made great efforts to recognize and respect MOSAO's role and prerogatives in the alliance. It is significant that the tensions within the alliance between MOSAO and the technical working group have been greater in recent years when the local threats and intimidation have been fewer.

The relatively smooth working relationships within the alliance were potentially threatened when the recently appointed Archbishop of Huancayo became interested in the situation in La Oroya. Influenced in part by the local media, he was initially suspicious of both the technical working group and Oxfam, perceiving them as being 'politically' motivated, and sought to establish an independent strategy focused on the Mantaro River valley, of which La Oroya formed a part. He sponsored a dialogue process in the city of Huancayo and created a church-affiliated NGO called Revive Mantaro Project with the aim of addressing the environmental issues of the valley as a whole. These potentially divisive moves were attenuated by the support received from Oxfam in connecting the Archbishop with the Catholic Bishops' Conference and important multilateral donors in the US and by the work of the Joining Hands Network's representative in Peru in brokering the relationship between the Archbishop and the technical working group and arranging for the School of Public Health of the Jesuit-run St. Louis University to undertake the study of heavy metals in the blood of La Oroya's inhabitants. These interventions converted a potentially divisive strategy into a complementary one, strengthening all parties and reinforcing the campaign.

Nevertheless, there were tensions between the components of the alliance. While MOSAO and the technical working group were appreciative of Oxfam's financial support and accompaniment and for the fact that it stuck by them despite receiving attacks in the media, they also felt that it could have and should have done more to influence DRP and its owner in the US. At one point, Oxfam representatives from the US talked about the potential of a class action suit in the US without any more being heard; at another point there was talk of involving the School of Public Health at Harvard University in addressing the health problems in La Oroya; there were also some discussions and initial research into the possibility of applying pressure through Doe Run's clients in the US; and there was a proposal to influence Doe Run's owner through contacts in the Jewish community in the US. None of these initiatives bore fruit and the reasons for their abandonment were never made clear to the campaign participants in Peru, creating a vague feeling of frustration at the apparent lack of commitment or capacity of Oxfam America in its home country.

Another support group for the campaign in the US, Friends of La Oroya, had moments of frustration with MOSAO and the technical working group. They felt that more could be done to mobilize public opinion in the US to influence DRP's owner. Together with Oxfam, they had generated interest and actions in the US media and organized reciprocal visits between members of the Herculaneum and La Oroya communities. They looked for specific suggestions from MOSAO and the technical working group about the sorts of campaigns they would like to see in the US and how the campaign messages should be framed and felt that they could not and should not launch initiatives without clear guidance from MOSAO. For their part, the members of MOSAO and the technical working group did not understand what information and directives their allies in the US needed and were unfamiliar with the campaign environment in the US and its potential and limitations. These difficulties were accentuated after the departure of Joining Hands Network's representative who had been acting as an intercultural broker.

These difficulties and tensions undermined the campaign's potential impact and underlined the importance of intercultural brokers in transnational advocacy campaigns that involve alliances stretching from the local to the global. When agencies like Oxfam hire exclusively local staff in their regional offices they acquire depth in local knowledge and understanding, but unless these staff members are also given the opportunity to gain knowledge and understanding of the organization's home base and country of origin some of the potential synergies from transnational cooperation may be lost. To some, having home office staff become familiar with regional conditions and regional staff and partners familiar with the home office and country may seem like 'illustrated tourism', but it may be a sound investment where transnational advocacy is involved.

At the time of writing, the situation in La Oroya had gained visibility and generated concern amongst public opinion both within Peru and in the US, which in itself was a major achievement. A network of international allies had been developed and they were willing and able to undertake campaigns within the US on behalf of their Peruvian allies. However, the steadfast opposition of the Renco Group to acknowledging their existence and the lack of clear points of leverage seemed to limit the possibility for achieving change from within the US. In Peru, there seemed to be more potential leverage points with greater supervision of DRP's compliance with its legal obligations by OSINERGMIN; a municipal environmental commission responsible for citizen monitoring that could potentially be strengthened; a regional government that was sensitive to environmental issues; and a newly created environmental ministry. However, MOSAO and the technical working group were in relative disarray and with limited capacity either to take advantage of these opportunities or of the goodwill of its allies overseas. This posed a challenge to the transnational coalition both to build on the capacities developed during the PAMA extension campaign and provide mutual support in order to be able to capitalize on the opportunities available to ensure the achievement of changes in the health and livelihood of the La Oroya population, which represented the 'bottom line' of the campaign.

Overall, in terms of Jordan and van Tuijl's four types of transnational NGO campaigns,[65] the La Oroya campaign could be classified as a cooperative one, where there was a high level of political responsibility toward the most vulnerable members of the alliance. However, there were also elements of a concurrent campaign, where there is coinciding representation of different but compatible objectives, in the relations between the original campaign alliance and Revive Mantaro Project.

One reason that the extractive industries staff in Oxfam America's home office did not place a high priority on the DRP campaign was that they were geared to influencing the international financial institutions and US Government based in Washington DC as their principal contribution to transnational advocacy. In this particular case, DRP did not have any relations with the international financial institutions and, as part of a group essentially owned by one person, it was singularly shielded from most of the pressure points (retail consumers, shareholders' meetings, stock exchanges) where advocacy may be exercised. This limited the opportunities for employment of the 'boomerang' strategy.

Nevertheless, the strategy was employed to some extent through reports on or reproductions of the stories in the international media to produce an 'echo' in the national media in Peru. The fact that the international media was reporting on the situation in La Oroya, especially the media in the company's home office in Missouri, served both as an encouragement to the embattled and intimidated activists in La Oroya and probably as a form of restraint on the actions that the company and its allies were prepared to undertake.

Accuracy of public messaging

While the campaign managed to paint Doe Run both in the US and Peru as a mining industry 'renegade' or 'black sheep', because of its ruthless corporate behaviour and the extraordinarily lavish expenditures of its owner, neither DRP nor the Renco Group were major political or economic actors in the US, whereas in Peru DRP was one of the country's major exporters and exercised considerable political influence in the Executive and Congress and even in the US Embassy. This meant that public messaging about the company and its activities could be more aggressive outside of Peru but had to be much more cautious within it.

Thus, aggressively critical articles, stories and messages originating from outside the country could be reproduced and distributed within Peru without fear of reprisals against local activists whereas those produced locally were much more careful and restrained. This situation meant that stories and articles produced for a foreign or international audience also had a strong impact on a secondary audience when reproduced and distributed in Peru. Nevertheless, the producers of materials for international media and audiences were encouraged to bear in mind that in all probability their eventual and perhaps most important audience would be in Peru and that this – and the possible repercussions – needed to be borne in mind. This constraint was especially relevant for Oxfam America's web page, which while primarily intended for a US audience, could be and was accessed by readers from government and industry in Peru.

The advocacy around the La Oroya case took place in a situation where there was a solid alliance between the mining industry and the national government and considerable hostility towards those who were critical of the industry and its role. This was especially so in the case of DRP, which had formed an alliance with the local municipality and trade union, controlled the local media and political authorities and was not above the use of violence and intimidation. In this context, Oxfam, as one of the principal targets of the industry and government media attack campaign, to some degree acted as a 'lightening rod', deflecting attacks and criticisms that might otherwise have been directed at its more vulnerable local allies, although this was resented as an 'unnecessary' cost by some members of the Oxfam family.

Likewise, the Presbyterian and Catholic Church organizations involved in the campaign not only loaned their legitimacy but also, together with the other elements of international solidarity, provided moral and psychological support to MOSAO and the technical working group and helped defend and maintain the advocacy space, limited in La Oroya but greater at the national level, which allowed the campaign to develop and achieve its objectives.

Notes

1 Water in the province of Yauli comes from the Mantaro, Yauli and Andaychagua rivers, into which various mining operations discharge effluents (UNES Consortium (2002) *Situación Ambiental del Aire, Aguas y Suelos en la Provincia de Yauli – La Oroya* (Lima: UNES Consortium).
2 D. Kruijt and M. Vellinga (1979) *Labor Relations and Multinational Corporations: The Cerro de Pasco Corporation in Perú (1902–1974)* (Amsterdam: Van Gorcum), p. 39.
3 R. Pajuelo (2005) *Medioambiente y Salud en La Oroya* (Lima: CooperAcción), p. 22.
4 S. Charpentier and J. Hidalgo (1999) *Políticas Ambientales en el Perú* (Lima: Agenda Perú), p. 26.
5 J. Aste (2005) *La Oroya: Responsabilidad Socioambiental de Doe Run Perú: Estudio Analítico del PAMA* (Lima: ECO-ANDES).
6 Interview with Maribel Chávez, NGO CooperAcción, La Oroya, 15 January 2005.
7 'In 2001, Doe Run released a study based on samples taken from 5,062 children and adults. The results of the study, which took samples from approximately 10 per cent of the entire population of La Oroya, essentially confirmed

the early findings of the studies by the Consortium and DIGESA: lead pollution levels in La Oroya exceeded internationally permitted limits, particularly affecting children living in La Oroya Antigua.' (R. Pajuelo (2005) *Medioambiente y Salud en La Oroya*, p. 55).

8   A. Cederstav and A. Barandiarán (2002) *La Oroya Cannot Wait: Analysis of the Environmental Pollution Caused by the Metallurgic Complex and their Health Impacts* (Lima: SPDA and AIDA); see also: R. Pajuelo (2005) *Medioambiente y Salud en La Oroya*, p. 55.
9   A. Cederstav and A. Barandiarán (2002) *La Oroya Cannot Wait: Analysis of the Environmental Pollution Caused by the Metallurgic Complex and their Health Impacts*.
10 Among the complementary actions, an international audit of the company was ordered, along with ongoing monitoring of its environmental commitments. In May 2003, the environmental consulting firms SVS Ingenieros S.A. and Golder Associates carried out an environmental assessment at the La Oroya smelter and made a number of detailed recommendations for further studies and monitoring and mitigation activities that the company should undertake. (J. Quijandría Salmón (2004) *Presentación del Programa de Adecuación y Manejo Ambienta (PAMA) de la Fundición de La Oroya*) (Lima: Ministry of Energy and Mines). In 2003, MEM fined the company for not submitting information for monitoring of the PAMA; the same occurred in 2004 (J. Aste (2005) *La Oroya: Responsabilidad Socioambiental de Doe Run Perú: Estudio Analítico del PAMA*).
11 *El Comercio*, 4 March 2006.
12 MEM press release, Lima, 26 November 2004.
13 *La República*, 20 February 2006.
14 CooperAcción (2006) *Informe de Conflictos Mineros: Los Casos de Majaz, Las Bambas, Tintaya y La Oroya* (Lima: CooperAcción).
15 *El Comercio* and *Perú 21*, 30 May 2006.
16 *El Comercio* and *Perú 21*, 30 May 2006.
17 'Intervienen a favor de pobladores de La Oroya', *El Comercio*, 29 June 2006.
18 E. Cruz, 'CIDH pide al Estado proteger a La Oroya ante contaminación causada por Doe Run', *La República*, 6 Sept 2007.
19 *Actualidad Minera del Perú*, June, 2008, p. 12.
20 'Doe Run asegura que plomo en sangre de niños de La Oroya bajó 50 por ciento', *Terra*, 11 June 2008.
21 'Reevaluarán a afectados por plomo', *El Comercio*, 4 August 2008; 'Evaluarán la contaminación', *El Peruano*, 4 August 2008; 'Evalúan la contaminación por minería', *Perú21*, 4 August 2008; and 'Peru's health minister and clergyman talk intervention and cleanup of contamination from Doe Run smelter', *Andean Air Mail and Peruvian Times*, 5 August 2008.
22 'Disminuye nivel de plomo en sangre de niños de La Oroya, según Doe Run', *Andina*, 16 October 2008; 'Doe Run Perú oculta información sobre plomo en la sangre de los niños', *Con Nuestro Perú*, 18 October 2008; and 'Mesa por la salud de La Oroya: Doe Run oculta información al afirmar que niveles de plomo en niños disminuyeron', *Ideeleradio*, 18 October 2008.
23 CONAM communiqué, 29 August 2006.
24 'Junín: Comité vigilará reducción de plomo en sangre de los niños', *CPN Radio*, 16 August 2006 (http://www.cpnradio.com.pe/html/2006/08/16/2/64_i.htm).

25 'Impiden instalación de comité ambiental en La Oroya', *La República*, 31 August 2006.
26 M. Salazar (2007) 'Plomo en la sangre de La Oroya', *Inter Press Service*, 4 October 2007, p. 2.
27 'Reciben propuestas para mejorar calidad de aire en La Oroya', *Coordinadora Nacional de Radio*, 12 September 2006 (http:www.cnr.org.pe/utiles/myprint/print.php).
28 M. Salazar (2007) 'Plomo en la sangre de La Oroya', p. 3.
29 M. Salazar, 'Doe Run será sancionada por contaminar', *Inter Press Service*, 18 April, 2008, p. 1.
30 'Plan de contingencia para La Oroya', *La Primera Huancayo*, 11 July 2008; and 'Movimiento Salud de La Oroya exige implementación de plan de contingencia para estados de alerta', *Pressperu* (http://www.pressperu.com/index2).
31 'Conam pide declarar en estado de alerta a La Oroya', *Correo de Huancayo*, 30 June 2008.
32 'El MINSA con los brazos cruzados en caso de La Oroya', *Correo de Huancayo*, 18 July 2008; and 'La Oroya exige estado de alerta', *La Primera*, 18 July 2008.
33 'Azufre en el aire de La Oroya superó los niveles históricos', *El Comercio*, 19 August 2008.
34 'Doe Run: Aire de La Oroya de mal en peor', *Con Nuestro Perú*, 16 August 2008.
35 'La Oroya: Sulfur contents in air exceed historical levels around Doe Run smelter', *Andean Air Mail and Peruvian Times*, 19 August 2008. See also: 'Quince metales tóxicos emanan de la planta industrial de La Oroya', *El Comercio*, 20 August 2008.
36 'Miércoles negro en La Oroya', *Perú Provincias*, 14 August 2008.
37 'Doe Run invertirá millones para mejorar ambiente peruano', *Univisión*, 24 August 2008.
38 'Alarmante situación el La Oroya', *Actualidad Minera del Perú*, No. 112, August, 2008, p. 3.
39 J. Bendezú, 'La Digesa cambia su forma de medición de la contaminación', *Correo de Cusco*, 19 September 2008.
40 'Doe Run inaugural segunda planta de ácido sulfúrico en Andes Perú', *Reuters*, 30 September 2008; and 'Doe Run Perú inaugurates $50 million sulphuric acid plant in La Oroya', *Andean Air Mail and Peruvian Times*, 1 October 2008.
41 'Doe Run recibe ISO', Peru.com, 23 August 2006 (http:www.peru.com).
42 'Doe Run Perú pierde su certificado ambiental ISO 14001', *Todo sobre La Oroya*, 9 April 2008. See also: http://www.blacksmithinstitute.org/projects/display/36 and 'Consejo directivo de Osinergmin resolvió apelación presentada por Doe Run Perú', *Agencia de Noticias ORBITA*, 12 November 2008.
43 M. Salazar, 'Doe Run será sancionada por contaminar', *Inter Press Service*, 18 April, 2008, p. 1.
44 'Minera Doe Run pierde ISO ambiental en La Oroya', *El Comercio*, 10 April 2008.
45 'La Oroya, 2007: Advocacy in review', *La Retama*, December, 2007, p. 3.
46 Red Muqui, 'Según AIDA informe de Blacksmith muestra imagen engañosa sobre situación de salud ambiental en La Oroya', *Nota de Prensa*, 10 September 2008.
47 G. Arauzo, 'Contaminación de La Oroya, Perú', *Con Nuestro Perú*, 25 October 2008 (http://connuestroperu.com/index2.php?option=com_content&task=v)

and 'Contaminación de La Oroya Perú', *Segui la Flecha*, 16 November 2008 (http://www.seguilaflecha.com/news_27229_CONTAMINACI%D3N-DE-LA-OROYA-PER%DA.html).
48 M. Perelman, 'Peruvian town's health goes up in smoke: Calls riser for Orthodox N.Y. billionaire to pay for pollution', *The Jewish Daily*, 27 June 2007.
49 'La Oroya, 2007: Advocacy in review', *La Retama*, December, 2007, pp. 2–3.
50 'Se posterga juicio contra Doe Run por contaminación con plomo en Perú', *Gestión*, 7 August 2008 (http://gestion.pe/?q=mode/15569) and 'Más sobre La Oroya', *Actualidad Minera del Perú*, No. 112, August, 2008, p. 9.
51 Red Muqui, 'Sobrevivir en plena contaminación', *Nota de Prensa*, 20 August 2008, p. 2; and 'El dueño de la empresa Doe Run Perú nombrado entre los más ricos de EE.UU.', *Red Uniendo Manos Perú*, 19 September 2008 (http://connuestroperu.com/index2.php?option=com_content&task=v).
52 Interviews with J. Aste, Advisor, Committee on Mining, the Environment and Indigenous Affairs, Peruvian National Congress, and former member Technical Working Group, Lima, 4 July 2008; C. Olivera and J. Coad, Joining Hands Against Hunger Network, Lima, 9 July 2008; R. Chacón, Independent Consultant and former member Joining Hands, Lima, 8 July 2008; and R. Ávila, Program Officer, Oxfam America, Lima, 16 July 2008.
53 *Actualidad Minera del Perú*, No. 86, June 2006, p. 13.
54 Interviews with E. Ames, former Coordinator, Technical Working Group, and former member, NGO Labor, Lima, 11 July 2008 and R. Ávila, Program Officer, Oxfam America, Lima, 16 July 2008.
55 Observatorio de Conflictos Mineros en el Perú, *Alerta Mensual*, March–April, 2008 (http://www.muqui.org/Observatorio_Marzo-Abril2008.htm) and Interviews with J. Aste, Advisor, Committee on Mining, the Environment and Indigenous Affairs, Peruvian National Congress, and former member, Technical Working Group, Lima, 4 July 2008; J. De Echave and M. Chávez, NGO CooperAcción, Lima, 8 July 2008.
56 Interview with R. Ávila, Program Officer, Oxfam America, Lima, 16 July 2008.
57 Interviews with E. Ames, former Coordinator Technical Working Group and former member NGO Labor, Lima, 11 July 2008; J. Aroca, Regional Program Coordinator, Oxfam America, Lima, 4 July 2008; J. De Echave and M. Chávez, NGO CooperAcción, Lima, 8 July 2008; and J. Aste, Advisor, Committee on Mining, the Environment and Indigenous Affairs, Peruvian National Congress, and former member, Technical Working Group, Lima, 4 July 2008.
58 M. Keck and K. Sikkink (1998) *Activists Beyond Borders* (Ithaca and London: Cornell University Press) p. 16.
59 Interviews with J. Aroca, Regional Program Coordinator, Oxfam America, Lima, 4 July 2008; J. Aste, Advisor, Committee on Mining, the Environment and Indigenous Affairs, Peruvian National Congress, and former member Technical Working Group, Lima, 4 July, 2008; C. Olivera and J. Coad, Joining Hands Against Hunger Network, Lima, 9 July 2008; and F. Vásquez, R. Camborda, P. Aquino and I. Gutiérrez, Environmental Affairs Office, Ministry of Energy and Mines, Lima, 21 July 2008.
60 J. Serrano (2006) *Estudio sobre la Contaminación Ambiental en los Hogares de La Oroya y Concepción y sus Efectos en la Salud de sus Residentes: Resumen de los Primeros Resultados Biológico*, (Huancayo: Universidad de San Luís and Arzobispado de Huancayo). See also 'Contaminación de La Oroya se extiende hasta Concepción', *El Comercio*, 22 August 2008; A. Mamani Mayta, 'Complejo

metalúrgico de La Oroya: Perú', *EcoPortal.net,* 9 September 2007 (http://www.ecoportal.net/content/view/full/64034); and G. Arauzo Chuco, 'La lluvia ácida en el centro del Perú', *EcoPortal.net,* 17 September 2007.

61 See 'Metal contaminants dumped by Doe Run's La Oroya smelter in Mantaro River threaten Peru's breadbasket', *Andean Air Mail and Peruvian Times,* 8 October 2008; R. Mayo, 'Metales en la cuenca del río Mantaro exceden límites tolerados por la OMS' (http://www.elcomercio.com.pe/edicion impresa/Html/2008-10-07/metales-cuenca-rio-mantaro-exceden-limites-tolerados-oms.html); and M. Salazar, 'Un río en coma profunda' *Interpress Service,* 17 November 2007.

62 Interviews with C. Olivera and J. Coad, Joining Hands Against Hunger Network, Lima, 9 July 2008 and R. Chacón, Independent Consultant and former member Joining Hands, Lima, 8 July 2008.

63 Interviews with J. Aste, Advisor, Committee on Mining, the Environment and Indigenous Affairs, Peruvian National Congress, and former member Technical Working Group, Lima, 4 July, 2008; E. Ames, former Coordinator, Technical Working Group, and former member, NGO Labor, Lima, 11 July 2008; J. De Echave and M. Chávez, NGO CooperAcción, Lima, 8 July 2008; R. Chacón, Independent Consultant and former member Joining Hands, Lima, 8 July 2008; F. Vásquez, R. Camborda, P. Aquino and I. Gutiérrez, Environmental Affairs Office, Ministry of Energy and Mines, Lima, 21 July 2008; and R. Ávila, Program Officer, Oxfam America, Lima, 16 July 2008.

64 M. Keck and K. Sikkink (1998) *Activists Beyond Borders* (Ithaca and London: Cornell University Press) p. 25.

65 L. Jordan and P. van Tuijl (2000) 'Political Responsibility in Transnational NGO Advocacy', *World Development,* vol. 28, number 12, pp. 2056–61.

9
Legitimacy, Accountability and Voice

Legitimacy in a democratic society

As CSOs and NGOs have become more active and influential in advocating for change and their voices more challenging, so also the reaction to them has become stronger, and the cry of 'by what right do these unelected bodies speak' becomes more strident. In response, NGOs in general and INGOs in particular will have to be very clear about how they answer that question. By what right do organizations like Oxfam speak? How exactly does their voice relate to that of those they are primarily concerned about, the poor of the developing world?

Academic Hugo Slim of Oxford Brookes University says that, before that question can be answered, NGOs have to answer another preliminary question – what status are they claiming for themselves; are they claiming to speak *as* the poor, *with* the poor, *for* the poor or *about* the poor?[1] How they answer that question will determine the nature of their legitimacy. If they are a community-based organization that is made up of poor people, then they can claim to be speaking *as* the poor. If an organization is working very closely with such people and speaks with their consent, as for example a labour union does for its worker members, then it can be said to be speaking *with*. If, as is often claimed, the poor or oppressed are for some reason unable to speak out and so are effectively 'voiceless' then the NGO might claim to be speaking *for* or on behalf of them. Finally, if an NGO is not speaking as, with or for a particular group of poor or victimized people, or is speaking quite generally, then it may claim to be speaking *about* the poor or oppressed.

In many situations, the CSO or NGO will be speaking in more than one of these capacities. It may, for example, be speaking *with* in one place and speaking *for* in another. A union supporting workers in a particular factory where there is a problem, for example in Sri Lanka, would be speaking *with* the workers in Sri Lanka and *for* them in international venues and meetings. Some CSOs, such as the organization MOSAO mentioned in Chapter 8, will always be speaking *as*, while others at the more policy end of the spectrum will always be speaking *about*. Oxfam in its advocacy around the WTO agreement on agriculture, in India and elsewhere, was speaking *about* the poor, in that case small and marginal farmers. In Peru it spoke *with* and *about* those whose rights were being abused in different arenas. It is important for NGOs to be clear on where their voice comes from in a given situation and to be transparent about it. As Slim says: 'The precise nature of their legitimacy will change depending on which mode of voice they are using. But they will lose all legitimacy if they are found to be masquerading – a sort of ventriloquist to the poor and oppressed'.

Where then do those NGOs that are not speaking *as* or *with* the poor, that are not the poor themselves or their representatives, obtain their legitimacy? By what right does an organization speak *for* or *about* the poor? For these, legitimacy comes from being effective and making useful contributors to democratic debate. As Clark says:

> Democracy no longer rests on the shoulders of a handful of elected politicians. Companies, NGOs, unions, the media, protest movements and intellectuals can join the deliberative process directly. It is no longer necessary to be elected, or have a constituency, or to be a large organization before one can speak; an individual can be as legitimate as an MP. We're all in the debating chamber now! If the British TV wildlife presenter David Attenborough were to proclaim on a conservation issue, he would have more clout than most MPs – yet no one voted for him, and he claims no members. The issue isn't legitimacy but advocacy effectiveness.[2]

But what then constitutes advocacy effectiveness? What characterizes an organization that can be regarded as legitimate, as usefully adding to the debate about issues in the South (or any other issue) from one that cannot? The characteristics would include having knowledge that is solidly based on research and/or experience, being recognized by other legitimate bodies as having useful knowledge or expertise to bring to the debate, and being sensitive to the views of those who are being spoken for or about. It should be stressed however that this route to legitimacy through democratic effectiveness or usefulness gives 'a voice but not a vote'. It conveys the right to speak, to have views heard, but not the right to take part in decision making. Academic Paul Wapner sets out how this applies to an organization like Oxfam:

> For example, the financial support that Oxfam receives from the public from 600,000 committed monthly givers, thousands of other additional occasional givers and from governments gives it a large claim to both popular and official legitimacy. In the UK, Oxfam gets massive voluntary support from around 20,000 volunteers. Such contributions in time and in kind are another hugely important element of support. So too is the kind of support that can come from the media, from opinion-formers and academics who support Oxfam's arguments or disagree with them from a position of recognition and respect. This kind of tangible support that is made manifest in money, time, intellectual agreement and shared conviction has to be actively generated by NGOs and human rights groups. It can reveal that a broad base of people and governments back an organisation as a morally important and practically effective operation, and one with which they actively seek to ally themselves. In Oxfam's case, such support generates a very tangible asset in Oxfam's legitimacy.[3]

But does this recognition in its own society as a useful contributor to democratic debate give a Northern-based NGO the right to a voice in another society, and in particular the right to advocate for certain views and positions in a Southern country? By what right do such foreign Northern organizations use their money and their influence to advocate for change in a Southern country? Is this Northern imperialism in disguise? The answer to that depends on two related issues – the foreign NGO's links into that society, and the values for which it stands.

First of all, one has to ask whether the Northern NGO is advocating its own ideas unilaterally, or is working with and supporting local groups and interests whose positions and views are already an element in the local political situation. Is it working with and supporting legitimate local organizations, such as ALaRM in Sri Lanka, or MOSAO and the technical working group in the La Oroya campaign in Peru, and gaining legitimacy through that association? Secondly, one has to ask whether the values or principles that the Northern NGO is promoting in that Southern society are peculiarly its own or represent values that are generally accepted in all societies. In most cases, one would hope, the Northern-based NGO and its chosen allies will be seeking change that amounts to the recognition of some fundamental right that most people would accept, and to which most governments, North and South, are already officially committed – for example, those set down in the Universal Declaration of Human Rights, such as freedom from arbitrary arrest, from being arbitrarily deprived of one's property, the right to just and favourable conditions of work, and to form or join a trade union, and the right to a standard of living adequate for health and well-being. These are not 'foreign' values, but universal ones. And as the Universal Declaration says 'every individual and every organ of society ... shall strive by teaching and education to promote respect for these rights and freedoms, and by progressive measures, national and international, to secure their universal and effective recognition and observance'.

In terms of values, Oxfam International (OI) says that it aims to promote the fundamental rights of those in the countries in which it works, and defines those as: the right to a livelihood, to basic services, to be safe from harm, the right to be heard, and the right to be treated as equal.[4] Once again, these are not foreign values or special interests that are being promoted, but fundamental rights that all human beings should be able to enjoy, wherever they live, and rights that most Southern governments have officially committed to. The basis on which NGOs claim legitimacy is perhaps best summed up in a charter agreed to in 2006 by a number of International Non-Government Organizations, which says: 'Our right to act is based on universally recognized freedoms of speech, assembly and association, on our contribution to democratic processes, and on the values we seek to promote. Our legitimacy is also derived from the quality of our work, and the recognition and support of the people with and for whom we work, and our members, our donors, the wider public, and governmental and other organizations around the world'.[5]

This legitimacy is now recognized by a wide variety of institutions – even the World Bank, one of the organizations least likely, one would have thought, to give such recognition given the amount of criticism and opposition it has received from NGOs over the years. And yet Jim MacNeill, Chairman of the Bank's Inspection Panel from 1999 till 2001, felt it necessary in 2004 to come to their defence:

> NGO's have strengthened the fabric of democracy in many fragile states, as I have witnessed personally in parts of Africa, Asia and, more recently, the Caucasus. They are indispensable agents of broader public participation and greater openness in private sector and gov-

ernment decision-making. In many countries they deliver essential services that weak governments will not or can no longer manage. And, yes, thanks to the computer, they are now able to network across borders and sometimes exert enormous influence. In the case of the Bank, local NGOs can enable the poorest and weakest of those affected by a Bank-funded project to voice their concerns and, through the Panel, the Bank's Board has provided a vehicle to investigate their claims while respecting the rights of all parties involved. International NGOs can augment local voices, strengthen local NGOs, and provide the sometimes much needed protection of a global spotlight.[6]

What then can we say about the case study campaigns? Are they examples of an INGO acting with legitimacy, as an effective and useful voice of the poor, or of an INGO exercising inappropriate influence in the South in an illegitimate manner? In terms of values, the campaign in Sri Lanka was basically advocating for the right to reasonable conditions at work, universal rights that are contained in the Universal Declaration and/or in the conventions of the International Labour Organization. In the case of the Indian campaign it was the right to a livelihood and to an adequate standard of living for farmers and rural people, although the connection was a little more difficult to make. The campaigns in Peru were about the right of those affected by extractive industries to be safe from harm to their health, to have their livelihoods respected and protected – whether as workers in a metallurgical complex, shopkeepers in a town economically dependent on a smelter, or indigenous hunters and fishers in the Amazon basin – and to have a voice in the decisions affecting their lives.

Legitimacy also depends on what status Oxfam was claiming *vis-à-vis* those it was trying to help, and whether its links to those groups justified that claim. In Sri Lanka, Oxfam and the ALaRM coalition were speaking *for* and *about* garment workers, based on the fact that they were either organizations that talked to and dealt with workers on a daily basis and were therefore directly answerable to them, or in the case of Oxfam an organization disciplined by its membership of a coalition with such organizations. The views expressed in the campaign came from and through ALaRM, and in some cases directly from workers themselves, for example, when individual women workers told their own stories at press conferences. In India, Oxfam could really only claim to be speaking *about* poor farmers and rural people, based on its years of experience working in rural India and its assessment of the effect of WTO agreements. It was not supporting views already circulating in Indian civil society, but introducing new ones. These were however apparently accepted by several (but not all) Indian NGOs, and by the large number of people who signed the 'Big Noise' petition. In the case of La Oroya in Peru, Oxfam and other international allies gained their legitimacy from their close association with MOSAO, an organization that comprised local CSOs who could claim to be speaking *as* and *with* those directly affected by contamination from the smelter. They supported the technical working group that worked with MOSAO. The company, through its allies in the trade union and local municipality, contested MOSAO's claims to representation, but it sustained its position and was eventually vindicated when both the union and the municipality broke ranks with the company. In the Camisea case, Oxfam's legitimacy was similarly based on its close links to organizations that represented those affected. The local and national indigenous organizations with whom it worked maintained their independence and were recognized as legitimate representatives of the majority of the communities affected by the natural gas project – although a few communities were affiliated to other smaller national indigenous organizations that were more accommodating in their demands. Oxfam's role was to link these organizations with their national and international NGO allies and ensure that their voice and concerns were present and heeded.

The case studies were also examples of an INGO together with its allies and partners being an effective contributor to democratic debate, by contributing useful knowledge and expertise to the local arena. In Sri Lanka and Peru, they raised issues that were being neglected and added new perspectives to the debate that would otherwise have not been heard, namely that of the affected groups. In Sri Lanka they also contributed the idea of a 'living wage' for workers. To Indian civil society Oxfam brought a clearer analysis of the links between rural development and international trade rules, and through its support for CENTAD the research and analysis that that organization produced. In all three countries Oxfam contributed an international perspective on the issues that were being debated nationally. In Sri Lanka this meant a global overview of what was happening to workers in the international garment trade, made available through OI reports, and of what was happening in terms of trade agreements and the phase-out of the MFA. In India likewise it was able to contribute to the Indian Government political intelligence from Geneva and other Northern capitals, analyses of what was happening in the WTO negotiations, and evidence and arguments that the Indian negotiators could use. In Peru it provided local groups impacted by a smelter owned by a US-based company information about that company's behaviour and operations in the US, and helped Amazonian indigenous leaders to understand the workings of international financial institutions.

Were these perspectives that it brought solidly based on research and experience? In almost every case they were, although there are issues around the impartiality of some of the research. Some pieces of research were undertaken locally, for example that on a 'living wage' in Sri Lanka, the CENTAD reports in India, and the reports on health in La Oroya. Others were international in nature and appeared as Oxfam International reports or briefing papers that were used around the world. These latter were mainly written by policy or advocacy staff of an Oxfam affiliate in the North, but based on research commissioned in the South. A potential problem with this type of 'advocacy research' is that it is research to gather evidence and arguments in support of a position that is to a large extent already determined. It is research with a purpose, to support an advocacy campaign, and as such its impartiality can be questioned. Some criticism of research methods was given by the independent evaluators who did an external evaluation of parts of the 'Make Trade Fair' campaign in 2006. They said that Oxfam's research 'can be selective in its sources and may not use the most up-to-date data; some research (in the main body of reports) was inconsistent with executive summaries, which appear to have been written to support campaigning messages'.[7]

Improving accountability

While NGOs can fairly readily defend themselves against challenges to their legitimacy, on the question of accountability they are more vulnerable. Of course, much of the criticism on this score comes from opponents who have perhaps been stung by NGO advocacy and would like to see them silenced, and the criticism is often overstated. But the accusations nevertheless need to be taken seriously. The overstatement is usually in the form of a comparison between NGOs that, it is said, are accountable to no one but themselves, and governments, that are accountable to their citizens through regular elections, and companies that are accountable to their shareholders. But of course not all governments are accountable to their citizens nor subject to democratic elections. And companies usually have no accountability to the many other groups apart from their shareholders whom they affect – for example the workers or growers who produce the products they sell, their employees, those who live near their plants, and so on.

There are two aspects to this issue of NGO accountability – accountability to those who fund and support them, and accountability to those whom they wish to help. In terms of the former, most have formal accountability to their boards and to those bodies that provide them with grants or other substantial funding. But even here they are open to criticism:

> Regrettably, most civil society groups have operated very limited and unimaginative accountability mechanisms in relation to their own activities. At best, the organizations have tended to have no more than loose oversight by a board (often composed largely of friends, who are in some cases paid), periodic elections of officers (with low rates of participation and sometimes dubious procedures), occasional general meetings (with sparse attendance), minimalist reports of activities (that few people read) and summary financial records (which often conceal as much as they reveal). Such pro forma accountability mainly addresses the bureaucratic requirements of governments and donors. It does not actively engage the association's stakeholders or promote genuine organizational learning.[8]

However there is also a significant and powerful informal accountability that civil society organizations in general and NGOs in particular have to the members of the public. Unless an NGO can maintain the trust and good-will of those who donate money to it or support its campaigns, its ability to function and its financial viability will be undermined. As one commentator put it: 'If CSOs do not perform on the basis of their stated vision and mission, they are likely to perish'.[9] This is also true for the wider general public in the sense that the NGO needs to maintain credibility in the eyes of the latter, and in the eyes of decision makers, if its arguments and positions are to be taken seriously. An NGO's credibility is one of its most valuable assets and it will guard it carefully for, without it, the NGO will be abandoned by its supporters and its ability to influence will disappear. As Jonathan Fox of the University of California in Santa Cruz has said:

> One of the most important sources of NGO accountability is the possible distance between the high standards they publicly set for themselves and their actual practices. If the distance between goals and practices becomes very large, or very obvious, then the NGO will have a credibility gap. This is a major potential source of accountability because most NGOs need credibility to survive. They need cred-

ibility with the media to have a public voice, with grassroots partners to have popular legitimacy, with elites to influence policy, and with funders to gain the material support essential for institutional survival.[10]

These then are the practical constraints on an NGO, including public scrutiny and the ability of supporters to vote with their wallets, that keep it in line with its values. It has no choice but to listen to the concerns of its members and supporters, and the public in general. This does not mean that NGOs always listen carefully or always act in ways that the latter would want, but it does mean that they are not completely free to act as they see fit. Like governments, they are bound by public opinion.

It is in the area of accountability to those whom they are attempting to help that INGOs are particularly weak. In 1999, a survey of the advocacy work of 32 UK-based development NGOs asked them 'To whom are you accountable for your advocacy work'? Almost half responded in terms of upward accountability to line-managers, donors, trustees and boards of governors, rather than downwards to those whose interests they claimed to promote. In fact several NGOs were actually surprised at the mention of downward accountability, and seemed unaware of the concept and unconvinced of its desirability.[11]

What formal accountability there is, tends to be in the other direction – financial accountability from Southern NGOs and CSOs that are the recipients of funding to their Northern funders. This relationship of donor and recipient tends to mask and undermine the need for accountability the other way as well, the obligation of donors to be accountable in non-financial ways to the Southern recipient, the people on whose behalf they advocate. This is the concept of 'political responsibility' outlined by Jordan and van Tuijl (see Chapter 2).

Instances of the non-accountability of Northern NGOs and INGOs to those they are supposedly helping are many. For example many organizations in South Asia believe that the campaigns by Northern NGOs to require certification on rugs imported into the North guaranteeing that they have not been manufactured using child labour have worsened the situation for child workers. Many children lost their jobs making rugs as a result, but were not able to go to school instead because their families could not afford to lose one extra income. Many found themselves in even worse jobs with lower wages and more unhealthy conditions. Likewise, a campaign by environmental groups in the US to ban the imports of Thai shrimps, on the grounds that the nets used to catch them in open seas were not equipped with escape flaps for sea turtles, aroused anger on the part of NGOs working with fishing communities in Thailand who insisted that there were no sea turtles in the areas where the shrimp fishing was carried out. These are examples of NGOs in the North (and sometimes the South) determining their own campaign agendas and messages without referring to those in the South who will be directly affected by their actions, without any sense of accountability for their actions to those who will be affected.

NGO accountability according to Slim might be defined as: 'the process by which an NGO holds itself openly responsible for what it believes, what it does, and what it does not do, in a way which shows it involving all concerned parties and actively responding to what it learns'. As such, he says, it deals in information that is both quantitative and qualitative, hard and soft, empirical and speculative, recording facts and making judgements. Different stakeholders, in the North and the South, will need to be accounted to in different ways. Some will want figures, others information about impact. But any accountability process must involve key stakeholders through representative meetings, assemblies or voting systems. Essential characteristics of any mechanism, Slim says, must be veracity and transparency. What an NGO is saying about itself, or what it reports others as saying about it, must be basically true, easily available and accessible to all. NGO accountability mechanisms must show clearly how the agency is responding to what it has learnt and what its stakeholders are telling it.[12]

This is a different concept from 'political responsibility' as defined by Jordan and van Tuijl but is compatible with it, in the sense that any NGO that was accountable in the way Slim defines it would also have a high level of 'political responsibility'. It would be communicating with its allies and network partners in the South on a regular basis and listening to what they had to tell it about its advocacy and campaigning.

Amongst the Oxfam affiliates, Oxfam Great Britain publicly says that its level of accountability could be improved. In a 'Statement on Legitimacy and Accountability' it says: 'We are working towards improved transparency and information sharing; more stakeholder participation in decision-making; and better evaluation and complaint mechanisms'. It identifies its stakeholders as 'the individuals and communities with whom we work; partners and allies; donors and supporters; staff and the wider public; and regulatory bodies in the UK and in countries where we operate'. For its donors and supporters it produces a number of reports, including an Annual Report and Accounts and an Annual Review, as well as other materials such as newsletters and email updates. In terms of accountability in its campaigning and advocacy to Southern allies and those whom it is seeking to assist, Oxfam Great Britain says:

> In developing countries in particular, we try to agree messages early in campaigns and to be respectful of partners' roles and relationships – for example, we make sure we do not take their place in lobbying their governments. Every two years, we hold the Oxfam Assembly or other forums, to which a number of partner agencies are invited. These Assemblies are not only to give us feedback, but also provide an opportunity to help shape future direction.[13]

INGOs are well aware of the need for accountability. As mentioned above, a group of 11 major organizations, including Amnesty, Greenpeace, Oxfam, Save The Children, YWCA and others, launched in 2006 the first global Accountability Charter for the non-profit sector, which they say is designed to 'enhance transparency and accountability, both internally and externally; encourage communication with stakeholders; and improve our performance and effectiveness as organizations'. While the INGO signatories to the charter include amongst their stakeholders 'people, including future generations, whose rights we seek to protect and advance', there is nothing specific in the charter about accountability to these stakeholders or how it might be manifested, apart from a promise to 'work in genuine partnership with local communities, NGOs and other organizations'. This is true of other INGO codes, such as that of the umbrella organization, the Australian Council for International Development, mentioned in Chapter 2, which is strong on accountability upwards to donors but a little vague on standards of accountability downwards to the poor of the developing world.

In the light of these short-comings, an argument has been put for having official certification systems for NGOs to ensure that acceptable standards of accountability, transparency, accuracy, internal democracy, etc are maintained and that NGOs are practicing what they preach. A number of United Nations organizations have such schemes in place for NGOs wishing to lobby within their processes, and there are already some examples of self-regulation and certification by NGOs. One example of the latter often quoted is that in the Philippines where a self-regulated code of conduct for NGOs was introduced in the early 1990s, and later transformed into a self-managed system that assesses NGO compliance with standards required for acceptance by the government as eligibility for tax exemption. The Philippines Council for NGO Certification can recommend withdrawal of registration and tax privileges from NGOs that fail to comply with these standards.

The World Bank in a major 1998 review of its relations with NGOs argued that the best way to ensure standards for NGOs was through self-regulation rather than legislation, and cautioned governments against over-regulating and micro managing.[14] One problem with government regulation is that a government will not always be impartial when it comes to making judgements about NGOs, particularly if it has been on the receiving end of an NGO campaign. In Peru, for example, there is legislation governing the activities of NGOs and a government agency that oversees it. But in recent years this agency has used its powers to audit and indeed harass local NGOs. Representatives from this agency attempted to intimidate Oxfam by threatening it with intervention, despite lacking any grounds for doing so, and struck CONACAMI from its register in what was a symbolic gesture of official displeasure.

Accountability in the case studies

In the case studies examined here the level of accountability to allies and partners, and to those whom the campaigns aimed to help, was quite high, with the exception of the campaign in India. In Sri Lanka, for example, there was active involvement and participation throughout the campaign by the allies who made up the ALaRM coalition, and priorities and messages were agreed from the beginning. Joint monitoring and evaluation took place from time to time, and the whole process was transparent. Oxfam did initially take its allies' place in lobbying the Sri Lankan government, but only at the request of those allies and only temporarily. Accountability to garment workers came through the workers' representative in the ALaRM coalition.

In Peru, Oxfam attempted to promote accountability in a number of ways. At the most elementary level, the South America regional office of Oxfam America pioneered the publication of annual reports in Spanish on its activities and funding in the region in an endeavour to be transparent and accountable to its partners, allies and the governments and civil societies of the region. These reports were read and commented upon, even by sections of the media hostile to Oxfam. At the national level Oxfam tried to encourage a sense of mutual accountability and recognition of shared risk and responsibility by promoting alliances between national organizations representing the affected groups (AIDESEP in the Camisea case and CONACAMI in the La Oroya case) and the national and international NGOs supporting them. At the local level Oxfam supported the creation of technical working groups, as in La Oroya, or stable coalitions, as in Camisea, which would be accountable to local representative organizations, such as MOSAO and COMARU.

In a frequently hostile political environment in Peru, Oxfam and its partners recognized that the need to develop a sense of mutual accountability and 'political responsibility' was critical. For example, a statement by Oxfam America on its website intended for a US constituency, which did not reflect the priorities or concerns of its partners, could open them to attacks in the media or reprisals by government, and put them at risk. Accountability worked the other way as well. The promotion of violence or radical statements by partners or allies in Peru could expose Oxfam to criticism for being 'anti-mining', 'anti-development" or even 'anti-systemic' (often used as a code word for 'terrorist'). This obliged Oxfam field staff to meet frequently with partners and allies to exchange information and coordinate actions and statements in the face of accusations in the media. This situation also generated tension between the Oxfams, as some were tempted to give credence to claims that Oxfam America was supporting violence and terrorism. This eventually led three of the other Oxfams to join Oxfam America in its extractive industries work and together develop agreed position statements and protocols.

In the India campaign, there was initially a high level of accountability as the views of potential allies and partners were sought regarding issues, priorities and approaches for the campaign, through the consultation process. But this was then dropped as the international agenda took over. There was no formal agreement on messages between Oxfam and the Indian NGOs with whom it worked, and attempts to form joint approaches to the government were not particularly successful so that Oxfam lobbied the Indian Government itself in its own name. There was no discernible accountability to farmers or rural people – and indeed there is the question of whether these were the groups to whom it should be accountable anyway. As mentioned in Chapter 5, the policies that Oxfam was advocating for with the Indian Government, and more generally in its global campaign around WTO rules, had implications for other groups in India as well, including the urban poor for whom preventing the importation of cheap food grains was not necessarily a good thing. As often happens in such campaigns, Oxfam had to choose between different groups with conflicting interests, in this case producers versus consumers of food crops.

A similar situation can arise in campaigns around extractive industries, such as the Peru cases, where NGOs choose to support those whose land has been taken or environment damaged by the company's operation, as against those who are benefiting from it and support it because it has provided jobs, business or highly valued infrastructure such as access roads, health clinics, and schools. In the case of the La Oroya operation, these differences of interest within the community were a critical aspect of the campaign, and were exploited by the company, which threatened to close down its operations, with consequent loss of jobs and benefits to the town, if it were obliged to make the investments demanded by Oxfam and its allies to reduce the contamination that was provoking the public health crisis. This obliged the workers in the smelter and the townspeople whose businesses depended on it to make a choice between their health and their jobs or businesses. In the face of this dilemma, the union and the town council opted to support the company, thus prioritizing their income sources, and putting themselves at odds with the groups that Oxfam and its allies were supporting. In response, the technical working group with support from Oxfam, undertook research to show that these divisions were unnecessary, that both jobs and health could be preserved. The research showed that the company did in fact have the financial resources needed to undertake the investments being demanded of them without having to close down. These results were subsequently corroborated by studies commissioned by the Ministry of Energy and Mines. It also helped that a period of high mineral prices undermined the company's arguments about its inability to pay. It is interesting to note that the fabulous wealth and extravagant purchases and donations of the company's sole owner in the US never carried weight in the discussions in Peru about the company's capacity to pay.

Dominance in advocacy networks

The issues considered so far in this chapter have been about the relationship of NGOs with the societies in which they operate. But there are other key issues concerning the relationships between NGOs themselves, and in particular between INGOs based in the North and their allies and advocacy network partners in the South.

In any network there are going to be power relationships, and this is certainly true of transnational advocacy networks. In a 1995 benchmark survey, some 350 NGOs from around the world who were attending an NGO Forum at the World Summit for Social Development in

Copenhagen, were asked whether they felt restricted by any of the following: larger NGOs, English-language NGOs, Northern NGOs, accredited NGOs, white-run NGOs, or male-run NGOs.[15] The answers were very consistent. The organizations of greatest concern to the respondents were the first three – larger NGOs, English-language NGOs and Northern NGOs. The majority of organizations, whether Northern or Southern, large or small, of whatever racial origin or gender, shared this perception. In other words, the issue as they saw it was not one of gender differences or racial differences but of large, resource-rich, English-speaking Northern NGOs versus smaller, resource-poor Southern ones. If these results still reflect the situation now, then this is a very worrying result for organizations who believe passionately in equality and for whom democratic participation is a core value. However, it is not totally unexpected. Larger NGOs based in the North simply do have better access to funds, to information, to key decision makers, etc, while Southern-based CSOs are typically reliant on them for these. In some cases, Northern advocacy organizations have better access to information about a country in question than organizations in the country itself – and better access to powerful governments and institutions that can influence the situation in that Southern country than they do.

There is also a concern that these larger Northern NGOs with their greater resources and influence might be pushing aside or marginalizing smaller NGOs and CSOs that focus on grassroots organizing and the empowerment of affected communities. These latter are not normally involved in the more public or dramatic types of campaigns that have short-term 'wins' in the form of policy changes, and high profile media-coverage that keeps them in the public eye. Instead they focus on longer-term, behind-the-scenes work with farmers' groups, workers, the urban poor, etc, developing their ability to analyse and find solutions to their own problems, and to take action themselves. This grassroots-level, people-centred, supportive work is important and potentially more sustainable and developmentally useful than high-level policy advocacy in that it empowers the affected groups to take control of their own situation and to act on their own accord, rather then being reliant on others to act for them. Building the collective power of those who have been excluded from political decision processes is not only positive in terms of social development, but also provides more sustainable and longer term solutions to problems than those that depend on NGOs coming in to assist, who may then move on. But this grassroots work can be inadvertently undermined by NGO and INGO advocacy. For example, an emphasis on the importance of research and 'information politics' can disempower local communities and organizers by conveying the notion that only NGO experts with their wide sources of information and their research reports can do advocacy effectively. Also large-scale campaigns such as 'Make Trade Fair' can have a similar effect by reinforcing the idea that smaller CSOs working locally are less than effective.

The larger, high profile NGOs need to be aware of this and sensitive to it. They need to take into account the fact that winning a positive change of policy or practice is not enough unless it also includes building the political clout of the affected groups, helping them to overcome their disenfranchisement from political processes and the feelings and structures of powerlessness. As Edwards and Gaventa have said:

> Northern NGOs have often concentrated on work at the international level with policy elites. While this work is necessary, it is insufficient if it is not reinforced by work at the national and grassroots levels. A key challenge for the future will be building new forms of global alliance that facilitate collaboration among levels while giving greater support and voice to the intended beneficiaries of a campaign and those working most closely with them.[16]

The campaign in India was a classic example of where this did not happen. The campaign concentrated on policy makers in the Indian Government rather than on the farmers who would be affected, and the only significant attempt to have the voice of the latter heard was the international 'Big Noise' petition, whose wording was written elsewhere. In the La Oroya campaign in Peru on the other hand the affected communities were intimately involved in determining the course of the campaign throughout and it was their voice that dominated. The work of Oxfam and its NGO allies was supportive and behind-the-scenes, undertaking research, providing training, linking MOSAO with contacts in the media and government, accompanying them in lobbying and generating international solidarity. Hopefully it will leave them more empowered than they were before the campaign.

Of all the factors that determine the relations within transnational advocacy networks between big and small, Northern and Southern members, it is the financial resources of the former and their role as funders that is probably the most significant. Northern NGOs often refer to the organizations that they fund in the South as their 'partners' while those on the receiving end tend to refer to these Northern organizations more accurately as their 'donors'. Calling the recipient a 'partner' implies a degree of equality in the relationship that does not exist when one is reliant on the other for funding, and the accountability is predominantly one way. Its role as the source of their funding gives the Northern NGO the power to influence the activities of the recipient organization, while the recipient can do nothing but respond accordingly or look for another donor.

The two South Asia case studies are examples of a Northern organization using its status as a funder to influence the work and priorities of local 'partner' organizations. In Sri Lanka it was Oxfam's status as their funder that induced the organization that later became ALaRM to come together at its request to discuss an issue of concern. The issue that they came together to talk about was one initiated by the funder, namely job losses due to the phase-out of the MFA. It is true that the Sri Lankan CSOs were not unwilling to be brought together like that, and that as the coalition developed Oxfam took a less pro-active role. But it did in those initial stages use its role as donor to drive the campaign in a certain direction. In the Indian campaign the influence was more extreme, in that Oxfam used its funds to simply buy the time, attention and services of local NGOs for its campaign around the WTO, and sub-contracted them to run its popular mobilization aspects and collect 'Big Noise' signatures. In its defence, however, it should be said that this was a different kind of campaign, in which centralized direction was perhaps necessary – a global campaign aimed at influencing an inter-governmental agreement, in which there needed to be a coordinated global strategy, centrally directed. A 2006 external evaluation of the 'Make Trade Fair' campaign as a whole said: 'Oxfam would benefit from more reflection on how it handles its power within alliances. Oxfam has become better, but has still not entirely learned to manage the sensitivities related to its size, the power of its brand, and the fact that it is often also a donor in its alliance work'.[17]

Even when the relationship within a transnational advocacy network is not one of donor and recipient, when Northern NGOs are working with allies and colleagues in relationships that do not involve funding, there is a tendency for those in the North to dominate, to not listen very well to those in the South and set their own agenda and priorities and perhaps unthinkingly expect those in the South to follow. In these circumstances Southern partners and allies can be left feeling like junior partners, welcomed as sources of information and legitimacy, but not treated as equals in the campaign. This point was made by the 2005 internal evaluation of the 'Make Trade Fair' campaign:

> A recurring issue continues to be the perception that Oxfam imposes its priorities and looks for collaboration with partners and allies, but is not pre-disposed to work on their priorities in turn, even when they have been working on trade for years.... Oxfam has generally adjusted its campaigning to better accommodate the various interests of its partners / allies, but at this stage Oxfam should be more adept at making these accommodations during campaign planning, rather than being negotiated as the campaign unfolds.[18]

Clark suggests that it might be beneficial if Northern organizations relinquished a little of their power, for example, by agreeing to expose themselves to peer pressure within international networks. They could even allow monitoring and evaluation to become a two-way process with Southern organizations and networks monitoring the activities of Northern funders and reporting to them on ethical, fiduciary, and governance issues and problems.[19] One method that could be used is 'social auditing', a process in which the various stakeholders in a project or campaign are involved in negotiating and periodically assessing a set of criteria through which the NGO or the campaign is to be judged. Another method is participatory budgeting, in which beneficiaries are directly involved in funding decisions. Large institutional donors in particular could try to develop approaches in which at least part of the money they disburse is controlled or influenced by the people they are trying to help.

It is worth mentioning here an interesting new development that may alter the dynamics of this relationship of Northern donor and Southern recipient – the emergence of funding organizations based in the South. It is no longer true that affluence is confined to the countries of Europe and North America and the rest of the world is poor. There are now significant affluent classes in countries like India, China, Mexico and Brazil, and given the size of these countries' populations these affluent classes are very large and their resources truly formidable. Why then, one may ask, do we need to raise funds in Europe and North America for development assistance projects (or advocacy) in India or Brazil when there are vast funds in the hands of affluent individuals and families in those countries that could be used. Some INGOs, particularly those that are structured as federations or co-federations, feel that this is a fair question and are looking at the possibility of tapping into these resources by establishing member organizations in these countries to raise funds domestically.

Oxfam International is one of them. It already has an affiliate based in China (Oxfam Hong Kong) that raises funds from its local population, has recently established another in India (Oxfam India) that does likewise, and is looking at the possibility of a Mexican affiliate, and perhaps some others. Although based in the South, these are international NGOs in that, as well as raising funds domestically for development and advocacy projects in their own countries, they are also obliged as Oxfams to fund activities in other countries and in other parts of the world. Thus Indian private donations could be used, for example, to fund development projects in Latin America, or to assist disaster victims in Africa, as well as funding development projects and domestic advocacy in India. For a Southern CSO, being dependent on a local domestic funding organization has a different dynamic from being dependent on a foreign one. One of the reasons for this new development is to address the accusation of foreign influence through foreign funding.[20] Instead of British or American or Australian money being used to fund advocacy in India, it would be Indian money raised for that purpose from the Indian population by an Indian organization registered with the government of that country. While Oxfam India carries a foreign-sounding name, and is linked to an international network of other Oxfams, the fact that it is so rooted in the local society will give it a greater legitimacy to undertake advocacy in India.

Yet to be explored, however, are the implications if such organizations become involved in funding or supporting advocacy outside their national borders. What are the implications, for example, of Indian civil society money being used to finance advocacy in neighbouring countries in South Asia, or of a Mexican INGO funding or supporting an advocacy organization or campaign in the United States? Also not yet explored are the implications for Oxfam International's advocacy priorities and style as its Northern-based affiliates are joined by an increasing number of Southern-based ones, with their own Southern focus and Southern priorities.

It was mentioned in Chapter 1 that there is a tendency among NGOs in recent years to come together into international confederations that involve Northern and Southern member organizations working together under a unified banner. Examples include Amnesty International with its 50 or so 'sections' spread around the globe, Friends of the Earth International that now has some 70 or so national member organizations, and Oxfam International with its 13 affiliates. As these confederations undertake unified advocacy campaigns, the internal North-South relations between the various components of the confederation can mean that it acts in many ways like a transnational advocacy network, and similar points about dominance can be made about the internal relations within this network.

For example, the various Oxfam affiliates involved in the 'Make Trade Fair' campaign and their field offices spread across Africa, Asia and Latin America could be said to have acted in many ways as a transnational advocacy network. It could be argued that Northern-based staff dominated the design and running of the campaign, particularly in the early stages, and that their colleagues in country and regional offices in the South had little influence. This is evidenced by, for example, the lack of proper representation of these Southern regions on the bodies that designed, planned and ran the campaign in its early years. The key body was the Trade Campaign Working Group (later Project Group), which in the beginning when many of the key decisions were being made, had no direct representation from the Southern regions – just one person representing them all. One can speculate on the reasons for this, but one possible factor was that Oxfam offices in the South were not organized or ready to provide input to such a campaign, as their focus was support for development programmes, and some advocacy at a national, local, even village level, rather than global campaigns. The experienced advocates on the Trade Campaign Working Group on the other hand would not have been keen to wait around for advice and input that was so slow in coming. However, as the campaign proceeded this changed, and eventually each region had its own representative on the Working Group. But by then the campaign was well under way and its shape and form well established – centrally planned, with only limited room for flexibility and variation at a regional or country level to take account of local situations and local priorities. Hence the tension in Sri Lanka between the global 'Play Fair at the Olympics' campaign and the local one which had its own quite different issues and strategies.

The only time that the Northern organizers and advocates were forced to listen to their colleagues in the South was when the 'Make Trade Fair' campaign threatened to affect the field programme. Whenever the advocates were planning to say something about a particular Southern country in which there was an Oxfam development assistance programme, the staff running that programme had the right to check and if necessary veto what was to be said, if it was going to create problems for the programme or threaten its continuance.

This raises another key issue for INGOs – the tension that can arise when an organization undertakes advocacy on an issue of concern in a country in which it has an operational on-the-ground programme. Does it give priority to the programme and ensuring that it continues to provide benefits to the poor, or does it speak out publicly and internationally, given that this might put the programme at risk? The usual response for most development INGOs is to continue programming and to speak out if and when they can, using whatever democratic space is available in the country concerned. The art is in judging what they can get away with in a particular political environment, and what is too dangerous. Even in the most repressive political environments there are always some areas in which public comment and criticism is possible, which is not seen as threatening to the regime (e.g. criticizing the World Bank's programmes in that country) and others where any comment by a foreign organization, in-country or internationally, would provoke an immediate strong reaction from the government. Most development INGOs find themselves having to navigate these dangerous political waters, often in a situation in which there are serious problems and urgent humanitarian needs that would be left unaddressed if they were thrown out of the country. This was an issue faced by Oxfam Great Britain in Colombia, where it had a large humanitarian programme in support of persons displaced by the political violence, and was concerned about the viability of the programme and the security of its local staff if other Oxfams or their partners spoke out against human rights violations by the security forces or their paramilitary allies.

But sometimes the ability to operate effectively becomes so restricted, or the need to speak out becomes so pressing, that it is decided that international advocacy will be more effective in assisting the poor or abused than trying to run an assistance programme in-country. This is the judgement that many agencies have made when deciding how best to help oppressed people in Burma. Where there is an existing programme, it is not often that an agency will close it down in order to speak out. But at least one Oxfam affiliate has done this in the past. In the late 1970s Oxfam Australia (then known as Community Aid Abroad) closed down its entire programme in Indonesia in order to publicly criticize the Suharto government over its actions in East Timor, where a brutal anti-rebel drive had disrupted rural life to such an extent that crops had not been planted and people were dying of starvation. The withdrawal was basically to protect its local staff and recipient organizations in Indonesia who would have been in serious trouble as a result of their association with an anti-government foreign organization. In the 1980s it similarly closed down its programme and withdrew from Somalia in order to speak out about the abuses of the then government in that country.

Relating to the poor

As well as the relationships between organizations within an advocacy network, there is also the question of the relationship of the latter to those they are attempting to help – the poor, the aggrieved, the abused, the unjustly treated. Cultural, social, economic, linguistic and other differences mean that this can at times be fraught with difficulty. Sometimes even making contact with such people can be difficult:

> [T]hey are typically unorganised, inarticulate, often sick, seasonally hungry, and quite frequently dependent on local patrons. They are less educated, less in contact with communications, less likely to use government services, and less likely to visit outside their home area ... They are relatively invisible, especially the women and children ... Visitors could easily spend a week in a village without either seeing or speaking to the poorer of its inhabitants; and without ever entering one of the colonies where many of the poorest live, visitors tend to see, meet, and interact with, only the more influential and better off rural people.[21]

A determining factor in the relationship between advocacy NGOs and those for whom they are advocating is the nature of the issue on which they are advocating and whether it came from the affected group or was initiated by the NGO. A significant difference between the campaigns in Peru described here and those in South Asia was that the former were about existing problems affecting specific groups who were asking for help, whereas the latter were about problems that had not occurred yet, but were anticipated by the INGO, and about which no one was yet asking for help. The affected groups in Peru were painfully aware of their problem and seeking outside assistance, and this formed the basis of the relationship with the organizations involved. The two campaigns in South Asia on the other hand were about an INGO trying to head off problems that it could see were about to happen if nothing was done, but of which the affected groups, the garment workers and farmers, were largely unaware, which meant a very different kind of relationship. Part of the task of the INGO and its allies in the South Asia cases was to raise awareness among these groups of the impending problem. But because these were large and diverse sectors of society, and the problems were not yet being felt, this was difficult. Their interaction with the affected groups on the issues of the campaign was therefore diffuse, sporadic and initiated by the advocating organizations themselves.

In cases such as those in Peru, where there is a specific group with a problem seeking assistance, the task of the NGOs involved is to take the group's issues and problems to the relevant political arenas in ways that will hopefully influence decision makers and help alleviate or rectify the situation. For the NGOs, this means listening to what the affected groups have to say about their problem and transmitting that as accurately and as forcefully as possible to the national government level and/or via international allies to centres of power in the North.

But sometimes this process does not work well and the story from the affected group gets distorted or filtered in the process, and the message that is given in the centres of power is not the one that the community wanted. Two examples of this are given in Chapter 2 – the campaign on behalf of the people of the Arun valley in Nepal where a huge dam was to be built, and the campaign against the operations of the Conoco oil company on the lands of the Huaorani people in Ecuador. In both cases what was advocated for in the South and North was not necessarily what the affected groups wanted. The views of the latter were lost to some extent in the campaigns. A similar thing nearly happened in the Camisea case, where there was a tendency in the NGO coalition to favour parks over people, because environmental organizations were in the majority, and for the rights of the affected indigenous people to be lost. However, the two perspectives were largely complementary rather than competing, as the indigenous people were as concerned about the environment as the environmentalists because it formed the basis of their livelihoods, and both the environmental and indigenous rights message were maintained on the campaign agenda.

As one author put it, in cases like this, 'it is not a question of Northern versus Southern NGOs, as is often portrayed: it is the poor versus both'.[22] In trying to explain why this is so, this same author, Warren Nyamugasira, who has worked in the development NGO sector in Uganda for over 20 years, points to the cultural and social differences that often exist between the staff of urban-based Southern NGOs and the poor communities with whom they are dealing. 'With all due respect', he says, 'many Southern NGOs do not qualify as "indigenous", in that they are not born out of the situations in which the poor live. Rather, they are modelled on the Northern NGOs who founded and/or fund them'.[23] Nyamugasira makes the point that it is a mistake to uncritically equate Southern NGOs with the voice of the poor. For Northern-based NGOs this is even more so.

As well as the social, cultural and economic differences that can make it difficult for NGOs to properly hear and convey what the affected groups are saying, gender differences can also be an issue. Can an NGO or CSO that is male-dominated or whose staff are predominantly male accurately represent the issues of women in an affected group? This was an issue in the Sri Lankan case, where the key members of the ALaRM coalition were organizations led by strong male figures, while the workforce that they spoke for was overwhelmingly female. The coalition took active steps to overcome this, however, by encouraging and facilitating the participation of women, particularly women workers and former workers in the coalition's decision-making processes. For example, it was established right at the start that each member organization would sent two representatives to the coalition's planning meetings, and that at least one of these would be female. Some organizations at first had difficulty finding a woman willing or able to attend, and those that did come to meetings were rather quiet. Part of the problem was a difference in levels of understanding, as the male members of the group were knowledgeable and decidedly more confident. Steps were taken to overcome this, for example, by providing background notes in the women's own language on the issues that were to be discussed, and by giving support and encouragement to female members to express their views and opinions. At times, women were specifically invited to express their views in meetings. At other times, in informal conversations outside the meetings (for example, while walking) women were encouraged to talk about a particular issue and then gently urged to express those views within the meeting. In the end, the situation changed and the voices of female workers were heard loud and clear within the coalition. By 2007 about two-thirds of those who came regularly to the coalition meetings were females, who were very actively and vocally involved in the discussions and decision making.[24]

If an NGO or advocacy network is to act effectively on behalf of an affected community or group, it needs to have either people from a similar background or those who can cross cultural, social, gender and other barriers and enter into the reality of other people's lives. This was an especially important issue in the Camisea campaign in Peru. The organization that was culturally close to those affected by the natural gas project was COMARU, a local indigenous federation. However, as mentioned above, the majority of the Peruvian and international NGOs working with them were environmental organizations whose primary concern was with biodiversity conservation. Even amongst the minority of indigenous rights NGOs in the coalition there were often differences between the 'grassroots' and national organizations. COMARU did not always see eye-to-eye with AIDESEP, the national indigenous organization. Because of the area's geographical isolation, it was rarely possible for COMARU's leadership to attend the campaign coalition meetings in the capital city of Lima. It fell upon Oxfam field staff and a small group of indigenous rights NGOs to act as mediators between the local and national, and between the indigenous and the environmentalists (who had a notorious history of conflict) to ensure that the voices of the indigenous people affected by the pipeline were clearly heard in the campaign.[25]

Every campaign needs people who can hear and sensitively understand what affected groups are saying about their lives and problems, and interpret or translate that into the kind of conceptual frameworks that the relevant policy makers can understand, and the specific changes that are required, without compromising the authenticity of the original message. This involves NGOs and their staff acting as what Nyamugasira calls 'accompaniers' for the affected groups:

> They can act as sounding boards, asking the kinds of question that enable people to identify the real issues and in turn formulate their questions to those in power. The accompaniers can be there as people discuss these questions with the policy-makers. They can also be there to help them evaluate their achievements and set higher objectives. They can use their contacts to gain access for them and give them confidence when walking in the corridors of power, which can indeed be daunting to the uninitiated. But they must never lose sight of the fact that they themselves are not the actors. They only accompany and act as temporary brokers.[26]

This particularly applies to the 'grassroots' CSOs and NGOs operating in the South, who are in direct contact with those who have the problem, who are their first link to an advocacy network. However, there is often a second link that must also occur, to NGOs in the North. For example, in the case of La Oroya this was the link to Oxfam America and the Presbyterian Church in the US and community groups in the company's hometown in the US. There is a need to ensure that this link works properly and effectively as well. In fact it did not work as well as it might have. La Oroya was never a high priority for the Oxfam America global extractive industries team in the US, because they did not see how it could be used to influence an important decision maker in the North, despite the fact that it was one of the emblematic cases defined as a priority by Oxfam's regional office and its partners in Peru. Another example of the link to the North not working well was the Sri Lanka case, where the involvement of Oxfam affiliates and other organizations in Europe to lobby the companies buying garments from Sri Lanka and/or the European Commission over market access could have been very useful, but did not happen in any effective way, because market access was not a priority in an international campaign that was basically about labour rights. The problem is that Northern-based NGOs and NGO staff have their own agendas and priorities, and whether or not an issue or request from a particular country or group is taken up will depend on the extent to which it fits into those Northern priorities and agendas.

In his book *The Marketing of Rebellion*, American academic Clifford Bob draws attention to this aspect of the relationship between affected groups and Northern NGOs, making the point that in the market-place of worthy causes, it is very much a buyers' market.[27] There are many hundreds of causes out there, vying for the attention and support of Northern advocates, but only a few ever get taken up. He uses as his examples insurgency movements such as those in China, contrasting the attention that the Tibetan case receives internationally with that of the Uygurs of western China who, like the Tibetans, have for generations resisted Han Chinese domination and cultural extinction, but have failed to inspire the broad-based international networks that support the Tibetans. His analysis, however, applies to any cause in the South (or the North for that matter) that is seeking international assistance.

> Challengers scramble for scarce resources in a setting thick with similar aspirants. Despite its promise, today's 'global civil society' is for many a Darwinian arena in which the successful prosper but the weak wither. At any one time, there is room for only a few challengers on any issue. Tacitly and at times openly, needy groups vie with one another for the world's sympathy, elevating themselves above their competitors and differentiating themselves from similar causes.

Aspirants must seek to make themselves heard beyond their borders, for example by getting themselves noticed by the international media, and then magnify their appeal by framing their situation and problem in a way that matches the interests and agendas of distant audiences. They must publicize their plight and portray their conflict as a righteous struggle, and craft their message so as to resonate abroad. For many this is a life and death situation, for in advertising themselves to the international community in this way, groups expose themselves to the wrath of the oppressing government, and if they then fail to win that international support they can be left very vulnerable.

This analysis by Bob attacks the idea that Northern or international NGOs always pick the most needy causes on which to bestow their support. Every aspiring cause, faced with a government crackdown or political exclusion will portray its troubles as the most deserving, but in practice, Clifford says, there is little or no connection between the worthiness or urgency of the cause and the level of international support it receives. Rather, Northern advocacy NGOs are inclined to choose those causes whose profile most closely matches their own requirements. 'Their principles are always important, but NGOs are apt to back causes that appear relevant, important, and understandable to their constituents or funders'. In particular, they will tend to support groups involved in issues that have potential to leverage social change beyond the particular conflict site – for example a particular World Bank supported problematic project that has the potential to spark fundamental changes in Bank procedures.

Northern and international NGOs cannot solve all the world's problems. They have very limited resources and the problems are overwhelmingly numerous and serious. All they can do is to pick an issue here and there, hopefully on the basis of it illustrating a wider problem or being able to leverage a wider effect, and focusing their limited advocacy and campaigning resources on that. This was the theory behind the global 'Make Trade Fair' campaign and its sub-campaigns on garment workers, agriculture, etc. The aim was not just to improve the conditions of workers or farmers in particular countries, but to use these as illustrations of a wider problem, an unfair trading system, and to press for acceptance of the idea that the potential of trade to lift people out of poverty was being frustrated because the rules and practices of trade were 'rigged' in the interests of rich and powerful countries and corporate interests and to the disadvantage of the poor and the weak. The aim in other words was nothing less than to make trade fair, using those cases as illustrative examples. Likewise, Oxfam America's global extractive industries campaign sought to achieve a series of changes in industry practices worldwide, typified by the 'ten golden rules' of the 'No Dirty Gold' campaign. To that end, they encouraged local partners to focus their campaigning on 'emblematic cases' which would typify or illustrate one or more of the issues contained in the 'ten golden rules'. In this way, they sought not only to resolve specific problems of concern to their local allies but to use them to drive a global change agenda.

Notes

1. H. Slim (2002) *By what authority? The legitimacy and accountability of non-government organizations* (International Council on Human Rights Policy). www.jha.ac/articles/a082.htm date accessed 14 April 2008.
2. J. Clarke (2003) *Worlds apart. Civil society and the battle for ethical globalisation* (Bloomfield, CT, USA: Kumarian Press) p. 176.
3. P. Wapner (2002) 'Defending accountability in NGOs', *Chicago Journal of International Law*, Spring, Academic Research Library, pp. 197–205.
4. Oxfam International website www.oxfam.org/en/about/why accessed 10 December 2008.
5. International Non-Governmental Organizations Accountability Charter. www.oxfam.org/files/INGO_accountability_charter_0606_0.pdf date accessed 17 August 2008.
6. J. MacNeill (2004) Letter to the editor, *Foreign Policy*, 1 October.
7. Anon (2006) *Promises to keep. Report on the evaluation of the implementation of Oxfam International's strategic plan 2001–2006*, Synthesis Report, p. 36. www.oxfam.org/en/about/accountability date accessed 17 August 2008.
8. J. A. Scholte (2004) 'Civil society and democratically accountable global governance', *Government and Opposition*, vol 39, issue 2, pp. 211–33.
9. K. Naidoo (2004) 'The end of blind faith. Civil society and the challenge of accountability, legitimacy and transparency', *Accountability Forum 2*, Special Issue on NGO Accountability and Performance (Greenleaf Publishing) p. 22.
10. J. Fox (2000) *Civil society and political accountability: Propositions for discussion.* Paper presented at University of Notre Dame, 8–9 May. http://kellogg.nd.edu/events/pdfs/Fox.pdf date accessed 7 September 2008.
11. A. Hudson (2001) 'NGOs transnational advocacy networks: from legitimacy to political responsibility?' *Global Networks*, vol 1, number 4, p. 338.
12. Slim (2002) *op cit.* www.jha.ac/articles/a082.htm
13. Oxfam Great Britain (2006) Statement of legitimacy and accountability. www.oxfam.org.uk/resources/accounts/legitimacy.html date accessed 17 August 2008.
14. World Bank (1998) *The Bank's relationship with NGOs* (Washington DC: World Bank).
15. Benchmark Environmental Consulting and Royal Ministry of Foreign Affairs (1996) *Democratic global governance: Report of the 1995 benchmark survey of NGOs* (Oslo, Norway).
16. M. Edwards and J. Gaventa (eds) (2001) *Global Citizen Action* (Boulder CO, USA: Lynne Rienner Publishers) p. 273.
17. Anon (2006) *Promises to keep. Report on the evaluation of the implementation of Oxfam International's strategic plan 2001–2006*, Synthesis report, p. 44. www.oxfam.org/en/about/accountability date accessed 17 August 2008.
18. L. Roper (2005) *'Make Trade Fair' internal evaluation*, report to Oxfam International, p. 66.

19 J. D. Clark (2001) 'Ethical Globalization: The Dilemmas and Challenges of Internationalizing Civil Society', in Edwards M. and Gaventa J. (eds) *Global Citizen Action* (Boulder CO, USA: Lynne Rienner Publishers) p. 27.
20 Although it was subsequently withdrawn, in November 2008 the President and Prime Minister of India sent a proposal to the national Congress under which international NGOs registered in the country could be disbanded if they attempted to influence national policies or decisions on the grounds that this would represent an interference with national sovereignty.
21 R. Chambers (1993) *Challenging the professions: Frontiers for rural development* (London: Intermediate Technology) p. 28.
22 W. Nyamugasira (2002) 'NGOs and advocacy: how well are the poor represented?' in Eade D. (ed.) *Development and Advocacy* (Oxford, UK: Oxfam Great Britain) pp. 11–12.
23 Nyamugasira (2002) *op cit.*, pp. 11–12.
24 J. Atkinson (2007) *Evaluation of the campaign on labour and trade in Sri Lanka 2002–2007*, Oxfam International, pp. 32–3.
25 On the conflict between indigenous and environmentalists, see for example Mac Chapin (2004) 'A challenge to conservationists', *World Watch*, vol 17, number 6, November/December, pp. 17–31.
26 Nyamugasira (2002) *op cit.*, p. 17.
27 C. Bob (2005) *The marketing of rebellion. Insurgents, media and international activism.* Studies in Contentious Politics (Cambridge: Cambridge University Press).

10
Conclusions

In recent decades, advocacy by national and international NGOs and other civil society organizations that challenges accepted views, provides alternative perspectives and promotes the voices of the politically excluded, has become an accepted part of the political scene. Environmental groups have pushed for recognition of global warming, and to stop the policies and practices of companies, international institutions or governments that damage the natural environment. Human rights organizations and peace groups have pressured for enhanced regimes of arms control and conflict management. Women's organizations have promoted increased gender sensitivity across the whole of global governance. Development NGOs have fought for relief from national debt, better policies by international financial institutions, fairer trade rules, improved food security, better health and educational services in the South, the rights of workers, children's rights, humanitarian relief, the rights of refugees, and so on.

Success, however, has been modest and there is much more that needs to be done. There is no doubt that this type of advocacy will increase in the future as NGOs continue to monitor the impacts on the poor and on Southern countries of the policies of governments and intergovernmental bodies and the practices of transnational corporations, and press them for greater transparency, more equitable policies, redress and correction of abuses, proper standards and monitoring mechanisms.

In the case studies in this book we have seen one particular INGO confederation, Oxfam International, working to improve the lot of garment workers and farmers in South Asia and to obtain redress for communities in Peru affected by the operations of companies. It did not of course do this by itself. Like all INGOs, it was only able to do what it did by working with other civil society organizations in both the North and the South, but in particular in the South, in informal networks that extended across national boundaries. It was able to take advantage of the unique situation of an INGO as an organization that has a presence and experience in the South, but also connections and influence in the North, plus the ability to generate resources to carry out such work.

One of the more useful roles it was able to play was making available politically useful information. Using its network of offices and contacts in Europe and North America, it was able to collect and provide relevant information and political intelligence on what Northern governments and companies were saying and doing and make it available in the South. It was also able to use its presence in a large number of countries in Africa, Asia and Latin America to research and provide an international or global overview of the issues of concern (for example, the situation of garment workers all around the world). All this research and information was analysed and processed, and provided to friends and opponents, to allies, governments, the media, etc in both the North and the South in forms that were as accessible as possible – ranging from simple brochures and media releases through to detailed reports, depending on the audience. It used in other words classic 'information politics' as defined by Keck and Sikkink, generating politically useful information and making it available where it would have most impact.[1]

It was also able to facilitate and assist with the provision of local research and analysis (for example the Living Wage report in Sri Lanka and the reports on lead levels in La Oroya). When local CSOs are fully stretched, as they so often are, fighting for basic rights or trying to survive in a hostile and repressive political environment, research and analysis is not usually very high on their list of priorities. But an INGO like Oxfam can in this situation bring in extra resources and/or skills to enable this to happen, which is what occurred in each instance.

By providing well-researched and authoritative reports like this, and skilfully publicizing and distributing them, an INGO can help change the terms of debate on a particular issue in a national context by providing alternative perspectives and giving a voice to those who would otherwise not be heard. This is basically what Oxfam and ALaRM did in Sri Lanka, for example, by providing reports that introduced a workers' perspective into the debate around the MFA phase-out – and in Peru by demonstrating that there were high levels of lead in the blood of pregnant women and children and that the source was Doe Run's lead smelter.

The fact that such high quality research and analysis is coming from local CSOs and NGOs can help change the attitude of governments and others towards them, from being regarded as marginalized radicals with shallow and ideologically driven agendas that are not worth listening to, to organizations with something worthwhile to say that needs to be listened to, whether or not one agrees with it. By providing such assistance and facilitating the distribution of high quality research and analysis, INGOs can help open up the democratic space available to local and national level CSOs to have their views heard.

As well as bringing information and analysis to advocates and others in the South, INGOs can also do the reverse: bring information and issues from the South, where the problem is, to the North where many of the decisions affecting that problem are made. A classic example of this was the Camisea case in Peru where the problems being experienced by the communities near the proposed natural gas pipeline were brought to the attention of the US government representatives on the boards of the Ex-Im Bank and the Inter-American Development Bank in Washington DC. Once again, this was a classic case of 'information politics' and of the 'boomerang strategy' outlined by Kerk and Sikkink.

The INGO's ability to do this depends on the influence it can exert on the targeted company or government in the North – and this in turn depends on its ability to generate active support from its members and other activists, and to access the media and the targeted decision makers in the North, skills that any INGO wishing to undertake advocacy successfully needs to develop and hone. It is also dependent on the nature of the target, on how sensitive the targeted company is to scandals that might damage its reputation or tarnish its brand name, or how sensitive the targeted government is to issues that can undermine its political position or its standing with the electorate.

Challenges

It is now well accepted by all except the most hardened critics that this type of activity by NGOs and other non-state actors is legitimate in a democratic society. They have a legitimate and useful role to play in contributing to debate in political processes. It is their ability to make a useful and effective contribution that gives NGOs legitimacy, the right to take part in those debates. But it does not give them the right to be involved directly in decision making. They have a voice but not a vote.

However usefulness and effectiveness demands that the positions taken by the NGO are based on thorough research and analysis and a sensitivity to the poor or affected groups whom they hope to benefit. It means being accurate and not oversimplifying an issue to the point of distortion in order to gain public support or rouse supporters to action. For a Northern-based INGO advocating or supporting advocacy in the South, that is, outside its own society, it also requires that the positions advocated for are based on universally held values and fundamental rights and do not represent special interests or foreign values not held by that society.

NGOs will continue to be challenged by those whom they are challenging, and their legitimacy called into question. They can minimize this to some extent by not claiming to be what they are not – by not claiming, for example, to speak on behalf of the poor when in fact all they are legitimately doing is speaking about the poor. INGOs that undertake advocacy need to be clear about their status. In most cases they will find themselves speaking *with* or *about* the poor, occasionally *for* the poor if they are not able to speak for themselves, but never *as* the poor. To claim a status that they do not have is merely to invite challenge.

Another challenge they will continue to face is that of accountability. INGOs have had some success in forcing international institutions to be more transparent and accountable for their projects, programmes, and overall policy approaches, and transnational companies to be more accountable for their operations and commercial practices. However, those who point the finger need to have a clean hand. Those who demand accountability of others need to be accountable themselves, and in this most INGOs are weak. In terms of accountability to donors and supporters, their formal mechanisms could generally be described as reasonable, and are significantly complemented by the need to maintain credibility in the eyes of the public and the trust and confidence of those who support them through donations or campaign actions. But in terms of accountability to those they are attempting to help most INGOs are quite weak.

There is a need to move beyond the view that accountability is primarily about the responsibility of 'partners' in the South to account for the grants they have been given to one that also includes the INGO's own responsibility and accountability to 'partners' and others in the South for the political, economic and other effects that advocacy done in their name has on them. This 'downwards' accountability needs to be incorporated into the various INGO codes and charters and used as a measure when accessing their performance. INGOs should undertake their advocacy in a way that reflects their democratic ideals, which means involving the affected parties as equal partners in determining positions, priorities and strategies, making sure they have equal access to information, and being accountable to them for the outcomes of their advocacy. It may also be desirable for INGO funders to relinquish some of their power over how the campaign funding is spent and allow this to be determined jointly by a coalition.

The giving of grants by INGOs to partner organizations in the South is a key determinant of the relationship between them. Most advocacy in the South requires financial resources to sustain it, and in many cases the only source of this is INGOs, particularly development INGOs like Oxfam. These have traditionally provided finance for development projects and programmes, but are increasingly also providing it for advocacy. While this funding may be very useful for organizations in the South seeking resources to carry on their work, it can also render them financially dependent on the Northern funder. For unlike the development grants that INGOs traditionally provide, which can be used to support activities that generate income and lead eventually to financial independence, advocacy funding is simply consumed and will not normally generate such independence.

The role of NGOs in networks

There will always be a tendency for Northern-based INGOs to be influential or even dominant in transnational advocacy networks because of their size, their better access to information, resources and influence and above all their role as funders. There are always going to be far more causes out there seeking assistance than there are INGO resources to support them, which means that INGOs are in a position to choose between worthy causes, to pick which organizations and causes they will support and which they will not. This they would hopefully do on the basis of greatest need or urgency, but there is no doubt that their own needs and priorities will also be a key factor. These will include 'campaignability', that is, how appealing the campaign will be or how readily understandable it is to the INGO's supporters, and also how strategic it is as an issue and its potential to leverage wider change.

A Southern CSO seeking the financial and political support of the INGO will be tempted to adjust or modify its cause in order to match the perceived priorities of the INGO. And even after a relationship has been established, the INGO will still be in a position to influence its

Southern allies and partners in the advocacy network because of its dominant position in terms of access to resources, information and influence.

There is a danger that the INGO will focus on the help that its Southern allies can offer it and its campaign in the North, rather than the help that it can offer them to achieve change directly in the South. This can lead to an 'extractive mentality', in which the Southern participants in the network are seen primarily as a source of legitimacy and of useful information, evidence, stories etc to support the campaign in the North. They can become, and feel themselves to be, merely supporting players in a campaign rather than as equals in a joint effort.

In taking an issue or cause into a Northern political arena, INGOs can and do sometimes filter or modify the issue, or express it in different terms in order to fit their own agendas. The classic examples of this are Northern environmental organizations portraying an issue such as the preservation of the Amazonian rainforest as a purely environmental one, neglecting the rights of those living in the affected area and depending on it for their livelihood. This distortion can lead to the affected groups losing control of the message and in some cases to the campaign resulting in outcomes that they do not want and that are not in their interests. There is a need in any transnational campaign for sensitive listening by INGOs to ensure that the messages of those affected are conveyed forcefully yet accurately, across cultural, social and political barriers to the centres of power where changes need to be made. INGOs should ideally see themselves as 'accompaniers', as temporary brokers, rather than as the main actors in this advocacy process. They need to be a little humble, and willing to listen to voices from the South, particularly those of their Southern allies, regarding advocacy messages, priorities and strategies.

Above all, there needs to be recognition that what they do in the North has political and other implications for those with whom they are working in the South. As Jordan and van Tuijl have put it, there needs to be a degree of political responsibility in the campaign, as reflected in the compatibility of its different objectives in different arenas, what happens with information within the network, and how strategies, risks and funds are managed.[2] In a truly participatory and democratically run campaign, the advocacy agendas and strategies will be set in close consultation with the groups who are to benefit from the campaign, and risks assumed only to the extent that they can be born by the most vulnerable. Such a campaign will be characterized by mutually supporting objectives by different NGOs in different political arenas; a continuous flow of information among all network members; periodic reviews of strategies by all parties involved; joint management of political responsibilities; and risk management based on the local realities in the political arena where campaign participants are most vulnerable.

Many NGO campaigns operate in different political arenas at the same time – at a local, national and international level, in the South and in the North. While overall strategies and campaign plans should be determined jointly by all members of the advocacy network, there also has to be recognition that different members will have expertise in different arenas, and that their advice should be listened to in terms of strategies and approaches to be taken within their particular arena. Thus a Nepalese CSO member of a campaign network based in Kathmandu is in a better position to determine the strategy to be adopted in Nepal than say a member based in Washington DC, who in turn is in a better position to advise on strategies *vis-à-vis* the US government. Each should be respected for advising on their own particular arena of expertise.

While all campaigns should be joint and run in a participatory and responsible way, the nature of the relationships within the advocacy network will also be determined by where the issue of the campaign originated, for example, from an affected group or from an INGO. An example of the former is the Camisea campaign, which started with the problems of a particular group of communities and involved CSOs and INGOs supporting them by taking their demands up to the national and international level. The WTO campaign in India was of course an example of the latter. These two different approaches could be characterized as 'supportive' on the one hand and 'directive' on the other. In fact there is a spectrum of approaches or campaign types ranging from the most supportive at one end to the most directive at the other.

In the global sub-campaign on the garment industry within Oxfam's international 'Make Trade Fair' campaign there were, as mentioned in Chapter 3, two approaches put forward, one of which was supportive and the other not. The original sub-campaign conceived by Oxfam ('Trading Away Our Rights') was one that built on and supported a number of national level labour campaigns for garment workers in a variety of countries – whereas the joint 'Olympics Campaign' was centrally organized, globally unified and much more directive. The global 'Make Trade Fair' campaign as a whole was an example of a campaign at the 'directive' end of this spectrum – planned, organized and directed from an international level and handed down to the country level, with affiliate offices, partner organizations and potential allies in the South having to fit in or find a connection as best they could with a campaign that was not of their design. Northern-based advocates in INGOs tend to gravitate towards the more directive type of approach as it puts them in a leadership role as against being merely the supporters of other people's campaigns. However directive campaigns are the least democratic or participatory, and the ones most likely to be out of touch with those whom the campaign is supposed to be helping.

But there are nevertheless some good reasons for running them in certain circumstances, for example when the campaign is aimed at influencing an international agreement, such as those on trade rules or emissions reductions, or influencing the policies and practices of a transnational company that operates over a range of countries. In such cases it makes sense for there to be an overall global strategy to influence the targeted agreement or company, and for individual country campaigns to fall in line with that for the sake of impact. But there will nevertheless always be a tension between the need to maximize impact by having a coordinated directive campaign, and the need to maximize relevance by having a more flexible approach in which Southern-based participants can take up an issue in their own way, in their own time, and with their own emphasis.

Supportive campaigns are not only more democratic; they are also more developmentally sound in that they tend to empower the affected group by giving them more control over their situation, rather than disempower them by having others act for them. They can also represent a longer term and more sustainable solution to problems in that, while the CSOs and INGOs will eventually move on to other issues and other campaigns, the affected groups remain and hopefully remain vigilant against the non-implementation of the policy or practice change won, or any repetition of the problem. On the down side however, supportive campaigns require a long-term commitment from the CSO or INGO, particularly if they involve the organizing or building of the capacity of the affected group, and the building of their confidence to speak out in a coherent way and face the harsh repression that often results. These are campaigns for the 'accompaniers', for the quiet behind-the-scenes supporters who are willing to stay and work with people on an issue over the long term. For INGOs that see themselves as primarily advocating in the North, who want to be able to take up new and important issues as they arise, or use new influencing opportunities in the North, this type of campaign will not be very appealing.

There is no doubt that international campaigning by civil society organizations will continue in the foreseeable future on a wide variety of issues, and that INGOs will play a key role in it, along with others in both the South and North. In doing so they are in a sense filling a gap in global governance. In a situation in which there are a growing number of issues that transcend national boundaries – environmental degradation, global warming, people trafficking, refugees and human rights abuses – and as yet no effective global governance to deal with them, there is a danger that critical issues will be neglected because governments and international institutions are not able or willing to deal with them. NGOs and other CSOs can raise issues that would otherwise be neglected in a way that hopefully ensures that attention is paid to them. On issues that are raised, they can provide alternative perspectives that add significantly to the richness of the debate. And they can provide an outlet and a voice to those suffering injustices of various kinds who are not being heard, whose fundamental rights are being abused, but whose government is perhaps part of the problem rather than the solution. While there are issues that need to be addressed and watched as set out in this and the previous chapter, this type of activity by civil society organizations needs to be not only recognized as legitimate, but encouraged and supported.

Notes

1 M. Keck and K. Sikkink (1998) *Activists Beyond Borders* (Ithaca and London: Cornell University Press) pp. 18–22.
2 L. Jordan and P. van Tuijl (2000) 'Political responsibility in transnational NGO advocacy', *World Development*, vol 28, number 12, pp. 2051–65.

Index

Acción Ecológica, 120
accountability, see under non-government organizations
accountability politics, see under campaigns, strategies
Accountability Charter, 27, 217
Action Aid International, 98
Activos Mineros S.A.C., 195
advocacy, 23–7, 120, 123–4, 160–1, 169–72, 196, 202, 213, 220–8, 236, 238–44
  people-centred, 44–6
  transnational networks, 23–7, 56–8, 103–4, 163, 166, 174, 196–7, 200, 220–8, 230–4, 240–4
Advocacy Institute, 123
Advocacy Learning Initiative (ALI), 123
agriculture, 94–115
Air Quality Technical Committee, 184
Ali, Lucky, 101
alliances, see under campaigns
Alliance for Energy, 43
Amazon Alliance, 8, 137
Amazon Watch, 137, 145
Ames, Eliana, 182
Amnesty International, 3, 9, 11, 217, 225
Andean Development Corporation (CAF), 136, 142
Anderson, Kenneth, 32–3
Anglican Church, 9
Anheier, H. K., 25
Apparel-Industry Labour Rights Movement (ALaRM), 72–4, 76–9, 209, 211, 218, 223, 230, 237
  Core Advisory Group, 70–1
Archbishop of Huancayo, 177–8, 183, 185, 187, 189, 197–9
Arun III Dam, 42
Arun Concerned Group, 43
Asháninka Communal Reserve, 147
Asics, 60

Association of Environmental Delegates (ADA), 170, 172, 193
Atkins, Chet, 173
Atlas, Steve, 173
audits, environmental, 168
Axworthy, Lloyd, 14
Australian Government, 23
Australian Council for International Development, 37, 217

Ballinger, Jeff, 41
Bank Information Centre (BIC), 7
Barandiarán, A., 173
Barreto, Pedro, S. J., see Archbishop of Huancayo
BHP Billiton mining company, 21, 129
Big Noise petition, see under campaigns
Bishops' Social Action Commission in Peru (CEAS), 188
Blacksmith Institute, 186
Blair, Tony, 16
Blitt, Robert, 36
Board of Investment (BOI), 73–4
Bob, Clifford, 232–3
Bono, 16
boomerang strategy, see under campaigns, strategies
British Parliament, 79
British Petroleum company (BP), 118
Brock, K., 109
Buenaventura mining company, 128
Bujagali Dam, 47–8

Caffrey, Patricia, 136–8, 158
Camisea Citizen Action (ACC), 153, 155, 157, 160–1, 163
Camisea Fund, 142–3, 151, 154, 160, 162
Camisea natural gas project, 44, 133–64
Camisea Ombudsman, 137

245

campaigns, 12–23, 37–46, 160, 169–72, 175, 177–82, 187–202, 211, 223
  achievements, 80–4, 103–9, 141–6, 189–91
  agricultural trade campaign, 61–3, 65
  alliances, 87–8, 110–11, 120, 138–46, 163, 172–7, 189, 191–4, 196–202, 212, 218–20, 223–4, 228–34
  Big Noise petition, 55, 79, 99–102, 106–7, 109, 212, 222–3
  Camisea campaign, 44, 127, 130, 133–64, 212, 218, 229–30, 238, 242
  Clean Clothes Campaign, 60–1, 80, 90
  democracy, 90–2, 114–15, 198–201, 208, 210–11, 243
  Education Now campaign, 53, 119
  garment trade campaign, 58–61, 64–5, 67–92
  infant formula campaign, 13–15, 18–19, 21, 23
  International Campaign to Ban Landmines (ICBL), 1–2, 9, 14–15, 19–20, 34
  Jubilee 2000 campaign, 9, 15–17, 19, 39
  La Oroya campaign, 127, 130–2, 166–202, 209
  Make Trade Fair campaign, 53–9, 67, 70, 72, 74, 82, 86, 88, 90–1, 94–5, 97, 99–101, 105–6, 115, 122, 213, 222–4, 226, 233, 242
  media, 83, 102, 104, 132, 144, 148, 154, 156, 158–9, 173–4, 176, 178, 181–2, 192, 194, 197–8, 201–2, 219
  No Dirty Gold campaign, 124–5, 233
  participation, 90–2, 114–15, 197–201, 243
  Play Fair at the Olympics campaign, 60–1, 79–80, 84, 91, 226, 242
  political responsibility, 46–9, 92, 215–16, 219, 241–2
  popular, 99–103, 102
  Publish What You Pay campaign, 125
  representation, 41–6, 46–9
  research accuracy, 37–9, 237–8
  Right to Know, Right to Decide campaign, 125
  Save La Oroya campaign, 187, 189
  small arms campaign, 15
  strategies, 18–23, 39–41, 107–9, 113–15, 158–9, 162, 174, 201, 241–2
    accountability politics, 107–8, 158, 194
    boomerang strategy, 22, 26, 86, 131–2, 162, 201, 238
    information politics, 107, 158, 194, 222, 237–8
    leverage politics, 158, 194
    symbolic politics, 159, 194
  Tambogrande campaign, 127–8
  Tintaya campaign, 127, 129–30
  Trading Away Our Rights campaign, 59–61, 83, 88
  Yanacocha campaign, 127–9
CARE, 7
Catholic Church, 9, 131, 178, 188, 192, 194, 198, 202
Cederstav, A., 173, 186
Centre for Advocacy and Research, 99
Centre for Community Economics and Development Consultants Society (CECOEDECON), 99–100
Centre for Economic and Social Rights (CDES), 120
Centre for Human Rights and the Environment (CEDHA), 182
Centre for International Environmental Law (CIEL), 193
Centre for the Development of the Amazonian Indigenous (CEDIA), 120, 137, 139, 144
Centre for Trade and Development (CENTAD), 95, 101, 105, 108, 112, 212–13
Centromin Peru, 167, 169, 195
Cerro de Pasco Copper Corporation, 167
certification, 124–5, 186, 217
Chandani, Badrika, 77

Chapman, Jennifer, 12, 56
Charveriat, Celine, 97–8
Cheatham, Craig, 173
Choudhary, Ramakrishna, 101, 109
Christian Aid, 35, 170
civil society organizations, 2–12, 18, 20, 23–7, 30–49, 98, 102, 109–10, 113, 139–40, 143, 146–9, 151, 153–6, 158–9, 161, 196, 207–8, 212, 214, 221–3, 225, 230–1, 236, 238, 240, 242–4
Clark, John, 9, 11–12, 18, 38, 43, 208, 224
coalitions, *see* campaigns, alliances
Committee of Neighbourhood Boards of La Oroya, 172
Confederation of Communities Affected by Mining in Peru (CONACAMI), 123, 129, 193, 197, 218
Confederation of Indigenous Nationalities of Ecuador (CONAIE), 120
Conoco oil company, 48–9, 229
Consumer Union & Trust Society (CUTS), 104
consent, free, prior and informed, 124–7
Conservation International (CI), 134, 137, 139
Constitutional Tribunal (Peru), 182–3, 190, 195
CooperAcción, 129–30, 170, 172, 193
Coordinator of Andean Indigenous Organizations (CAOI), 5
Coordinator of Indigenous Organizations of the Amazon Basin (COICA), 5, 8
Core Advisory Group, *see under* Apparel-Industry Labour Rights Movement (ALaRM)
Covenant Centre for Development (CCD), 99, 102

Dabindhu Collective, 76, 86
Das, Palash Kanti, 104
Delhi University, 101
democracy, *see under* campaigns

Doe Run Peru (DRP), 166, 169, 173–7, 180–7, 189, 191–202, 237
Doe Run Resources Corporation, 169, 173, 187
Doha Development Round, 96

Earthjustice, 182, 186, 193
EarthWorks, 124
Eco-Andes, 170, 172, 193
Economist, The, 30
Education Now campaign, *see under* campaigns
Edwards, Michael, 15, 26–7, 34–6, 222
Ekta Parishad, 102
Energy Investment Supervisor (OSINERG), *see* Peruvian Government, Energy and Mining Investment Supervisor (OSINERGMIN)
environmental impact assessments (EIAs), 136, 148, 152, 168
environmental management and adjustment programmes (PAMAs), 168–9, 175–80, 182, 187–9, 192, 198, 200
Environmental Defense, 137, 145
Environmental Law Institute (ELI), 124
E-Tech International, 154, 158
European Commission, 56, 74, 86, 232
European Parliament, 79
European Union, 62, 74, 95–7
Export Credit Agencies (ECAs), 145, 160
Export Processing Zones (EPZs), 67–8, 76, 79–80
Export-Import Bank (Ex-Im Bank), *see under* US government
extractive industries, 118–64, 166–202, 211, 220
Extractive Industries Transparency Initiative, 125
extractive industries working group, *see under* Oxfam International

farming, contract, 95, 98
Fifth Avenue Synagogue, 187
Filomena Tomaira Pacsi, 170, 172

248 *Index*

Flannery, Dennis, 140–1, 151–2
Focus on the Global South, 8
Ford Foundation, 124
Fox, Jonathan, 214–15
Free Trade Zone Workers Union (FTZWU), 86
Freeport copper mine, 21
Friends of La Oroya, 199
Friends of the Earth Indonesia (WALHI), 3
Friends of the Earth International (FoEI), 3, 9, 225
Friends of the Earth South Africa (GroundWork), 3
Fujimori, Alberto, 134–5

Gaventa, John, 34, 222
Global Alliance for Workers and Communities (GA), 41
global union federations (GUFs), 4
Global Village Engineers (GVE), 145, 158
Goodland, Robert, 137, 139–40
Graffiti, 186
Grameen Bank, 5
Graña y Montero, 135
Green Cross, 187
Greenpeace, 3, 9, 11, 37–8, 217
Group of eight countries (G8), 16, 19
Group of twenty countries (G20), 63, 97, 112

Handicap International, 1
Harper, Caroline, 38
Harvard University, School of Public Health, 199
Highly Indebted Poor Countries Initiative (HIPC), 15–16
Hong Kong Ministerial meeting, 98–9, 102–4
Hudson, Alan, 6
Human Rights Committee of the Parish of La Oroya, 172
human rights organizations (HROs), 36–7
Human Rights Watch, 1, 9
Hunt oil company, 135

India, 94–115
Indian government, 97–8, 101, 103–5, 107–12, 212, 219, 222
  Commerce and Industry Minister, 104, 109, 111
  Commerce Secretary, 109
indigenous peoples, 120, 134
  Amahuaca, 134
  Asháninka, 134
  Huaorani, 48–9, 229
  Machiguenga, 134, 138
  Nahua, 135
  Yaminahua, 134
  Yine (Piro), 134
Industrias Peñoles S.A., 169
infant formula campaign, *see under* campaigns
information politics, *see under* campaigns, strategies
Institute for Policy Studies, 137
Interamerican Association for Environmental Defense (AIDA), 172, 182, 186, 191
Inter-American Development Bank (IDB), *see under* World Bank
Interamerican Human Rights Commission (CIDH), 176, 182–3, 190, 192–3, 196
Interethnic Association for the Development of the Peruvian Jungle (AIDESEP), 120, 137, 139, 143, 153, 161, 218, 231
Inter-institutional Technical Coordination Group (GTCI), *see under* Peruvian Government
International Baby Food Action Network (IBFAN), 9, 13–14, 23
International Campaign to Ban Landmines (ICBL), *see under* campaigns
International Confederation of Free Trade Unions (ICFTU), 61, 90
International Development Association, *see under* World Bank
International Labor Organization (ILO), 22, 73–4, 81, 83, 87
  Task Force, 73–5, 81–2, 84, 211
International Monetary Fund (IMF), 15–16, 25, 53, 119

Index 249

International Nestlé Boycott Committee, 14
International Olympic Committee (IOC), 80
International Rivers Network (IRN), 47–8
International Textile, Garment and Leather Workers Federation, 4
Inuit Circumpolar Council, 5

Joining Hands against Poverty Network, 172–4, 177, 188–9, 199
Joint Apparel Associations Forum (JAAF), 73
Jordan, L., 45–9, 92, 114, 200, 215–16, 241
Jubilee 2000 campaign, *see under* campaigns
Junín regional government, 183, 185, 190–1, 200

Kaldor, Mary, 22
Kategari, Walter, 159
Keck, M., 18–26, 81–4, 107–8, 158, 160, 194, 196, 237–8
Kisan Seva Samiti Mahasangh, 107
Knight Piesold consulting company, 145
Kugapakori-Nahua State Reserve, 134, 144
Kumudini, Sunitha, 77

Labor (NGO), 172, 188, 193
labour unions, 4, 58–61, 78–9, 82, 85–7, 89, 176, 191, 202, 207–8, 210, 212, 220
  global union federations (GUFs), 4
Lamy, Pascal, 102
La Oroya Antigua Defence Committee, 172
La Oroya Chamber of Commerce, 172
La Oroya Provincial Civil Defence Committee, 185
Legacy 13, 187
legitimacy, *see under* non-government organizations

leverage politics, *see under* campaigns, strategies
licence, social, 178–9
livelihoods, 98–9, 104

Machiguenga Communal Reserve, 147, 153
Machiguenga Council of the Urubamba River (COMARU), 120, 137–9, 141, 143–4, 153–4, 157, 159–60, 219, 230–1
Machiguenga Indigenous Communities Federation (CECONAMA), 137, 139, 153–4
Majot, Juliette, 47–8
MacNeill, Jim, 210
Make Trade Fair campaign, *see under* campaigns
Manu National Park, 134
Marks and Spencer, 59
McGee, R., 109
Medecins Sans Frontieres, 7
media, *see under* campaigns
Medico International, 1
Megantoni Sanctuary, 147
Menon, Shri S. N., 109
Metaloroya S. A., 169
Mineral Policy Centre, *see* Earth Works
Mines Awareness Group, 1
Mining Dialogue Group, 175–6
Mining, Minerals and Sustainable Development Initiative, 180, 193
mining ombudsman, *see under* Oxfam Australia
monitoring, 152, 154, 160, 163, 171, 188, 196–7, 200
Movement for the Health of La Oroya (MOSAO), 130–1, 172–9, 181–4, 187–94, 196–200, 202, 208–9, 219, 222
Multi-Fibre Agreement (MFA), 69–71
  phase-out, 69–71, 73, 75, 77, 79, 80, 84, 87–8, 212, 237
Multi-Sector Committee for the Economic and Historical Relevance of La Oroya, 179, 181
Municipality of La Oroya, 184, 191, 202, 212, 220

Nath, Kamal, 101, 109
National Indigenous Confederation of the Ecuadoran Amazon (CONFENIAE), 120
National Mining, Petroleum and Energy Society (SNMPE), 179
Natural Protected Areas (ANPs), 134, 137, 147
Nestlé corporation, 13–14, 19, 23
New Economics Foundation, 12
New York Times, 30
Newmont mining company, 128
Nike sportswear company, 23, 41, 59–60
non-government organizations, 1–12, 23–7, 30–49
  accountability of, 30–2, 35–7, 46–9, 163, 213–20, 223, 239–40
  advocacy, 38, 89, 228
  development oriented, 5, 24, 112, 215, 236
  environmental, 193
  indigenous rights, 231
  international, 24, 27, 32, 34–5, 37, 88–90, 98, 108, 113, 193, 207, 210, 212, 215, 217, 219–21, 224–5, 227–8, 230, 236, 238–44
  legitimacy of, 32–5, 88–90, 111–13, 161–2, 198, 207–13, 225, 238–9
  policy and advocacy, 7
Nyamugasira, Warren, 229, 231

O'Neill, Paul, 16
Organization for Economic Cooperation and Development (OECD), 23
Otishi National Park, 147
Overseas Development Institute, 40, 113
Overseas Private Investment Corporation (OPIC), 21
Oxfam, 6, 11
  America, 118–26, 129–30, 172–3, 189, 199–200, 202
  Global Extractive Industries Team, 119, 123–4, 189, 231
  Australia, 64, 118–19, 129–30, 227
  mining ombudsman, 119, 129
  Great Britain, 64, 74, 118–22, 216–17, 227
  Hong Kong, 225
  India, 64, 225
  Intermon, 118
  International, 7, 9, 52–3, 55–8, 89, 102, 104, 107–8, 118, 120, 122–3, 210, 213, 225, 236
    extractive industries working group, 119, 123
    Media Group, 57
    Regional Strategic Teams, 57–8, 122
    South America, 122–3
    South Asia, 64–5, 94, 98
    Regional Trade Advisor, 104
    South Asia Labour and Trade Team (SALT), 65
    Trade Campaign Working Group, 57, 226
    Trade Policy Group, 57
  Novib, 64, 119
  South Asia Trade and Agriculture Group, 65

Paniagua, Valentín, 193
Paracas Bay, 136, 140–1, 147, 150–1, 159
Paracas National Marine Reserve, 133, 136, 140, 159
participation, *see under* campaigns
Peru/LNG, 155–6, 160
Peruvian Environmental Law Society (SPDA), 124, 140–1, 143, 171–2, 182, 188, 192–3
Peruvian government, 130, 135–6, 138–9, 142–3, 147–51, 153–4, 156, 160–4, 189
  Energy and Mining Investment Supervisor (OSINERGMIN), 137, 142, 144–5, 147, 152, 196, 200
  Inter-institutional Technical Coordination Group (GTCI), 137, 140, 142, 152

Ministry of Energy and Mines (MEM), 137, 142, 152–3, 155, 168, 175–82, 184, 187, 190–1, 192, 194–5, 197, 220
Office of Environmental Affairs (DGAA), 168, 177–8
Ministry of Health, 168, 174, 180, 182–5, 190–2, 195
Office of Environmental Health (DIGESA), 168, 177, 184–5
National Civil Defence Institute, 185
National Congress, 154, 174, 174–6, 183, 190, 192, 201
National Environmental Council (CONAM), 183–5, 190–1
Ombudsman's office, 144, 154, 156, 190
Truth and Reconciliation Commission, 159
Philippines Council for NGO Certification, 218
Physicians for Human Rights, 1
Plan International, 7
Pluspetrol oil company, 135–6, 139, 142, 144, 147, 149–50, 159
Popular Assembly of La Oroya, 172
Popular Mobilization Group, 57
Presbyterian Church, 131, 172–3, 192, 194, 198, 202, 231
public opinion, *see* campaigns, media
political responsibility, *see under* campaigns
Public Service International (PSI), 4, 9
Puma, 60

Quijandría, Jaime, 149

Red Muqui, 188
Renco Group, 130–1, 169, 174, 187, 189–90, 200–1
Rennert, Ira Leon, 169, 174, 187, 189, 199
representation, *see under* campaigns
research accuracy, *see under* campaigns
Revive Mantaro Project, 188, 195, 198, 200
Rio Tinto, 21

Saint Louis University, School of Public Health, 177–8, 191, 195, 199
Salamon, L. M., 25
Salazar, Milagros, 184
Save the Children Fund, 6, 7, 35, 38, 217
Schnayerson, Michael, 174
Scholte, Jane Aart, 35
Serrano, Fernando, 178
Sharma, Shefali, 106, 111
Shell oil company, 118, 134–7, 163
Shinai Serjali, 137, 144
Shuar People's Interethnic Federation of Ecuador (FIPSE), 120
Sikkink, K., 18–26, 81–4, 107–8, 158, 160, 194, 196, 237–8
SK Corporation, 135
Slim, Hugo, 207–8, 216
small arms campaign, *see under* campaigns
Smithsonian Institution, 134
social movements, 9–11
Social Watch, 9
Sonatrach, 135
special and differential treatment (SDT), 96–7
Spiro, Peter, 36
Sri Lanka, 67–92
Sri Lankan government
Department of Labour, 73, 75, 84–5, 87–8
Ministry of Finance, 73
Ministry of Industries, 74
Ministry of Trade, 74
strategies, *see under* campaigns
subsidies, 95–6, 98, 100, 102–3, 110
symbolic politics, *see under* campaigns, strategies

Tambogrande Defence Front, 127
Tapia, Hildebrando, 174
Techint Group, 135
technical working group, 172–6, 179, 181–2, 187–9, 192, 197–200, 202, 209, 212, 219–20
Tecpetrol of Peru, 135
Texaco oil company, 120
TGP, 135, 144–5, 150, 152, 154

252 *Index*

The Nature Conservancy, 137, 139
Third World Action Group, 13, 19
Third World Network, 7–8, 11
Tikait, M. S., 107
Toledo, Alejandro, 147, 193
trade unions, *see* labour unions
TÜV Rheinland Industrie Service GmbH, 186

Umbro, 60
UNES Consortium, 170–3, 191
Union of International Associations, 24
United Nations Children's Fund (UNICEF), 13
United Nations (UN), 36, 56, 217
United States Catholic Bishops' Conference, 199
United States government, 62, 95–7, 103, 118–19, 130, 146, 155–6, 158, 160, 162, 201, 238, 242
  Center for Disease Control, 191
  Embassy in Peru, 201
  Export-Import Bank (Ex-Im Bank), 130, 133, 136, 142, 144, 146–7, 149–50, 156–7, 159–60, 162, 238
  Treasury Department, 146–7, 161
Universal Declaration of Human Rights, 23, 210–11
Universidad ESAN, 180

van Tuijl, P., 45–9, 92, 114, 200, 215–16, 241
Verma, Samar, 97, 104–5, 112, 115
Vietnam Veterans of America Foundation, 1
Voluntary Action Network of India (VANI), 99

wage, living, 72, 77–8, 80–1, 212–13, 237
Walmart, 59, 78

Wapner, Paul, 209
War on Want, 13
White Band Day, 99
Wiesel, Elie, 187
Workers' Councils, 78–9, 82
World Bank, 15–16, 25, 42–3, 47–8, 53, 56, 73, 118–19, 127–8, 136–7, 180, 210, 218, 227, 233
  Inspection Panel, 42–3
  Inter-American Development Bank (IDB), 130–1, 133, 136, 138, 140–8, 150–6, 158, 160–3, 238
  International Development Association, 44
  International Finance Corporation (IFC), 128, 155
World Development Movement, 7
World Federation of Sporting Goods Industries, 79
World Health Organization (WHO), 13, 166, 183, 185
World Social Forum, 10
World Summit for Social Development, 220
World Trade Organization (WTO), 7, 10, 25, 32, 35, 53–4, 56–7, 61–3, 69, 94–114, 208, 212, 219
World Vision, 6, 7
World Wide Fund for Nature (WWF), 9, 136–7, 139, 145

Yine Yane Indigenous Communities Federation (FECONAYY), 137, 154
Young Women's Christian Association (YWCA), 217
Youth for Unity and Voluntary Action (YUVA), 99

Zelms, Jeffrey L., 173
Zimbabwe Human Rights Association (ZimRights), 3